THE CATHOLIC BIBLICAL QUARTERLY

MONOGRAPH SERIES

11

A SEPTUAGINT TRANSLATION TECHNIQUE IN THE BOOK OF JOB

by

Homer Heater, Jr.

A Septuagint Translation Technique in the Book of Job

BY

HOMER HEATER, JR.

The Catholic Biblical Association of America
Washington, DC 20064
1982

A SEPTUAGINT TRANSLATION TECHNIQUE IN THE BOOK OF JOB

by Homer Heater, Jr.

© 1982 The Catholic Biblical Association of America
Washington, DC 20064

PRODUCED IN THE UNITED STATES

Library of Congress Cataloging in Publication Data

Heater, Homer.
  A Septuagint translation technique in the
Book of Job.

  (The Catholic Biblical quarterly. Monograph
series ; 11)
  Bibliography: p.
  Includes index.
  1. Bible. O.T. Job—Translating. 2. Bible.
O.T. Job. Greek—Versions—Septuagint.
I. Title. II. Series.
BS1415.2.H4   223'.1048   81-10085
ISBN 0-915170-10-8   AACR2

DEDICATED TO
MY WIFE
PATRICIA

קמו בניה ויאשרוה בעלה ויהללה

Prov 31:28

CONTENTS

ACKNOWLEDGMENTS

This monograph is a revision of a doctoral dissertation originally submitted to the faculty of the Semitics Department of the Catholic University of America. I am deeply grateful for the generous contribution in assistance provided by my original committee consisting of the late Msgr. Patrick W. Skehan, Fr. Alexander A. DiLella, O.F.M., and Bro. Aloysius Fitzgerald, F.S.C. I am especially grateful to Msgr. Skehan for his patient instruction and example of diligent scholarship while I was undertaking a program of studies in Semitic languages.

I have carried on a teaching responsibility at the Capital Bible Seminary during the entire time this project was underway. Much encouragement in every way has come from the President, Mr. George A. Miles. His cheerful fellowship and patient leadership have been greatly appreciated.

My thanks go also to Fr. Bruce Vawter, C.M., Chairman of the CBQMS Editorial Board, for his diligence in editing the manuscript for publication and to Fr. Joseph Jensen, O.S.B., for his technical assistance.

Though I assume full responsibility for the contents of this monograph, I am grateful for the contribution made by all those mentioned above. I trust that this publication will be a worthy successor to the scholarly works that have preceded it in the CBQMS.

PREFACE

The Book of Job was contrived by its nameless writer to be a challenge; and in the communities of faith, it has been understood through the centuries that Providence willed it so. Like any deliberate challenge to thought and conscience on a complex range of problems, it has been faced and evaluated on many levels, over and over again. Within the nascent Christian community (Jas 5:11) the person of Job was made the challenge, as he had been in the days of Ezekiel (14:14, 20). The ground had shifted somewhat, however; for Ezekiel, Job had been a type for the virtuous man. In the Epistle of James, he is the example of steadfastness, of enduring hope—some have even said, of patience! The change was because of the Book; and the lesson is a valid one. But if the human author of the Book of Job, sitting under a palm tree in the Arabian oasis of Teima in the days of Nabonidus—which, with apologies, is where the present writer thinks to put him—were given to foresee what the author of James would say, he might easily conclude: he read the story; but did he read the speeches?

Reading Job has never been easy; and for the trained scholar of today, the reference materials multiply, but many a problem on the basic level of language, or of integrity of a word, a phrase, a line in the text, remains with shadowy answers. Prof. Heater, with his fine control of Greek, and with no little courage, turned his attention for purposes of this monograph to the earliest reader of Job with whom we have had direct contact: the "Septuagint" Greek translator of the 2d century B.C. In the Greek book as we have it, the task of separating out the work of that translator from a reviser no more than a century later (the poet from the pedant...) has become both easier and more fruitful since D. Barthélemy's making of the reworked 1st century A.D. Greek Minor Prophets scroll from Wadi Khabra in Palestine the touchstone for distinguishing levels of revision before Origen. The reviser is now easier to know well than is the translator whose work he fleshed out; but he is far less interesting for the understanding of the Book. Helpful in many a detail, but not nearly as provocative in the insights it seems to promise for illuminating the Hebrew text of Job, is the fragmentary Aramaic targum from the 11th cave at Kh. Qumrân. It is by a translator less gifted but more sober in his approach to the text than the oldest Greek translator, with whom he may have been contemporary. That oldest translator retains his fascination for the textual critic, for the literary critic, for the student of theological currents in the Judaism of the period. All these interests are reflected in the literature surveyed by Prof. Heater as he probes into the identifiable written sources, elsewhere in Job and elsewhere in the Old Testament, which were drawn upon by that translator, whether to amplify and to highlight the message he saw in his text, or whether at times to veil over difficulties in the text that resisted any more direct approach. When in the near future, it is hoped, the first critically established text of the Greek Job, based on the full manuscript tradition, appears in the Göttingen series, the data gathered in this monograph will provide a most useful accompaniment for it, illustrating how that ancient translator went about his task.

Patrick W. Skehan

ABBREVIATIONS
Biblical Books (with the Apocrypha)

Gen	Genesis	Add Esth	Additions to Esther
Exod	Exodus	Bar	Baruch
Lev	Leviticus	Bel	Bel and the Dragon
Num	Numbers	1-2 Esdr	1-2 Esdras
Deut	Deuteronomy	4 Ezra	4 Ezra
Josh	Joshua	Jdt	Judith
Judg	Judges	Ep Jer	Epistle of Jeremiah
1-2 Sam	1-2 Samuel	1-2-3-4 Macc	1-2-3-4 Maccabees
1-2 Kgs	1-2 Kings	Pr Azar	Prayer of Azariah
Isa	Isaiah	Pr Man	Prayer of Manasseh
Jer	Jeremiah	Sir	Sirach
Ezek	Ezekiel	Sus	Susanna
Hos	Hosea	Tob	Tobit
Joel	Joel	Wis	Wisdom of Solomon
Amos	Amos		
Obad	Obadiah	Matt	Matthew
Jonah	Jonah	Mark	Mark
Mic	Micah	Luke	Luke
Nah	Nahum	John	John
Hab	Habakkuk	Acts	Acts
Zeph	Zephaniah	Rom	Romans
Hag	Haggai	1-2 Cor	1-2 Corinthians
Zech	Zechariah	Gal	Galatians
Mal	Malachi	Eph	Ephesians
Ps, Pss	Psalm(s)	Phil	Philippians
Job	Job	Col	Colossians
Prov	Proverbs	1-2 Thess	1-2 Thessalonians
Ruth	Ruth	1-2 Tim	1-2 Timothy
Cant	Canticles	Titus	Titus
Eccl	Ecclesiastes	Phlm	Philemon
Lam	Lamentations	Heb	Hebrews
Esth	Esther	Jas	James
Dan	Daniel	1-2 Pet	1-2 Peter
Ezra	Ezra	1-2-3 John	1-2-3 John
Neh	Nehemiah	Jude	Jude
1-2 Chr	1-2 Chronicles	Rev	Revelation

א   Codex Sinaiticus of the LXX
A   Codex Alexandrinus of the LXX
AB   Anchor Bible
ALUOS Annual of Leeds University Oriental Society
B   Codex Vaticanus of the LXX
BA   *Biblical Archaeologist*
BASOR *Bulletin of the American Schools of Oriental Research*
BDB   Brown-Driver-Briggs, *A Hebrew and English Lexicon of the Old Testament*
BHK   *Biblia Hebraica*, Kittel-Kahle edition
BHS   *Biblia Hebraica Stuttgartensia*
Bib   *Biblica*
CBQ   *Catholic Biblical Quarterly*
DJD   Discoveries in the Judaean Desert
Exp   *Expositor*
HAT   Handbuch zum Alten Testament
HTR   *Harvard Theological Review*
HUCA *Hebrew Union College Annual*
ICC   International Critical Commentary
IEJ   *Israel Exploration Journal*
JAOS   *Journal of the American Oriental Society*
JB   *Jerusalem Bible*
JBC   *Jerome Biblical Commentary*
JBL   *Journal of Biblical Literature*
JTS   *Journal of Theological Studies*
KJV   *King James Version*
LUÅ   Lund Universitets Årsskrift
LXX   The Septuagint
MBib   *Miscellanea Biblica, II.* Twenty-fifth Anniversary Volume of Pontificio Istituto Biblico (Vol. I is *Biblica* 14)
Mus   *Muséon*
NAB   *New American Bible*
NEB   *New English Bible*
RB   *Revue biblique*
RSV   *Revised Standard Version*
SBLMS Society of Biblical Literature Monograph Series
VTSup Vetus Testamentum, Supplements
ZAW   *Zeitschrift für die alttestamentliche Wissenschaft*
ZNW   *Zeitschrift für die neutestamentliche Wissenschaft*

CHAPTER I

INTRODUCTION

The last few decades have witnessed a resurgence of interest in Septuagintal studies, stimulated not a little by the Qumran finds, which have also promoted the use of the Septuagint for textual criticism.[1] These new materials have provided fresh insight into the complex history of the Septuagintal text.[2] In addition, there have been new endeavors to determine the nature of the translation of the various parts of the Septuagint. This latter, happily, has led away from a tendency in the past to use the Septuagint almost uncritically to emend the Hebrew text.

The purpose of this monograph is to contribute to these ongoing studies by showing a technique used by the Septuagintal translator of Job, which, when properly understood, should assist in evaluating some of the Septuagint readings that diverge from the Masoretic Text.

I. The Problem

A. THE TEXT FORMS OF THE SEPTUAGINT OF JOB

The first issue that confronts one who works with the Septuagint translation of Job is the matter of two entirely different types of Greek translation. There is an old or original Greek that is quite loose in the way it handles the Hebrew text, even to the point of omitting an appreciable amount of Hebrew throughout the book, and there is a later Greek designed to fill these lacunae. This later Greek translation will not be discussed in this monograph because it is quite literal and therefore not subject to the same type of technique addressed here.[3]

B. THE OLD GREEK OF JOB

1. The Length of the Original Translation.

Most discussions on the Greek of the Book of Job begin with this quotation from Origen:

---

[1]This is especially true in Samuel and Isaiah. See F. M. Cross, Jr., *The Ancient Library of Qumran and Modern Biblical Studies* (rev. ed.; Anchor; Garden City, N.Y.: Doubleday, 1961) 168-194.

[2]See, e.g., D. Barthélemy, *Les devanciers d'Aquila* (VTSup 10; Leiden: Brill, 1963).

[3]I have discussed this later Greek and applied the characteristics of the KR (proto-Theodotion) with positive results. See Heater, "A Septuagint Translation Technique in the Book of Job" (Ph.D. diss., Catholic University of America, 1976) 22-53.

1

Again there are many passages throughout the whole of Job which, though present in the Hebrew, are lacking in our own, mostly amounting to four or three lines [or "verses" (ἔπη)], but from time to time fourteen or fifteen.[4]

The old Greek is actually shorter, by about 350 lines or one sixth, than the Hebrew text. The extant Greek codices have been expanded to about 2200 lines.[5] The assumption is almost universally held that the shorter Greek text represents an abbreviated, not an originally short, Hebrew text. Hatch argued for the latter almost a century ago, and Orlinsky in modern times has defended the shorter Hebrew, but he stands virtually alone.[6]

2. The Characteristics of the Old Greek Translation.

The old Greek of Job has long been criticized for its approach to the Hebrew text. Swete and Dhorme believe that the original translation of Job was for a general readership and not for synagogue use.[7] Hellenistic influence is evident in the introduction into the text of Hades (33:22) and the Horn of Amalthea (42:14).[8] The old Greek is quite idiomatic as opposed to the later additions, which are of an altogether different character.[9] Dhorme provides extensive examples of explanation, harmonization, theological speculation, or theological scruples, and places where certain liberty was taken in the use or suppression of metaphors and comparisons. To this he adds license, errors, redundancies, and omissions.[10]

The old Greek has a tendency to abridge two cola of a bicolon apparently in the interest of providing a single Greek colon containing

---

[4]Quoted by S. Jellicoe, *The Septuagint and Modern Study* (Oxford: Clarendon Press, 1968) 136.

[5]S. R. Driver and G. B. Gray, *A Critical and Exegetical Commentary on the Book of Job* (ICC; Edinburgh: T. & T. Clark, 1921) lxxiv. This work was begun by Driver and finished by Gray, but to the latter belongs the major portion of the work.

[6]E. Hatch, *Essays in Biblical Greek* (Oxford: 1889; reprinted, Amsterdam: Philo Press, 1970); H. M. Orlinsky, "Studies in the Septuagint," *HUCA* 28 (1957) 53-74. E. Dhorme (*A Commentary on the Book of Job* [London: Nelson, 1967; originally *Le livre de Job*, Paris: J. Gabalda, 1926] cciii) stated firmly before Orlinsky's work was published: "No critic now accepts the hypothesis advanced by Hatch in 1889 according to which the Septuagint version was produced on the basis of an original Hebrew text, of which the present text is only an amplification. Bickell attempts to exploit this thesis in the interest of his strophic theory. He has done so only at the cost of innumerable inconsistencies."

[7]H. B. Swete, *An Introduction to the Old Testament in Greek* (rev. R. R. Ottley; Cambridge: University Press, 1902; reprinted, New York: Ktav, 1968) 256; Dhorme, *Book of Job*, cxcvi.

[8]Dhorme, *Book of Job*, cxcvi.

[9]H. St. J. Thackeray, *A Grammar of the Old Testament in Greek* (Cambridge: University Press, 1909) 3-4.

[10]Dhorme, *Book of Job*, cxcvi-cxcix.

elements from both Hebrew components,[11] which is one reason for a shorter text in the old Greek. In other places cola are omitted in their entirety (see, for example, chap. 28).

3. The Issue of Theological Bias.

In conjunction with the matter of translation style, the question of whether the translator allowed a theological bias to influence his work must be addressed. This issue of theological tendencies, posited by Dhorme, has given rise to several studies on the nature of the translation of the Septuagint of Job. In 1946 G. Gerleman published his *Studies in the LXX. I, The Book of Job.*[12] Three years later, H. S. Gehman published an article in *JBL* called "The Theological Approach of the Greek Translator of Job 1-15."[13] Both men argued that the Greek translators altered the text materially because of theological predilections. D. H. Gard, a student of Gehman, presented his doctoral dissertation in a monograph in 1952 titled *The Exegetical Method of the Greek Translator of the Book of Job.*[14] H. M. Orlinsky[15] indicates that the works of all three contain much un-attributed material from earlier scholars.[16]

Since some of our examples of the translator's technique coincide with passages referred to by Gerleman, Gehman, and Gard as instances of theological bias, a few of their examples will be set out at this point. One category is what Gerleman calls toning down of language:

> Nor in the description of Job himself has the Greek translator given us an entirely faithful picture of the complex meditator portrayed by the Hebrew poet. It is chiefly in the description of the controversy between Job and God that one notices a distinct difference. The most violent outbursts on the part of Job, where he sees in God a demonic enemy, and where he denies the whole moral order of the world, have been modified in the LXX in several places.[17]

He then gives Job 19:6 as an example. In that verse, עותני is translated ὁ ταράξας. What Gerleman has failed to note is that there is an inner Job

---

[11]For a similar phenomenon in LXX-Isaiah, see Ziegler, *Untersuchungen zur Septuaginta des Buches Isaias* (Münster: Verlag des Aschendorffschen Verlagsbuchhandlung, 1934) 46-47, 51-52.

[12]G. Gerleman, *Studies in the LXX. I, The Book of Job* (LUÅ, N.F.1. 43.2, 1946).

[13]H. S. Gehman, "The Theological Approach of the Greek Translator of Job 1-15," *JBL* 68 (1949) 231-240. See also his "Exegetical Methods Employed by the Greek Translator of I Samuel," *JAOS* 70 (1950) 292-296.

[14]D. H. Gard, *The Exegetical Method of the Greek Translator of the Book of Job* (SBLMS 8; Philadelphia: Society of Biblical Literature, 1952).

[15]Orlinsky, "Studies in the Septuagint," *HUCA* 28 (1957) 70-71.

[16]Orlinsky, "Studies in the Septuagint," *HUCA* 28 (1957) 53-74; 29 (1958) 229-271; 30 (1959) 153-167; 32 (1961) 239-268; 33 (1962) 119-151; 35 (1964) 57-78; 36 (1965) 37-47.

[17]Gerleman, *Studies in the LXX*, 53.

treatment of this word. Job (alone in the Septuagint) translates עות with ταράσσειν three times and at least once under the influence of another passage.

Gerleman's inconsistency in the use of the evidence is demonstrated by the following argument: "Unduly anthropomorphic expressions also give rise to dogmatic misgivings in the translator. It may suffice to mention a few examples." He then cites Job 26:13 where Hebrew "hand" is changed to "command."[18] However, when the translator reproduces "hand" literally (10 of 14 occurences!), Gerleman tries to defend his position by saying that these are "less concrete" situations.[19] Orlinsky has reviewed these arguments and others from Gerleman in a devastating fashion.[20]

Gerleman gives 10:13 as a case where the Septuagint avoids the accusation that God has hidden evil designs against Job in his heart.[21] However, the Greek of 10:13 has been imported directly from 42:2 where it translates the Hebrew. Furthermore, the entire tenth chapter of Job *in Greek* precludes the idea that the translator is trying to exonerate God.[22] Gerleman also assumes that the translator of Job was offended by the expression "sons of God" and substituted "angels of God," but this practice was in vogue for more than a century prior to the translation of Job.[23]

Gehman's article in *JBL* three years later picked up the same general theme.[24] Gard merely compiled examples from other writers without providing a genuine critical analysis of the material.[25] Orlinsky has been particularly devastating in his critique of Gard's work.[26] The material in Gard's book is secondary and so noncritical as to be virtually worthless.

Orlinsky's outstanding work on the style of the Septuagint of Job has thoroughly refuted the idea of a broad theological or philosophical bias on the part of the translator. He has demonstrated that many of the divergences (called anti-anthropomorphisms, etc.) are nothing other than stylistic Greek.[27] Some of them, however, are the result of the translation technique presented in this monograph.

---

[18] Ibid., 58. I discuss the reason for "command" in conjunction with 40:19. It has nothing to do with anti-anthropomorphism.

[19] Ibid., 59. See further my discussion in Chapter II, §14.

[20] Orlinsky, "Studies in the Septuagint," *HUCA* 30 (1959) 153-167.

[21] Gerleman, *Studies in the LXX*, 54.

[22] See my discussion at 10:13.

[23] See my discussion at 38:7.

[24] Gehman, "The Theological Approach of the Greek Translator of Job 1-15," *JBL* 68 (1949) 231-240.

[25] Gard, *Exegetical Method*.

[26] Orlinsky, "Studies in the Septuagint," *HUCA* 28 (1957) 70-71.

[27] Ibid. For a complete list of the series in *HUCA*, see above note 16.

4. Value for Textual Criticism.

A shift in attitude in textual criticism has taken place both in the area of conjectural emendation and in the use of versional evidence. Jellicoe's conservative statement on the former bears this out:

> Conjectural emendation, so common half a century or more ago, and carried to extremes, for example, by Duhm, and to the point of eccentricity in the later work of Cheyne, is today in some circles virtually rejected, a reaction which is altogether too radical. The main objection, which certainly has validity, is on grounds of subjectivism. Used with discretion, however, it will always have a place.[28]

More relevant to this monograph is his statement regarding the use of versions. His caution is particularly relevant to the Book of Job:

> Formerly when the intrinsic trustworthiness of the Massoretic text was held in lesser esteem, it was the practice of commentators copiously to emend their text on "the authority of the Septuagint" as preserving an earlier and more reliable reading. Though it would be mistaken to abandon the hypothesis entirely, it must be applied with a greater degree of caution than was formerly exercised. As we have seen, translation involves interpretation, and this may in some cases suggest prima facie a different Hebrew text, a supposition which further investigation fails to support.[29]

Orlinsky argues that, though the critical use of the Greek of Job has been primarily reserved for places in the Hebrew text where help was desperately needed, the nature of the old Greek has not been sufficiently apprehended by many of those who have used it.[30]

This monograph is proceeding on the assumption, borne out by study, that the Hebrew *Vorlage* of the old Greek of Job was essentially that presently contained in the Masoretic Text.[31] Therefore, any use of the Greek text to emend the Hebrew text must be made with great care. The

---

[28] Jellicoe, *Septuagint and Modern Study*, 320.

[29] Ibid., 321.

[30] Orlinsky, "Studies in the Septuagint," *HUCA* 28 (1957) 71-72, and throughout the series in *HUCA* (see above, note 16). He says, "Such commentators as A. Merx, Franz Delitzsch, A. Dillmann, C. Siegfried, B. Duhm, K. Budde, A. B. Ehrlich, E. König, S. R. Driver-G. B. Gray, M. Buttenwieser, P. Dhorme, N. Peters, E. J. Kissane, and W. B. Stevenson make practically no mention of the Septuagint where the masoretic text presents to them no difficulty. It is only when their opinions of what the author of Job may or should have written are upset by the preserved reading that they resort to the Septuagint, and even then only when it can—on their view—be made to support their opinions."

[31] See Orlinsky ("Studies in the Septuagint," *HUCA* 28 [1957] 53-74), who holds to a shorter *Vorlage* and often opts for a different reading. In spite of this, Orlinsky assumes that the Greek was working from a Hebrew text very similar to that contained in the Masoretic Text. See also Jellicoe, *Septuagint and Modern Study*, 317.

more cautious approach of *BHS* as opposed to *BHK* is to be applauded, but emendation should never be undertaken without a full appreciation of the approach of the Greek translator. The body of our study will show that several emendations made on the basis of the Greek must be given up, because the different Greek has been imported from another place.

5. The Anaphoric Translation Technique.

This monograph presents in detail a practice of the Greek translator that goes beyond the matter of style. It is the technique of interpolating material from some other part of the Septuagint, although usually from within Job itself, into the passage with which he is working. I am calling this technique "anaphoric translation." The term "anaphoric" has been adopted from the Greek grammar for the sake of convenient designation and for want of a more suitable term. It refers in Greek grammar to the use of the definite article with a noun referring back to "what is known or assumed to be known."[32] As a translation technique, "anaphoric translation" refers to the interpolation or adaptation of words or phrases from other passages of Scripture where the underlying idea is the same or similar. Suggestions on the reason for this editorial work are made in the conclusion of this monograph.

Ziegler has observed similar practices in the Septuagint of Isaiah where he has shown smoothings and harmonizations.[33] P. W. Skehan has pointed out the same technique in the Hebrew text of the 1QIsa[a] scroll.[34] T. Muraoka presents illustrations for this practice from several OT passages.[35] The tendency to introduce words from other passages has already been observed in Job. For instance, Kissane says of the Greek of this book: "The translator had a predilection for certain words and phrases, and he is sometimes influenced by the reading of a parallel passage in which the wording of the Hebrew is entirely different."[36]

In this monograph, we select those cola which contain words or phrases identifiable from other parts of the Septuagint. Some examples will be included that will not be as obvious as others, but to have as comprehensive as possible a presentation of the data, they will be included with appropriate qualifications.

---

[32]F. Blass and A. Debrunner, *A Greek Grammar of the New Testament and Other Early Christian Literature* (tr. and rev. R. W. Funk; Chicago: University of Chicago Press, 1961) 132.

[33]J. Ziegler, *Untersuchungen zur Septuaginta des Buches Isaias* (Münster: Verlag des Aschendorffschen Verlagsbuchhandlungen, 1934).

[34]P. W. Skehan, "The Qumran Manuscripts and Textual Criticism," *Volume du Congrès. Strasbourg 1956* (VTSup 4; Leiden: Brill, 1957) 148-160; see also Heater, "Textual Harmonizations in 1QIs[a] and LXX" (M.A. thesis, Catholic University of American, 1967).

[35]T. Muraoka, "Literary Device in the Septuagint," *Textus* 8 (1973) 20-30.

[36]E. J. Kissane, *The Book of Job* (Dublin: Browne & Nolan, 1939) xlv.

6. Modern Translation Theories.

There has been an extensive amount of work in recent years in the area of translation theories. The United Bible Societies have spearheaded a number of studies that they have called "Helps for Translators."[37] J. de Waard faults Jellicoe for his treatment of "translation techniques." He argues that Jellicoe's work shows serious shortcomings owing to the failure to take into account modern translation theory and adequate linguistic terminology.[38] De Waard then turns to an area that has direct bearing on this monograph:

> We should no longer speak of "interpretative additions" in translation when we mean to say that implicit source information has been made explicit. In such a case nothing has been added to the source text. Only when we have to do with the making explicit of information which is *not* implicit in the source . . . we can talk of additions which presuppose, of course, a wrong interpretation.[39]

De Waard is lending a much needed precision to the terminology of translation practices, but it must be remembered that these modern methodologies are highly sophisticated and represent an effort to analyze every aspect of translation including psychological as well as linguistic phenomena. In approaching the Greek translation of the OT, however, and especially the Book of Job, much care should be exercised in applying modern linguistic description to the practices of the ancient translator.

The "technique" under discussion in this monograph is most certainly "addition" by anyone's definition, and the practice is consciously followed by the translator. It is not a philosophy of translation, but could perhaps be better described as a mentality.[40] Owing to the unique nature of this "technique," the modern discussion of theories or philosophies has little bearing on the issue, and there will be little reference to them.

II. Methodology and Materials Used

A. DETERMINATION OF THE OLD GREEK

Current codices do not differentiate between the old Greek and the new. Thus, some system must be followed to ascertain the original text. Eusebius attributed to Origen the practice of adding in his Hexapla the missing Greek from "Theodotion's" translation and indicating it with an

---

[37] Eight volumes have been published; see especially E. A. Nida and C. R. Tabor, *The Theory and Practice of Translation* (Leiden: Brill, 1969) vol. 3.

[38] J. de Waard, "Translation Techniques Used by the Greek Translators of Ruth," *Bib* 54 (1973) 499-515. See his bibliography on the subject.

[39] Ibid., 515.

[40] See further B. Kedar-Kopfstein, "The Interpretative Element in Transliteration," *Textus* 8 (1973) 55-77 and his bibliography.

asterisk.[41] These signs are imperfectly preserved in two Greek manuscripts, two Latin manuscripts, and the Syro-Hexapla (a Syriac translation based on Origen's fifth column).[42] The Copto-Sahidic translation of the Septuagint did not preserve the "Theodotionic" passages.[43] The signs can be recovered from these sources with a relative amount of accuracy.[44] Rahlfs has included these signs in his hand edition.[45]

B. THE MANUSCRIPTS

Codex Vaticanus (B) will be used as the text for comparison with the Hebrew. Orlinsky summarizes the position of Margolis on Joshua, Montgomery on Daniel (in this case "Theodotion's" text) and Kings, Rahlfs on Ruth and Psalms, and Ziegler on Isaiah, Minor Prophets, Ezekiel, Jeremiah, and Daniel, by saying that in spite of its faults B appears to represent generally the best preserved text of the original Septuagint translation. With reference to Job, he writes: "Bearing in mind that G^B is but a single manuscript and only a member of a recension and with many faults ... the

[41] H. B. Swete, *Introduction to the Old Testament in Greek*, 64.

[42] The two Greek MSS are the Colbertinus (Paris #1952) and the Codex 248 (Holmes-Parsons=Codex Vaticanus, 346). See Field, *Origenis hexaplorum quae supersunt* (2 vols.; Oxford: Clarendon Press, 1875) 2.i. For the Latin version, the two MSS with obeli and asterisks are that of Oxford (Bodleian 2426) and that of Tours (Turonensis 18). See G. Beer in *ZAW* 1896, 297-314; 1897, 97-122; 1898, 257-286. The Syro-Hexapla was published in facsimile by A. M. Ceriani (*Codex Syro-hexaplaris Ambrosianus*, Milan, 1874).

[43] G. B. Gray (*Book of Job*, lxxii) says "edited by Ciasca in *Sacrorum Bibl. fragmenta Copto-Sahidica*, Romae, 1889, ii. 1-68. From mutilation of MSS., cc. 39:9-40:8 of this version are missing. The lower Egyptian, or Bohairic, version of G was edited and translated by H. Tattam (*The ancient Coptic Version of the book of Job*, London, 1846); but this version contains the Hexaplaric additions and is of relatively little interest." See also Orlinsky, "Studies in the Septuagint," *HUCA* 28 (1957) 56. The *absence* of the "Theodotionic" passages should indicate a translation from a pre-hexaplaric text, but some disagree. Dhorme (*Book of Job*, cci-ccii) writes: "It had been supposed, and this was the thesis of Ciasca, followed by Bickell, that this Sahidic version, lacking the passages added by Origen on the basis of Theodotion, represented the original text of the Septuagint. But the fact is that certain passages, which, in accordance with the witnesses as a whole and even according to style, would appear to belong to Theodotion, nevertheless have a place in the Sahidic version. Thus 9:15b of the Septuagint certainly comes from Theodotion, as is attested by the Greek, Latin, and Syriac traditions. But it is found in the Sahidic version (9:14). The latter again contains 17:16b; 20:3-4a; 25:6b, which likewise belong to Theodotion. Hence we cannot do otherwise than associate ourselves with the reservations of Burkitt as regards the pre-hexaplar character of the Sahidic version. The fact which seems to us undeniable is that the Coptic translator has deliberately omitted the stichs marked by asterisk. In a few cases his perspicacity has failed him."

[44] F. Field (*Origenis hexaplorum quae supersunt*) has rendered a valuable service by gathering Origenian material from the various sources.

[45] A. Rahlfs, *Septuaginta id est Vetus Testamentum Graece iuxta LXX interpretes* (Stuttgart: Württembergische Bibelanstalt, 1935) vol. 2.

present writer has found it to be the best single representative of the Septuagint text to work with in the Book of Job."[46] Dhorme's position is the same.[47]

It must still be kept in mind that even if the pre-hexaplaric text can be determined the recensional activity before Origen's time was quite extensive. It is in light of this that Jellicoe, after quoting favorably Swete's opinion that B represents on the whole the oldest form of the Septuagint in any extant manuscript, also issues Swete's caveat: 'It would be an error to suppose B to reflect consistently the oldest and the best text....'"[48]

Codex Alexandrinus cannot be used because it is too far removed from the original. Dhorme agrees, and L. Dieu argues that Alexandrinus is a member of the Lucianic recension.[49]

C. THE PRINTED TEXT

As indicated above, Rahlfs' two volume edition of the Septuagint will be used for the text of Codex B and the restoration of the diacritical marks of Origen.[50] Orlinsky says again of his own work in Job: "Rahlfs' handy two-volume edition of the Septuagint (really=G[B]) was employed, the well-known edition by Swete being too prone to error."[51] In view of the fact that Rahlfs does not always follow B readings, variants will be controlled by referring to Swete, Dhorme, and when deemed necessary, the facsimile. Holmes and Parsons will be used primarily for minuscule evidence.[52]

D. THE USE OF THE HEBREW TEXT

Unless the Hebrew text impinges upon the translation technique in some way, no attempt will be made to deal with it. This is not to preclude the possibility or probability that the Septuagint at times represents a better reading; the Hebrew text, as such, is simply beyond the scope of this discussion. By virtue of this fact, few commentaries on the Book of Job will make much contribution to this study, with the notable exceptions of the classic works of Dhorme and Gray.[53]

---

[46]Orlinsky, "Studies in the Septuagint," *HUCA* 33 (1962) 123.

[47]Dhorme, *Book of Job*, cciv.

[48]Jellicoe, *Septuagint and Modern Study*, 156; Swete was quoting Hort.

[49]Dhorme, *Book of Job*, cciv; L. Dieu, "Le texte de Job du Codex Alexandrinus et ses principaux témoins," *Mus* 13 (1912) 223-274.

[50]Rahlfs, *Septuaginta*.

[51]Orlinsky, "Studies in the Septuagint," *HUCA* 33 (1962) 123.

[52]H. B. Swete, *The Old Testament in Greek According to the Septuagint* (Cambridge: University Press, 1896) vol. 2; Dhorme, *Book of Job*; R. Holmes and J. Parsons, *Vetus Testamentum Graecum cum variis lectionibus* (Oxford: Clarendon Press, 1823) vol. 3.

[53]Dhorme, *Book of Job*; Gray, *Book of Job*.

E. AN EXPLANATION OF TERMS AND ABBREVIATIONS USED

The phrase "old Greek" refers to the original, abbreviated translation of the Book of Job. The expanded speech of Job's wife (2:9) will be considered a part of this old Greek translation even though it was probably inserted subsequently to the original translation. By "new Greek" is meant the later translation of the Hebrew cola left untranslated by the original Septuagint which have been inserted at the appropriate places.[54] "G" refers to the Greek translation of Job only, whether new or old. LXX is used for all the rest of the OT in Greek. The traditional *sigla* A′Θ′Σ′ are used for Aquila, Theodotion, and Symmachus, but Θ′ is used only when quoting others or referring to a marginal *scholium*. What has been traditionally referred to as "Theodotion" or "proto-Theodotion" will be called KR in this monograph when used by the writer; KR is an abbreviation for Καίγε Recension. MT refers to the Masoretic Text and will be quoted from Kittel's *Biblia Hebraica*.[55] When the word "Hebrew" is used, it refers to the MT unless otherwise noted.

[54]Sometimes they are inserted in the wrong places.
[55]R. Kittel, *Biblia Hebraica* (3rd. ed.; Stuttgart: Württembergische Bibelanstalt, 1951); now appearing, of course, in the reedited form of *Biblia Hebraica Stuttgartensia* (Stuttgart: Deutsche Bibelstiftung, 1977). These are being referred to as *BHK* and *BHS* respectively.

CHAPTER II

ANAPHORIC TRANSLATIONS

Examples of anaphoric translation technique will now be presented. The procedure will be to work from the beginning of the book to the end citing passages that appear to contain material interpolated from other Scriptures.

§1. Job 1:1c

This technique is encountered in the very first verse in the book.

καὶ ἦν ὁ ἄνθρωπος ἐκεῖνος	1:1b	והיה האיש ההוא
ἀληθινός ἄμεμπτος δίκαιος		תם וישר
θεοσεβής		וירא אלהים
ἀπεχόμενος ἀπὸ παντὸς	1:1c	וסר מרע
πονηροῦ πράγματος		

And that man was genuine, blameless, just, God-fearing, and avoiding every evil act.

And that man was blameless and upright, and one who feared God and avoided evil.

This phrase is repeated with minor variations in 1:8 and 2:3. The Hebrew and G have in those places:

ἄνθρωπος ἄμεμπτος ἀληθινός	1:8d	איש תם וישר
θεοσεβής		ירא אלהים
ἀπεχόμενος ἀπὸ παντὸς	1:8e	וסר מרע
πονηροῦ πράγματος		

A man blameless, genuine, God-fearing, and avoiding everything evil.

A man blameless and upright; one who fears God and avoids evil.

ἄνθρωπος ἄκακος ἀληθινός	2:3d	איש תם וישר
ἄμεμπτος θεοσεβής		ירא אלהים
ἀπεχόμενος ἀπὸ παντὸς	2:3e	וסר מרע
κακοῦ		
ἔτι δὲ ἔχεται ἀκακίας	2:3f	ועדנו מחזיק בתמתו

A man guileless, genuine, blameless, God-fearing, and avoiding all evil, and yet he maintains his guilelessness.

A man blameless and upright; one who fears God and avoids evil. And yet he maintains his blamelessness.

The additions of interest in both 1:1c and 1:8e are παντὸς and πράγματος; 2:3e differs in having κακοῦ instead of πονηροῦ and in omitting πράγματος. The expanded παντὸς may reflect Deut 23:10b.

καὶ φυλάξῃ ἀπὸ παντὸς ῥήματος πονηροῦ	Deut 23:10b	ונשמרת מכל דבר רע
And you shall keep away from every evil thing.		And you shall keep yourself from every evil thing.

The literal translation of דבר by ῥήμα is not particularly unusual, but Codex A has πονηροῦ πράγματος as in Job.

Muraoka's explanation of this addition is not convincing. He argues that παντὸς πονηροῦ πράγματος is an alliterative device. He notes that no such device for this idiom is employed outside Job, nor at Job 28:28 where a similar phrase appears. He includes 2:3 in his list, apparently failing to note that its reading is unique.[1] A more likely explanation is that "keeping oneself from every evil act" easily lends itself to an aphorism, and the expansion in Job may have been stimulated by the memory of this often recurring phrase.[2] The following verses may have affected the translation before us. They at least illustrate that this phrase is relatively commonplace.

τὸ δὲ ἀπέχεσθαι ἀπὸ κακῶν ἐστιν ἐπιστήμη	Job 28:28b	וסור מרע בינה
And to avoid evil is understanding.		And to avoid evil is understanding.

ὁ ἄγγελος ὁ ῥυόμενός με ἐκ πάντων τῶν κακῶν	Gen 48:16a	המלאך הגאל אתי מכל רע
The angel who delivers me from all evils.		The angel who has redeemed me from all evil.

ὃς αὐτός ἐστιν ὑμῶν σωτὴρ ἐκ πάντων τῶν κακῶν ὑμῶν	1 Sam 10:19b (LXX 1 Kgdms 10:19b)	אשר הוא מושיע לכם מכל רעותיכם
Who is himself your savior out of all your evils.		Who himself has saved you out of all your evils.

φοβοῦ δὲ τὸν θεὸν καὶ ἔκκλινε ἀπὸ παντὸς κακοῦ	Prov 3:7b	ירא את יהוה וסור מרע
Fear God and turn away from all evil.		Fear Yahweh and turn away from evil.

[1] T. Muraoka, "Literary Device in the Septuagint," *Textus* 8 (1973) 29.

[2] Bar 2:33 has καὶ ἀποστρέψουσιν . . . ἀπὸ πονηρῶν πραγμάτων αὐτῶν. G-Job is probably too early to have been influenced by Baruch, but the converse is possible and would show that this was a popular thought.

The statement in 1:1c, 1:8e, and 2:3e apears to have been influenced by the stock wisdom saying. There was probably less of a conscious borrowing than an unconscious expansion.[3] The reason for the translation of (מרע) by κακοῦ, and the omission of the expansion πράγματος in 2:3e is not obvious. It may be that the lexical choice of ἄκακος for תם in 2:3d influenced ἀκακίας for בתמתו in 2:3f. The translator perhaps then departed from πονηροῦ and used κακοῦ because of the presence of ἄκακος and ἀκακίας. In the four cases where סר מרע appears in Job (28:28 is the fourth), סור is consistently translated by ἀπέχειν. Of the many times סור appears in the Bible (15 in Job), only these four are translated with ἀπέχειν. This is a good indication that the translator thought these passages to be one idea, even though he was not entirely consistent in his treatment of them.

§2. Job 1:3f

This verse involves a double reading and an interpolation.

καὶ ὑπηρεσία πολλὴ σφόδρα 1:3e		ועבדה רבה מאד
καὶ ἔργα μεγάλα ἦν αὐτῷ ἐπὶ 1:3f τῆς γῆς		
And he had a very large number of servants and extensive holdings in the land.	And very many servants.	

τὰ ἔργα τῶν χειρῶν αὐτοῦ 1:10c εὐλόγησας		מעשה ידיו ברכת
καὶ τὰ κτήνη αὐτοῦ πολλὰ 1:10d ἐποίησας ἐπὶ τῆς γῆς		ומקנהו פרץ בארץ
You have blessed the works of his hands and multiplied his possessions on earth.	You have blessed the work of his hands, and his herds are spread over the land.	

The hexaplaric signs are indicated by Dhorme: "The translation καὶ ὑπηρεσία πολλὴ σφόδρα was marked by an obelus, according to Chrysostom. It figures however in Sah. and has no obelus in Jerome, nor in Syro-hex."[4] The doublet is probably original. There are no variants listed in Holmes and Parsons.[5] The translator chooses to read עבדה both as עֲבָדָה (ὑπηρεσία) and עֲבֹדָה (ἔργα). Apparently, the doublet arose from a desire to produce harmony between the statement about Job in 1:3 and

---

[3]See further Prov 15:27; 16:30; Wis 16:8. Note the addition of παντός in Prov 3:7b.

[4]E. Dhorme, Book of Job, 3.

[5]R. Holmes and J. Parsons, Vetus Testamentum Graecum cum variis lectionibus (Oxford: Clarendon Press, 1823) vol. 3, ad loc.

Satan's observations about him in 1:10. In 1:10c, the translator renders
מעשה as ἔργα, and מקנהו becomes κτήνη. By means of a double translation of עבדה in 1:3e, he is able to maintain the Hebrew (עֲבֻדָּה) and
harmonize with 1:10c by translating עבדה the second time as if reading
עֲבָדָה and using the word ἔργα found in 1:10c.[6] It remains only to bring in
בארץ (ἐπὶ τῆς γῆς) from 1:10d to complete the harmonization.

§3. Job 1:5d

| καὶ προσέφερεν περὶ αὐτῶν
θυσίαν κατὰ τὸν ἀριθμὸν
αὐτῶν
καὶ μόσχον ἕνα περὶ ἁμαρτίας
περὶ τῶν ψυχῶν αὐτῶν | 1:5c

1:5d | והעלה עלות מספר כלם |
| And he offered a sacrifice for them according to their number and one calf for a sin offering for their souls. | | And he offered burnt offerings according to the number of them all. |

Dhorme says: "The addition which G makes after כלם . . . is a gloss
on the previous phrase and imputes to the children of Job a fault which is
hypothetical only. This addition is marked by an obelus in Syro-hex. and
Jerome."[7] Gray argues: "The clause *may* rest on a Hebrew original
(. . . cf. *e.g.* Lv. 16:3, Nu. 15:28); but even if so, the words are secondary
and due to the interpolator failing to realize that to the author of the book,
as to the Hebrews of an early period, the עולה had by itself sufficient
expiating virtue."[8] The source of this gloss lies in the Pentateuchal instructions for sacrifice. עלות (θυσίαν) is not sufficient for the translator. He
goes to the Pentateuch for a different type of offering more appropriate to
the needs of the context.

| καὶ πᾶν τὸ στέαρ τοῦ
μόσχου τοῦ τῆς ἁμαρτίας
περιελεῖ ἀπ᾽ αὐτοῦ | Lev 4:8a | ואת כל חלב פר החטאת
ירים ממנו |
| And he shall take from it all the fat of the calf of the sin offering. | | And he shall remove all the fat from the ox of the sin offering. |

---

[6]G. Beer (*Der Text des Buches Hiob Untersucht* [Marburg: N. G. Elwertsche Verlagsbuchhandlung, 1897] 1-2) suggests that ἔργα μεγάλα ἦν αὐτῷ is original and καὶ ὑπηρεσία πολλὴ
σφόδρα is Theodotion. He reasons further that ἐπὶ τῆς γῆς comes from באדמה(ר)=בה. This
requires quite a bit of rearrangement and does not explain ἦν αὐτῷ, which was probably
supplied simply to make the interpolation ἐπὶ τῆς γῆς complete.

[7]Dhorme, *Book of Job*, 4.

[8]S. R. Driver and G. B. Gray, *Book of Job*, Pt. II, 4.

καὶ ποιήσει τὸν μόσχον ὃν τρόπον ἐποίησεν τὸν *μόσχον* τὸν *τῆς ἁμαρτίας*	Lev 4:20a	ועשה לפר כאשר עשה לפר החטאת
And he shall do to the calf as he did to the calf of the sin offering.		And he shall do to the ox as he did to the ox of the sin offering.
καὶ τὸν *μόσχον* τὸν περὶ τῆς ἁμαρτίας	Lev. 8:2b	ואת פר החטאת
And the calf for the sin offering.		And the ox for the sin offering.
οὕτως ποιήσεις τῷ *μόσχῳ* τῷ ἑνὶ	Num 15:11a	ככה יעשה לשור האחד
Thus you shall do to the one calf.		Thus shall it be done for each ox.

These verses account for both the type of offering and the number of animals to be offered.[9] Beer generally agrees, although he does not refer to it as a specific borrowing.

G has added the sin-offering because in his understanding of the priestly legislation of the Pentateuch, the sin-offering was needed in addition to the burnt-offering to expiate sins which Job's children may have committed.[10]

The phrase περὶ τῶν ψυχῶν αὐτῶν is rare enough, and in the Pentateuch it is always related in a technical sense to כפר.[11] There are six occurrences in the Pentateuch.[12] At Num 6:11 and 15:28, the sin offering is involved.

καὶ ποιήσει ὁ ἱερεὺς μίαν περὶ ἁμαρτίας καὶ μίαν εἰς ὁλοκαύτωμα	Num 6:11a	ועשה הכהן אחד לחטאת ואחד לעלה
καὶ ἐξιλάσεται περὶ αὐτοῦ ὁ ἱερεὺς περὶ ὧν ἥμαρτεν περὶ τῆς ψυχῆς	Num 6:11b	וכפר עליו מאשר חטא על הנפש
And the priest shall offer one for a sin offering and the other as a whole burnt offering, and the priest shall		And the priest shall offer one as a sin offering and the other as a burnt offering and shall make atonement for

---

[9]See further Lev 8:14; 16:3; Num 28:12, 14.

[10]My translation of Beer, *Der Text*, 2.

[11]For uses of this Greek phrase without reference to sacrifice see Josh 9:24; Esth 7:7 (א^{c.a}); 9:16 (א^{c.a}); Prov 7:23; Sir 4:20; 1 Macc 3:21; 12:51.

[12]Exod 30:15, 16 (ὑμῶν not αὐτῶν); Lev 17:11 (ὑμῶν); Num 6:11; 15:28; 35:31. The last three have no pronoun.

make atonement for him for the sin he committed by reason of the dead person.		him for the sin he committed by reason of the dead person.

καὶ ἐξιλάσεται ὁ ἱερεὺς περὶ τῆς ψυχῆς τῆς ἀκουσιασθείσης   Num 15:28a   וכפר הכהן על הנפש השגגת בחטאה

And the priest shall make atonement for the soul of the one who sinned ignorantly.

And the priest shall make atonement for the person who sinned inadvertently.

Even though περὶ τῆς ψυχῆς in Num 6:11a has a different meaning from Num 15:28a, the phrases are identical in both Hebrew and Greek. It would appear that the stylistic περὶ τῶν ψυχῶν αὐτῶν which would translate על נפשיהם, has been brought into Job 1:5 to complete the technical terminology for the specific offering Job presented. Gerleman calls this an explanatory addition, but it is interesting to note that the particular offering that has been added is the sin offering (Lev 4:14), which covers the sin of ignorance in keeping with the situation in Job 1.[13]

§4. Job 1:7c

This verse contains an amplification influenced by other passages in Job.

περιελθὼν τὴν γῆν καὶ ἐμπερι-   1:7c   משוט בארץ ומהתהלך בה
πατήσας τὴν ὑπ᾽ οὐρανὸν πάρειμι

I have come from going through-out the land and walking back and forth on the earth.

From going up and down the land and walking in it.

The parallel passage in 2:2 is treated quite differently in G, which shows that the G-translator does not feel the need to make the same lexical choices for the same Hebrew words, a characteristic of later revisers.

διαπορευθεὶς τὴν ὑπ᾽ οὐρανὸν   2:2c   משט בארץ ומהתהלך בה
καὶ ἐμπεριπατήσας τὴν σύμ-πασαν πάρειμι

I have come from going through-out the earth and walking back and forth in the entire land.

From going up and down the land and walking in it.

---

[13]G. Gerleman, Studies in the LXX. I, The Book of Job (LUÅ, N.F.I. 43.2, 1946) 12.

The unique treatment of ὑπ' οὐρανόν in Job calls for an examination of its occurrences throughout the book. Dhorme notes that this phrase normally paraphrases הארץ.[14] The old Greek of Job does indeed paraphrase ארץ by the definite article and ὑπ' οὐρανόν six times out of 12 (2:2; 9:6; 18:4; 38:18; 38:24; 38:33). In addition, the בה of 1:7c has ארץ for its antecedent and is translated τὴν ὑπ' οὐρανόν. There is a Hebrew phrase, however, that has been translated literally in G and has in turn become the stock phrase used eight times for ארץ. In Job 41:3b, תחת כל השמים לי הוא is translated εἰ πᾶσα ἡ ὑπ' οὐρανὸν ἐμή ἐστιν. This Hebrew phrase appears also in 28:24b. The G and Hebrew equivalents are difficult to determine, but an examination of the elements will clear them up.

αὐτὸς δὲ οἶδεν τὸν τόπον αὐτῆς	28:23b	והוא ידע את מקומה
αὐτὸς γὰρ τὴν ὑπ' οὐρανὸν πᾶσαν ἐφορᾷ	28:24a	כי הוא לקצות הארץ יביט
εἰδὼς τὰ ἐν τῇ γῇ πάντα	28:24b	תחת כל השמים יראה
And he knows its place. For he sees everything under heaven, knowing all the things in the earth.		And he knows its place. For he looks to the ends of the earth and sees all that is under the heavens.

Parts of cola 24a and 24b have been reversed. Ἐφορᾶν translates ראה in Job (five times outside this passage). Εἰδεῖν appears quite frequently in Job under various forms and usually translates ידע (never נבט). The εἰδὼς of 24b is surely translating ידע of 23b a second time. The reason for the reversal is probably to give the first position to heaven and the second to earth.[15]

The Hebrew phrase תחת השמים also appears in Exod 17:14; Deut 25:19; 29:19.[16] All three texts refer to blotting out a name מתחת השמים, for which the LXX has ἐκ τῆς ὑπὸ τὸν οὐρανόν. Τὴν ὑπ' οὐρανόν has a good ring to it for the translator, who uses it in the Book of Job for the dwelling place of man. He has a precedent for the idea expressed in Hebrew by תחת השמים in Job itself and in the Pentateuch. Therefore, he has not coined a phrase but borrowed one.

§5. Job 1:14b

An interpolation occurs here to harmonize parallel passages.

τὰ ζεύγη τῶν βοῶν ἠροτρία καὶ	1:14b	הבקר היו חרשות

---

[14]Dhorme, *Book of Job*, 6.
[15]Yet the translator has no problem with earth-heaven in 1:7; 5:10; 34:13.
[16]Other later references are Eccl 1:13; 3:1; Dan 9:12; and in Greek Bar 5:3.

αἱ θήλειαι ὄνοι ἐβόσκοντο   1:14c   והאתנות רעות
ἐχόμεναι αὐτῶν   על ידיהם
The yokes of oxen were plow-   The oxen were plowing, and
ing, and the she-asses were   the she-asses were grazing be-
grazing beside them.   side them.

ζεύγη βοῶν πεντακόσια   1:3c   וחמש מאות צמד בקר
ὄνοι θήλειαι νομάδες πεντα-   1:3d   וחמש מאות אתונות
κόσιαι
Five hundred yoke of oxen and   And five hundred yoke of oxen
five hundred she-asses of the   and five hundred she-asses.
pastures.

ζεύγη βοῶν χίλια   42:12d   ואלף צמד בקר
ὄνοι θήλειαι νομάδες χίλιαι   42:12e   ואלף אתונות
A thousand yoke of oxen and   A thousand yoke of oxen and
a thousand she-asses of the   a thousand she-asses.
pastures.

Beer has already noted the source of this addition, "τὰ ζεύ. = צמד ist aus 1, 3,"[17] but he does not mention its occurrence in 42:12. The restoration of Job's fortunes in chap. 42 is stated in doubled terms. His five hundred yoke of oxen become a thousand, and the number of female asses increases twofold. The presence of צמד in these two places (and only these two) in conjunction with בקר and a list of animals prompts the translator to harmonize by inserting ζεύγη in 1:14b.

§6. *Job 1:15a, 17b, c*

The treatment of this passage by the G-translator is probably not a direct interpolation. The influence of Hebrew phraseology elsewhere, however, has apparently affected his dealing with the words under consideration.

καὶ ἐλθόντες οἱ αἰχμαλωτεύ-   1:15a   ותפל שבא ותקחם
οντες ἠχμαλώτευσαν αὐτάς
And when the despoilers came,   And the Sabaeans fell upon
they carried them off.   them and captured them.

Gerleman argues tht the translator of Job has simplified or adapted certain words to make them more meaningful to non-Semitic readers. He then gives 1:15 as a case in point. "The two nomad tribes the Sabaeans and the Chaldeans, who robbed Job's herds, are apparently unknown to the

[17]Beer, *Der Text*, 7.

Greek translator, and he simplifies the matter for himself and for his readers by generalization."[18] How Gerleman can say that the Sabaeans were unknown to the translator, when in 6:19 he treats שבא as a *nomen gentilicum* (Σαβῶν), is strange indeed. He points this out himself but explains its transliteration there on the basis of the parallel תמא.[19] Gerleman could have spared himself this contradiction had he taken note of Dhorme's observation long ago: "G connects שבא with שבה 'to take captive.' Hence οἱ αἰχμαλωτεύοντες."[20] Schleusner also has: "שְׁבָא, i.e. *Sabaei*. Job I, 15. Οἱ αἰχμαλωτεύοντες. Appellativum pro proprio reddiderunt: nam שְׁבָא est *abducere in captivitatem*. Eckermanno שֹׁבָה legisse videntur, vel שָׁבָה, *caterva praedonum homines captivos abducentium*. שָׁבָה- *in captivitatem abduco*."[21]

    G handles 1:17 in a similar manner.

οἱ ἱππεῖς ἐποίησαν ἡμῖν κεφαλὰς γ´	1:17b	כשדים שמו שלשה ראשים
καὶ ἐκύκλωσαν τὰς καμήλους καὶ ᾐχμαλώτευσαν αὐτάς	1:17c	ויפשטו על הגמלים ויקחום
The horsemen divided into three groups against us, encircled the camels, and took them away.		The Chaldaeans divided into three groups, seized the camels, and took them away.

The reason שבא is transliterated in 6:19 is that it there represents the country. The treatment of שבא as οἱ αἰχμαλωτεύοντες in 1:15 and כשדים as οἱ ἱππεῖς derives from the designation of these as types of marauders. As Dhorme points out, "The Sabaeans of v. 15 denote rather Arabic plunderers, whereas the Chaldaeans are Aramaean plunderers. The former came up from the south, the latter spring from the east and north."[22] At the same time, the choice of the substantive οἱ αἰχμαλωτεύοντες for שבא has come about, as Dhorme suggests, because of its association by the translator with שבה. Likewise the verb ᾐχμαλώτευσαν in both 1:15a and 1:17c for לקח was chosen because of the Hebrew idiom relating "capturers" and "capturing." 2 Chr 6:36 gives an example of this idiom.

παραδώσεις αὐτοὺς κατὰ πρόσωπον ἐχθρῶν καὶ	2 Chr 6:36b	ונתתם לפני אויב ושבום שוביהם אל ארץ רחוקה

[18]Gerleman, *Studies in the LXX*, 33.

[19]Ibid.

[20]Dhorme, *Book of Job*, 9.

[21]I. F. Schleusner, *Novus thesaurus philologico-criticus sive lexicon in LXX et reliquos interpretes graecos ac scriptores apocryphos Veteris Testamenti* (5 Vols.; Leipzig: In Libraria Weidmannia, 1821) 1. 102.

[22]Dhorme, *Book of Job*, 11. In light of what G did with שבא/שבה, כשדים may also have been read פרשים. Cf. Ezek 23:6, 12, 14-19; 26:7; Hab 1:6-8.

αἰχμαλωτεύσουσιν οἱ αἰχμαλωτεύοντες αὐτοὺς εἰς γῆν ἐχθρῶν εἰς γῆν μακρὰν ἢ ἐγγύς	או קרובה
You will deliver them before their enemies, and their captors will carry them off to a hostile land, to a land far or near.	And you deliver them up to the enemy, so that their captors carry them off to a land far or near.

Variations on this construction are found in several places in the OT.[23] The Hebrew expression is common enough to justify its inclusion here by the translator as an explanation of שבא and the complementary verb ᾐχμαλώτευσαν for לקח.

§7. *Job 1:16b*

The approach to this verse is a little different in that it deals with an omission rather than an addition.

πῦρ ἔπεσεν ἐκ τοῦ οὐρανοῦ 1:16b καὶ κατέκαυσεν τὰ πρόβατα	אש אלהים נפלה מן השמים ותבער בצאן
Fire fell from heaven and burned up the sheep.	The fire of God fell from heaven and burned up the flock.

אש אלהים is translated simply by πῦρ. This omission is taken by Gerleman as a theological preoccupation. He says:

> The translator does not content himself with denouncing Satan as the ulterior cause of Job's suffering, by his incitement of God. According to him, it was from beginning to end, Satan's own work. A similar tendency to acquit God is manifested in 1,16, where it is related how "the fire of God" fell from heaven and consumed Job's sheep and servants. The LXX for אש אלהים, have only πῦρ.[24]

Gard argues in the same way under the chapter heading, "Portrayals of God as the Agent of Destruction or the Persecutor of Man Avoided or Changed by the Translator."[25] The description of this omission as a theological tendency will not stand up. Fire from or of Yahweh occurs in a judgmental sense at Gen 19:24; Lev 10:2; Num 11:1, 3. It also occurs in the confrontation between Elijah and the prophets of Baal in 1 Kgs 18:38. In each case, the LXX translates fully, indicating no hesitancy in attributing such judgment to God.

---

[23]See 2 Chr 6:36; 28:5, 11, 17; Ps 68:19; Isa 14:2; Judg 5:12; 1 Kgs 8:46 (parallel to 2 Chr 6:36).

[24]Gerleman, *Studies in the LXX*, 58.

[25]Gard, *The Exegetical Method*, 61.

The only place in Hebrew outside this passage where אש אלהים occurs is 2 Kgs 1:12. The story there involves the sending of captains to capture Elijah. Three times the statement is made that ותרד אש מן השמים ותאכל אתו. Fire from heaven is mentioned in this passage a total of five times, but only once is אלהים used with אש (1:12). Some Hebrew manuscripts do not have אלהים.[26] The five occurrences of אש מן השמים are translated uniformly as πῦρ ἐκ τοῦ οὐρανοῦ. The one occurrence of אלהים with אש is not present in G. The only Greek available for this passage is a member of the KR recension (γδ′). If there had been an אלהים present in the *Vorlage*, it surely would have been translated. Among sources dependent on the Greek, אלהים is reflected only in the Armenian (a hexaplaric witness) and the Syro-hexapla. In the latter, "God" is under an asterisk.[27] This is quite strong evidence that the אלהים has come in through dittography or confusion with אש אלהים.[28] For this reason Gray argues that אלהים may have been originally absent at both Job 1:16b and 2 Kgs 1:12:

> With the combination of the two definitions of the lightning-fire found here in H, but not in G, from which אלהים is absent, cf. 2 K. 1:12b in most Hebrew MSS (but 11 MSS and also G T V om. אלהים), 1 K. 18:38 (G L, but not H); . . . As in 2 K. 1:12b, so here the shorter text of G may be the original.[29]

This opinion may indeed be correct, but it is also possible that Job 1:16b is shorter because the translator of Job was thinking of the vivid description of fire falling from heaven at Elijah's command (in Hebrew) and accordingly followed a shorter text there in omitting אלהים.

§8. *Job 1:20b*

One word has been added in this verse.

οὕτως ἀναστὰς 'Ιὼβ διέρρηξεν τὰ ἱμάτια ἑαυτοῦ	1:20a	ויקם איוב ויקרע את מעלו
καὶ ἐκείρατο τὴν κόμην τῆς κεφαλῆς	1:20b	ויגז את ראשו
So Job arose, tore his garments, and shaved the hair of his head.		Then Job arose, tore his garment, and shaved his head.

---

[26] Kittel, *BHK*, 557.

[27] Brooke, *et al.*, *The Old Testament in Greek*, 2. 300. See also A. Rahlfs, *Septuaginta-Studien* (Göttingen: Vandenhoeck & Ruprecht, 1904) 1. 48.

[28] Is Rev 20:9, καὶ κατέβη πῦρ ἐκ τοῦ οὐρανοῦ καὶ κατέφαγεν αὐτούς, following this KR rendering?

[29] Gray, *Book of Job*, Pt. II, 8.

Beer believes the addition of κόμην is to explain the Hebrew, but the Greek idiom does not require it.[30] Gerleman calls κόμην a "pedantic addition," but there may be more behind this than mere spontaneous expansion by the translator.[31]

There are two Pentateuchal passages that involve treatment of the hair.

οὐ ποιήσετε σισόην ἐκ τῆς Lev 19:27a   לא תקפו פאת
κόμης τῆς κεφαλῆς ὑμῶν   ראשכם
(For translation, see discus-   (For translation, see discussion.)   sion.)

τρέφων *κόμην* τρίχα κεφαλῆς Num 6:5b   גדל פרע שער ראשו
Caring for the long hair of   He shall let the hair of his
his head.   head grow long.

The Hebrew of Lev 19:27a says literally, "You shall not go around the sides of your head." The *NAB* has "Do not clip your hair at the temples." G is more difficult because of the word σισόην. Liddell-Scott have only: "LXX *Le*. 19.27; Phaselite word acc. to Hsch."[32] Lee-Brenton translates, "Ye shall not make a round cutting of the hair of your head . . . ."[33] The LXX of Lev 19:27a has made ראשכם more explicit. In Num 6:5b, κόμην stands for פרע and τρίχα for שער.

The word κόμης appears in Job 16:12 where G and Hebrew have:

λαβών με τῆς κόμης διέτιλεν 16:12b   ואחז בערפי ויפצפצני
He took me by the hair and   He seized me by the neck and
plucked it out.   dashed me to pieces.

The translation of ערף by κόμης prompts Schleusner to say: "עֹרֶף, *cervix*. Job. XVI, 12. Λαβών με τῆς κόμης, ubi aequipollentes formulas metaphoricas, *prehendere cervicem alicuius*, ac *tenere aliquem coma*, pro more suo, de sensu tantum solliciti, permutarunt."[34] The translator, however, may be reading a transposition of this word ערף (פרע) and, therefore, translating as in Num 6:5b. Κόμης is supplied in Lev 19:27a as it is in Job 1:20. In Num 6:5b, a section dealing with the Nazarite vow, κόμην is an interpretation of פרע. The same is probably true in Job 16:12 as well. The translator

---

[30]Beer, *Der Text*, 8. Jer 7:29 has κεῖρε τὴν κεφαλήν σου for the Hebrew גזי נזרך. The Hebrew should mean something like, "Shave off your consecrated hair."

[31]Gerleman, *Studies in the LXX*, 12.

[32]Liddell-Scott-Jones-McKenzie, *A Greek-English Lexicon* (9th ed.; Oxford: Clarendon Press, 1940) 1601.

[33]L. C. Lee-Brenton (trans.), *The Septuagint Version of the Old Testament* (London: Bagster, 1844) 155.

[34]Schleusner, *Novus thesaurus*, 3. 354.

of Job may be adding this word simply for explanation, but the two passages in the Pentateuch and one in Job may have influenced his thinking. Certainly the practice had already been followed before the translator of Job did his work.

§9. Job 1:21d

The translator has added a full line to this verse.

ὁ κύριος ἔδωκεν ὁ κύριος ἀφείλατο	1:21c	יהוה נתן ויהוה לקח
ὡς τῷ κυρίῳ ἔδοξεν οὕτως ἐγένετο	1:21d	
εἴη τὸ ὄνομα κυρίου εὐλογημένον	1:21e	יהי שם יהוה מברך

The Lord gave; the Lord has taken away. As it seemed good to the Lord, so it has come to pass. May the name of the Lord be blessed.	Yahweh has given and Yahweh has taken. May the name of Yahweh be blessed.

This statement forms a little homily on the sovereignty of God.[35] The impersonal use of δοκεῖν for ישר בעיני appears in Josh 9:25 and Jer 27:5.

ὡς ἀρέσκει ὑμῖν καὶ ὡς δοκεῖ ὑμῖν ποιήσατε ἡμῖν	Josh 9:25b	כטוב וכישר בעיניך לעשות לנו עשה
As it pleases you, and as it seems right to you, do to us.		Do to us as it appears good and right in your sight to do.
καὶ δώσω αὐτὴν ᾧ ἐὰν δόξῃ ἐν ὀφθαλμοῖς μου	Jer 27:5b (LXX 34:5b)	ונתתיה לאשר ישר בעיני
And I shall give it to whomever it seems right to me.		And I give it to whomever it seems right to me.

Δοκεῖν is used for אם על המלך טוב in Esth 1:19; 3:9; 5:4; 8:5; and for כטוב בעיניכם in Esth 8:8. In Θ-Daniel, δοκεῖν is used to translate צבא four times (4:14, 22, 29; 5:21).[36] The old Greek at Dan 4:17 has καὶ ὅσα ἂν θέλῃ ποιεῖ ἐν αὐτοῖς. This idiom appears to have gained more currency by the time of the translation of some of the later books into Greek. The translation of Job in old Greek is generally contemporary with the

---

[35] Beer (Der Text, 8) says: "In M bilden יהי שם יהוה מברך und יהוה נתן ויהוה לקח einen Vers, in dem לקח u. מברך mit einander reimen. Das + Gs nach לקח ist ein innergriechischer Zusatz."

[36] See Heater, ("A Septuagint Translation Technique," 46-53) for a discussion of the nature of "Theodotion"-Daniel.

"Theodotion"-Daniel.[37] God's sovereignty over human affairs is being presented in Daniel 4 and 5. and the same idea is set forth in Job 1:21.

The second half of the colon, οὕτως ἐγένετο, should represent כן היה, if there were Hebrew behind it.[38] This phrase is similar to Gen 1:9 where ויהי כן is translated καὶ ἐγένετο οὕτως. There is probably no direct borrowing at this point, but the influence of Gen 1:9 and Daniel 4 and 5 is very possible. To the G-translator, God's power was being displayed in these destructive events just as surely as in the creation events of Genesis 1 and in the control of Nebuchadnezzar's kingdom in Daniel 4 and 5. This gloss alone should discourage scholars from attempting to find evidence that the G-translator was trying to avoid the attribution of such works to God.

§ 10. Job 1:22

ἐν τούτοις πᾶσιν τοῖς συμβε-βηκόσιν αὐτῷ	1:22a	בכל זאת
οὐδὲν ἥμαρτεν Ἰὼβ ἐναντίον τοῦ κυρίου	1:22b	לא חטא איוב
καὶ οὐκ ἔδωκεν ἀφροσύνην τῷ θεῷ	1:22c	ולא נתן תפלה לאלהים

In all these things that happened to him, Job did not sin before the Lord, nor did he say anything disrespectful to God.

In all this, Job did not sin, nor did he say anything disrespectful to God.

The first addition, τοῖς συμβεβηκόσιν αὐτῷ, shows up also at 2:10 and 42:11.

ἐν πᾶσιν τούτοις τοῖς συμβε-βηκόσιν αὐτῷ	2:10d	בכל זאת
οὐδὲν ἥμαρτεν Ἰὼβ τοῖς χείλεσιν ἐναντίον τοῦ θεοῦ	2:10e	לא חטא איוב בשפתיו

In all these things that happened to him, Job did not sin with his lips before God.

In all this, Job did not sin with with his lips.

ἤκουσαν δὲ πάντες οἱ ἀδελφοὶ αὐτοῦ καὶ αἱ ἀδελφαὶ αὐτοῦ	42:11a	ויבאו אליו כל אחיו וכל אחיתיו
πάντα τὰ συμβεβηκότα αὐτῷ	42:11b	
καὶ ἐθαύμασαν ἐπὶ πᾶσιν οἷς	42:11f	וינחמו אתו על כל הרעה

[37] For other lexical choices common to both the old and new Greek of Job, see Heater, "A Septuagint Translation Technique," 41.

[38] כן היה does appear in Gen 41:13 but is translated in a different way.

ἐπήγαγεν αὐτῷ ὁ κύριος   אשר הביא יהוה עליו

Then all his brothers and sis- / Then all his brothers and sis-
ters heard all that had happened / ters came to him, and they com-
to him, and they marvelled at / forted him about all the evil
all that the Lord had brought / that Yahweh had brought upon
upon him. / him.

ἀκούσαντες δὲ οἱ τρεῖς φίλοι   2:11a   וישמעו שלשת רעי
αὐτοῦ τὰ κακὰ πάντα τὰ ἐπελ-   איוב את כל הרעה הזאת
θόντα αὐτῷ   הבאה עליו

And when his three friends / And Job's three friends heard
heard of all the evil that had / of all this evil that had come
come upon him. / upon him.

Dhorme believes G has interpreted בכל זאת wrongly:

> We have here the author's judgment on Job's conduct. The expression בכל זאת
> "in all that" is ambiguous. G implies that it is a question of all the circumstances
> which have just been narrated. This is also the opinion of Schlottmann, Hitzig,
> and Duhm. But in 2:10 the complement "by his lips" proves that the author has
> in view the sin of the spoken word, and that consequently "in all that" is an
> allusion to what immediately precedes, i.e. to the words of Job. Moreover, Satan
> has spoken about the possibility of bringing a curse to the lips of the holy man.
> His failure is evident.[39]

But the context of 2:10 is different from that of 1:22, for in 2:10 Job is
responding to his wife's urging to curse God, the very thing Satan had said
he would do under the right circumstances (1:11). In 1:22, on the contrary,
he is responding to the calamitous news of the destruction of his family and
goods. Thus the בכל זאת of 2:10 has a different antecedent from that of
1:22, but G has made the antecedent uniform for 1:22 and 2:10, and has
interpolated the whole phrase into 42:11.

     The question now arises: Why has the translator introduced this
phrase? It may have been inserted in 1:22 simply as a literary device and
then placed in the other two passages to harmonize. If so, it would be what
de Waard calls implicit statements in the source language becoming explicit
statements in the receptor language.[40] Yet it is also likely that the Hebrew
כל הרעה הזאת הבאה עליו of 2:11a is being anticipated at 1:22a, from
which it was then apparently borrowed for 2:10 and 42:11.[41]

[39]Dhorme, Book of Job, 14.
[40]J. De Waard, "Translation Techniques Used by the Greek Translators of Ruth," Bib 54
(1973) 503-506.
[41]Beer (Der Text, 9) says: "Nach זאת G + τοῖς συμβεβηκόσιν αὐτῷ s. ⸗ [Syriac] (bei
[Jerome]¹·² nur his s. ⸗ =הבאה עליו vgl. 2,11." This phrase is used elsewhere. Gen 42:29 has
πάντα τὰ συμβάντα (D^{sil}EFLM rell) and πάντα τὰ συμβεβηκότα (Adhlp). Josh 2:23 has πάντα
τὰ συμβεβηκότα (B) and πάντα τὰ συμβάντα (Ngn).

The second addition, ἐναντίον τοῦ κυρίου, occurs also in 2:10e as ἐναντίον τοῦ θεοῦ. Gard's explanation of this addition in 2:10e is that:

> The translator felt that there could be the possibility of Job's having sinned inwardly in his thoughts. He therefore eliminates such a possibility by adding the phrase ἐναντίον τοῦ θεοῦ "in the presence of God" to show that Job's integrity is without blemish and that sin is an offence before God.[42]

Gray refers to it merely as an amplification.[43] Gard's treatment of ἐναντίον has not taken into consideration its use elsewhere in the LXX. Liddell-Scott do give for the preposition the first meaning of "opposite, face to face" or "before." The second meaning, however, has the hostile sense of "opposing" or "contrary." Both meanings also exist in the adverbial usage.[44] There are thirteen passages in the LXX where ἁμαρτάνειν ἐναντίον τοῦ κυρίου (twice τοῦ θεοῦ) occurs. The normal translation is "against." Israel's theology did not include a concept of sin in the presence of God which was not also against him.[45]

Gard's whole point is based on the presence of בשפתיו in 2:10e, but that point is blunted by the fact that ἐναντίον is introduced at 1:22b without the presence of בשפתיו, at least in the majority of the manuscripts of the MT. The G-translator is not at all trying to make sure that Job has not sinned inwardly in his thoughts as opposed to external speech. He is simply pointing in the direction of the sin. The addition at 1:22b and its harmonistic insertion at 2:10e probably reflect the same stylistic usage employed elsewhere in the LXX. It is of further interest that of the thirteen references mentioned above which have a Hebrew *Vorlage* only one has לאלהים. The rest have ליהוה or ביהוה. The one exception is Gen 39:9 where Joseph refuses to sin against God (לאלהים, ἐναντίον τοῦ θεοῦ). It may be possible that the לאלהים in 1:22c reminded the translator of the well-known Joseph story and thus had some bearing on the addition.

§11. Job 2:3

The first item in this verse is not an interpolation but a method of translating.

προσέσχες οὖν τῷ θεράποντί μου 2:3b 'Ιώβ	השמת לבך אל עבדי איוב
Therefore, have you considered my servant Job?	Have you considered my servant Job?

---

[42]Gard, *Exegetical Method*, 28.
[43]Gray, *Book of Job*, Pt. II, 10.
[44]Liddell-Scott, *A Greek-English Lexicon*, 554-555.
[45]Gen 39:9; Deut 1:41; 9:16; 20:18; 1 Sam 7:6; 2 Chr 12:2; Jer 3:25; 8:14; 14:20; 16:10; Bar 1:17; 3:2, 4; cf. Ps 51:6.

προσέσχες τῇ διανοίᾳ σου κατὰ 1:8b   השמת לבך על עבדי איוב
τοῦ παιδός μου ʼ Ἰώβ
Have you set your mind against   Have you considered my servant
my servant Job?   Job?

Προσέσχες τῇ διανοίᾳ in 1:8b is good classical idiom (though often
with τὸν νοῦν). It is also true that προσέχειν alone is used with the
sense of "to regard" or "take heed" (as in 2:3; 7:17), but more rarely.[46]
However, the LXX normally translates the various constructions of the
Hebrew phrase שים לב in a number of ways such as νοεῖν . . . καρδία
(Isa 47:7), λαμβάνειν . . . εἰς τὴν διάνοιαν (Isa 57:11), ἀναλαμβάνειν . . .
ἐν καρδίᾳ (Job 22:22), τάσσειν εἰς τὴν καρδίαν (Ezek 44:5), τιθέναι τὰς
καρδίας (Hag 1:7), ὑποτάσσειν τὰς καρδίας (Hag 2:18), ἐφιστάναι τὸν
νοῦν (Isa 41:22), τιθέναι ἐπὶ ψυχήν (Isa 42:25), ἐκδέχεσθαι τῇ καρδίᾳ (Isa
57:1). The only two places outside of Job where שים is translated by
προσέχειν are Pentateuchal passages.

δς δὲ μὴ προσέσχεν τῇ δια- Exod 9:21a   ואשר לא שם לבו אל
νοίᾳ εἰς τὸ ῥῆμα κυρίου   דבר יהוה
And whoever did not regard   And whoever did not regard
the word of the Lord.   the word of Yahweh.

καὶ εἶπεν πρὸς αὐτοὺς προσ- Deut 32:46a   ויאמר אלהם
έχετε τῇ καρδίᾳ ἐπὶ πάντας   שימו לבבכם
τοὺς λόγους τούτους   לכל הדבוˮים
And he said to them, "Set   And he said to them, "Take
your heart on all these   to heart all the words."
words."

The paraphrase in Exod 9:21a is much like Job 1:8b. The Egyptian who did
not "carefully consider" the word of Yahweh lost his cattle in the plague of
hailstones. The translator of Job may have had these passages in mind
when he rendered 1:8b and 2:3b into Greek. He has chosen a Greek idiom,
but one that is used elsewhere in the LXX for this particular Hebrew
construction.

The differences in G between 1:8b and 2:3b are interesting. השמת לבך
is treated fully in 1:8b with προσέσχες τῇ διανοίᾳ, and the Hebrew על is
rendered κατά. G is saying: "Have you set your mind against my servant
Job?"[47] The use of κατά, incidentally, indicates that the G-translator was

---

[46]Liddell-Scott, *A Greek-English Lexicon*, 1512.

[47]Lee-Brenton (*The Septuagint Version of the Old Testament*, 665) ignores the κατὰ τοῦ
of 1:8b translating as he does 2:3b. Κατά with the genitive can indeed mean "in respect of,
concerning" (Liddell-Scott, *A Greek-English Lexicon*, 883), but that meaning is normally
reserved for κατά with the accusative as found in the very next colon. Admittedly, "against"
does not make as much sense, but it must be correct. The same thing probably holds true in
42:8 despite the Hebrew כעבדי.

reading על not אל, which shows up in fifteen manuscripts.[48] The reduction of the Greek question from προσέσχες τῇ διανοίᾳ (1:8b) to προσέσχες (2:3) and the addition of οὖν have probably come about because G sees progression between the two confrontations involving God and Satan.

There is an additional expansion at 2:3g.

| σὺ δὲ εἶπας τὰ ὑπάρχοντα αὐτοῦ 2:3g
διὰ κενῆς ἀπολέσαι
And you have told me to destroy
his material goods for no reason. | ותסיתני בו לבלעו חנם

Though you incited me against
him to destroy him without
cause. |

The G-translator has treated ותסיתני as σὺ δὲ εἶπας and expanded בו to τὰ ὑπάρχοντα αὐτοῦ. Gerleman has taken this as an effort on the part of the translator to soften the attribution of the incitement of Satan to God.[49] Dhorme argues along the same line: "G σὺ δὲ εἶπας τὰ ὑπάρχοντα αὐτοῦ διὰ κενῆς ἀπολέσαι softens the final phrase ותסיתני . . . חנם."[50] The Hebrew says literally, "And you incited me against him to swallow him up for no reason." בלע is usually treated literally in the LXX.[51] Job 2:3g is the only place in the LXX where the metaphorical significance is spelled out as ἀπολλύειν.[52] This, of course, is a valid translation, and the English versions have used similar phraseology.[53]

The problem with which the G-translator is faced is the fact that בלע is applied to Job. Whether it is translated literally (καταπίνειν) or meta-phorically (ἀπολλύειν), Job has not actually been swallowed up or destroyed. His oxen and asses have been destroyed (1:15), as have his flocks (1:16), and his camels (1:17), and his children (1:19), but not Job. The translator must provide a more appropriate object of this verb. He finds it in v 4.

| ὅσα ὑπάρχει ἀνθρώπῳ ὑπὲρ τῆς 2:4c
ψυχῆς αὐτοῦ ἐκτίσει
Whatever a man has he will give
as a ransom for his life. | וכל אשר לאיש
יתן בעד נפשו
And all a man has he will give
for his life. |

---

[48] B. Kennicott, *Vetus Testamentum Hebraicum cum variis lectionibus* (Oxford: Clarendon Press, 1780) 2. 478.

[49] Gerleman, *Studies in the LXX*, 57-58.

[50] Dhorme, *Book of Job*, 15.

[51] Some form of καταπίνειν or καταπονίζειν, 36 times of 48. Job has the greatest variety: ἀπολέσαι (2:3); ἔπαισας (10:8); οὐ γεύσεται (20:18); κατασιωπήσω (κατεπιώσω?) (37:20).

[52] Schleusner (*Novus thesaurus*, 5. 373) says: "Sed ibi ὑπάρχοντα αὐτοῦ de suo addidisse videntur, ut tolleretur ambiguitas, quae est in hebr. בלע et gr. ἀπολέσαι."

[53] *NAB:* "Although you incited me against him to ruin him without cause." *RSV* and *KJV:* "to destroy."

Satan provides an inclusive expression when he says וכל אשר לאיש. The
LXX elsewhere often translates כל אשר ל with πάντα τὰ ὑπάρχοντα
αὐτοῦ or a similar expression.[54] The translator has linked בו of v 3 with
כל אשר לאיש of v 4. In 2:3g, the G-translator applied it specifically to Job
(τὰ ὑπάρχοντα αὐτοῦ). In 2:4c, he follows the Hebrew in making it more
general (ὅσα), to be applied as a general principle to anyone. This insertion
of τὰ ὑπάρχοντα, therefore, provides a paraphrase to clear up the problem
of the object of ἀπολέσαι. It is not the translator's intention to exonerate
God but to harmonize this verse with the context.

§ 12. Job 2:8a

καὶ ἔλαβεν ὄστρακον ἵνα τὸν 2:8a
ἰχῶρα ξύῃ
καὶ ἐκάθητο ἐπὶ τῆς κοπρίας 2:8b
ἔξω τῆς πόλεως

ויקח לו חרש להתגרד בו

והוא ישב בתוך האפר

And he took a potsherd to scrape
away the pus and sat on the
dunghill outside the town.

And he took a potsherd to scrape
himself, and he was sitting in the
midst of the ashes.

φύρεται δέ μου τὸ σῶμα ἐν 7:5a
σαπρίᾳ σκωλήκων
τήκω δὲ βώλακας γῆς ἀπὸ 7:5b
ἰχῶρος ξύων

לבש בשרי רמה וגיש עפר

עורי רגע וימאס

My body is covered with the
corruption of worms, and I waste
away, scraping dirty scabs from
the pus.

My flesh is clothed with worms
and dirty scabs. My skin cracks
and festers (1. וימס).

The words ξύειν and ἰχῶρος appear only in these two verses in the
LXX. Ἀποξύειν occurs only in Lev 14:41, 42, 43 as a translation of קצע,
קצה.

καὶ ἀποξύσουσιν τὴν οἰκίαν Lev 14:41
ἔσωθεν κύκλῳ καὶ ἐκχε-
οῦσιν τὸν χοῦν ἔξω τῆς
πόλεως εἰς τόπον ἀκάθαρτον
καὶ λήμψονται λίθους ἀπε- Lev 14:42a
ξυσμένους στερεούς

ואת הבית יקצע מבית
סביב ושפכו את העפר אשר
הקצו אל מחוץ לעיר אל
מקום טמא
ולקחו אבנים אחרות

And they shall scrape off
the house all around the inside and empty the dust outside the city in an unclean

Then the inside of the house
shall be scraped round about,
and the plaster that has been
scraped off shall be emptied

[54]Cf. Gen 12:5; 13:6; 14:16; Job 15:29; 17:3; 18:7.

place. And they shall take
scraped foundation stones.

in an unclean place outside
the city. And other stones
shall be taken.

ἐὰν δὲ ἐπέλθῃ πάλιν ἀφὴ
καὶ ἀνατείλῃ ἐν τῇ οἰκίᾳ
μετὰ τὸ ἐξελεῖν τοὺς λίθους
καὶ μετὰ τὸ ἀποξυσθῆναι τὴν
οἰκίαν καὶ μετὰ τὸ ἐξαλειφ-
θῆναι

Lev 14:43

ואם ישוב הנגע
ופרח בבית
אחר חלץ את האבנים
ואחרי הקצות את הבית
ואחרי הטוח

And if the plague returns
and breaks out again in the
house after the stones have
been removed, the house
scraped and replastered.

And if the disease breaks
out again in the house after
the stones were taken away,
and the house scraped and
replastered.

Leviticus 13 deals with the subject of leprosy (צרעת) in humans. In the
latter part of Leviticus 14 instructions are given for the removal of a plague
in the walls of a house. The treatment is to scrape off the mortar or plaster
(עפר) and carry it to an unclean place outside the city. It would appear that
the translator considers Job's ailment to be in some way related to the
disease in Leviticus 13 and 14. This has influenced his translation of 2:8,
which has in turn affected his treatment of 7:5. Dhorme has already
discussed the fact that in 7:5, G takes ויגיש עפר from the first colon and
puts it in the second, translating βώλακας γῆς; רגע, he says, is being read
גרע and translated as ξύειν.[55] However, the reason רגע is being read גרע is
the desire of the translator to harmonize 7:5b with 2:8a and Lev 14:41. The
presence of the Hebrew להתגרד in 2:8a and יקצע in Lev 14:41 provides the
basis for the scraping, which is introduced from 2:8a into 7:5b. In the
leprosy context, the עפר had to be scraped off. Likewise, Job is made to
scrape off the גיש עפר in 7:5a, and this is accomplished by supplying ξύειν
from 2:8a.[56]

Ἰχῶρος is more difficult to explain. Beer wonders: "Ist für ἰχῶρος
([Jerome] saniem), dem in M nichts entsprechen würde, vielleicht χρωτὸς =
עורי zu lesen?"[57] Dhorme follows Beer on this point.[58] The word is used in
the LXX only at Job 2:8a and in 7:5b. Ἰχῶρα is supplied at 2:8a to provide
an object for the scraping. בו refers to the potsherd, and להתגרד, as a

[55] Dhorme, *Book of Job*, 100; so also Beer (*Der Text*, 45), who says: "Mit ξύω
([Syriac] ܘܢ ?ܐ. übersetzt G 2,8 גרד. Hier ist aber ξύων = גרע d.i. M רגע vgl. G Jer.
48,37 גרעה = ξυρηθήσεται."
[56] J. Ziegler ("Der textkritische Wert der Septuaginta des Buches Iob," *MBib* 2 [1934] 290)
has already noted the connection between 2:8 and 7:5.
[57] Beer, *Der Text*, 45.
[58] Dhorme, *Book of Job*, 100.

reflexive, needs no object. G has turned the reflexive into an active and provided an object in the "pus." From 2:8a, it is then imported to 7:5b as an interpretation of עורי, and Beer is not correct in assuming an original χρωτός for ἰχῶρος.

§13. Job 2:9

The addition inserted between the first and second half of v 9 has long intrigued students of the LXX. In spite of the fact that the expansion is neatly woven into the Greek text based on the MT, the evidence points to a hand later than that of the translator. Gray argues that the vocabulary "points strongly to a different hand" from that of the translator.[59] There are indeed five words, which, though they appear elsewhere in the LXX, occur only at 2:9 in Job, and three *hapax legomena*. Vocabulary counts are always a tenuous method for determining authorship, but they can form part of a cumulative argument.[60]

The most common attitude about this addition is to assign it to the imagination of the G-translator or later editor who, as Davidson says, felt "no doubt, nature and propriety outraged, that a woman should in such circumstances say so little."[61] Beer's position is: "Woher dieses + Gs, ist schwer zu sagen. Stammt es etwa aus dem selben Midrasch oder Targum, worauf der Zusatz Gs nach 42,17 zurückgeht?"[62] An examination of the passage, however, shows a general affinity to the rest of Job, and though the composition is probably by a later editor, the ideas come from the Book of Job. Gray points out that although the composer could have been working out of his overall knowledge of Hebrew-Job (cf. 7:2; 14:6; 39:3), the curious rendering of 7:5 shows a subsequent worker familiar with G-Job.[63] (In the phrase-by-phrase discussion that follows, the colon enumeration does not follow Rahlfs.)

χρόνου δὲ πολλοῦ προβεβη-   2:9a   ותאמר לו אשתו
κότος εἶπεν αὐτῷ ἡ γυνὴ αὐτοῦ

---

[59] Gray, *Book of Job*, lxxiii; "The Additions in the Ancient Greek Version of Job," *Exp* 19 (1920) 422-438. Gray gives words or phrases, one of which, εἰς τὸ κενόν, should not be included since κενά, διὰ κενῆς, εἰς κενόν, etc., appear 21 times in Job. The same is true of διανυκτερεύειν since νυκτερινός occurs four times in Job.

[60] Including up-to-date use of the computer, which has been employed in Pauline writings and most recently in the Book of Isaiah.

[61] A. B. Davidson, *A Commentary, Grammatical and Exegetical on the Book of Job with a Translation* (London: William and Norgate, 1862) Vol 1 (quoted in Gray, *The Book of Job*, Pt. I, 25).

[62] Beer, *Der Text*, 11.

[63] Gray, "The Additions in the Ancient Greek Version of Job," 435. Swete (*An Introduction to the Old Testament in Greek*, 256) assumes it to be original.

| And after much time had passed, his wife said to him. | And his wife said to him. |

This phrase is good classical idiom for the passing of time, but it is not so used in the LXX. A relatively common expression is that which occurs in Gen 18:11.

'Αβραὰμ δὲ καὶ Σάρρα πρεσ-	Gen 18:11	ואברהם ושרה
βύτεροι προβεβηκότες		זקנים באים
ἡμερῶν		בימים
And both Abraham and Sa-		And both Abraham and Sa-
rah were old, advanced in		rah were old, advanced in
days.		days.

Προβαίνειν is not used in the LXX with χρόνος except at 2:9a. The only reason for this insertion is the abruptness of the Hebrew. Job's wife speaks suddenly and harshly. This genitive absolute is added to soften her entrance on the stage and to provide a transition from Job's miserable situation to his wife's remarks.[64]

| μέχρι τίνος καρτερήσεις λέγων | 2:9b | עדך מחזיק בתמתך |
| How long will you be patient saying . . . ? | | Are you still holding to your innocence? |

G of 2:9b is a paraphrase of the Hebrew. There is a precedent in 2:3 where the same Hebrew phrase is translated ἔτι δὲ ἔχεται ἀκακίας, but the translator or editor has not chosen to use it. His rendering is a looser one.

ἰδοὺ ἀναμένω χρόνον ἔτι μικρὸν	2:9c
προσδεχόμενος τὴν ἐλπίδα τῆς	2:9d
σωτηρίας μου	
Look, I am waiting yet a little while,	
expecting the hope of my deliverance.	

The main thrust of this clause is that Job hopes to be delivered from his present situation. This hope is expressed in 13:16.

καὶ τοῦτό μοι ἀποβήσεται εἰς	13:16a	גם הוא לי לישועה
σωτηρίαν		
And this will result in deliverance for me.		This also will be my deliverance.

---

[64]A. Dillmann (Hiob [Leipzig: Hirzel, 1891] 18) says: "Die LXX, erklärend, schicken χρόνου δὲ πολλοῦ προβεβηκότος voraus."

Job argues that his ability to come before God and present his case is proof of his innocence. He will be vindicated in it. Paul's use of this clause in conjunction with his own trial (Phil 1:19) is a good commentary on the intent of this context in Job. Even though the point of 2:9d is somewhat different from that of 13:16a, the composer is putting into the mouth of Job's wife words Job will later use himself.

The idea of waiting for a period of time shows up also at 7:2, 3.

ἢ ὥσπερ μισθωτὸς ἀναμένων τὸν μισθὸν αὐτοῦ	7:2b	וכשכיר יקוה פעלו
οὕτως κἀγὼ ὑπέμεινα μῆνας κενούς	7:3a	כן הנחלתי לי ירחי שוא

Or as a hired servant waiting for his pay, thus I also have endured empty months.	As a hired servant waits for his pay, thus I am alotted months of emptiness.

In chap. 7, Job bemoans the life of humanity. He likens it to a term of military service, the days of a mercenary, a slave, and a hireling who waits (in 7:2 יקוה) for his pay.[65] Ἀναμένειν appears only in 7:2b and 2:9c. As in the case of 13:16, the intent in 2:9c is different from that in 7:2b, but the words are used against Job which he will later use of himself. Job will say in 7:3a: "I also have endured empty months as a hired servant *waiting* for his pay." In 13:16a, he avows: "This also will be my *deliverance*." In 2:9b, Job's wife says: "How long will you be patient saying, 'Look, I am *waiting* yet a little while, expecting the hope of my *deliverance*.'"

ἰδοὺ γὰρ ἠφάνισταί σου τὸ μνημόσυνον ἀπὸ τῆς γῆς	2:9e
υἱοὶ καὶ θυγατέρες ἐμῆς κοιλίας ὠδῖνες καὶ πόνοι	2:9f
οὓς εἰς τὸ κενὸν ἐκοπίασα μετὰ μόχθων	2:9g

For behold, your memorial
has disappeared from the earth,
even your sons and daughters,
the pains and labors of my
womb that I bore with sorrows
in vain.

When Bildad describes the plight of the wicked in chap. 18, he uses a number of calamities that inevitably befall those who sin against God. One of those is in 18:17a.

τὸ μνημόσυνον αὐτοῦ ἀπόλοιτο ἐκ γῆς	18:17a	זכרו אבד מני ארץ

---

[65]See Dhorme (*Book of Job*, 97) for a discussion of the Hebrew.

	18:17b	ולא שם לו על פני חוץ
May his memory perish from the earth.		His memory perishes from the earth, and he has no name in the land.

Although 18:17b does not appear in old Greek, the critical word μνημόσυνον is in 18:17a. The only other occurrence of this word in Job is at 2:9e. It would appear that 18:17a lies behind the line in 9e.

σύ τε αὐτὸς ἐν σαπρίᾳ σκω-   2:9h
λήκων κάθησαι διανυκτερεύων
αἴθριος
And you yourself are sitting
outside all night long in rot-
tenness of worms.

In chap. 7 Job is describing his own unhappy lot. That 7:5 forms a backdrop for G of 2:8 has already been indicated (§12).

φύρεται δέ μου τὸ σῶμα ἐν	7:5a	לבש בשרי רמה וגיש עפר
σαπρίᾳ σκωλήκων		
And my body is covered with the coruption of worms.		My flesh is clothed with worms and dirty scabs.

The corruption of worms is an expansion of the Hebrew רמה. Διανυκτερεύειν occurs in the LXX only here, but νυκτερινός is found four times in Job. In 7:3, 4, Job says:

νύκτες δὲ ὀδυνῶν δεδομέναι	7:3b	ולילות עמל מנו לי
μοί εἰσιν		
ἐὰν κοιμηθῶ λέγω πότε ἡμέρα	7:4a	אם שכבתי ואמרתי מתי
ὡς δ᾽ ἂν ἀναστῶ πάλιν πότε	7:4b	אקום ומדד ערב ושבעתי
ἑσπέρα		נדדים עדי נשף
And nights of pain have been appointed to me. When I lie down, I say, "When will it be day?" And when I rise up again, "When will it be evening?"		And nights of misery are appointed to me. If I lie down I say, "How long before I rise up?" But the night continues. I am full of restlessness until dawn.

The composer has drawn from 7:3, 4 the picture of dismal Job spending the night restlessly and covered with worms. Job's wife is thus made to taunt him with the misery he expresses in chap. 7.

κἀγὼ πλανωμένη καὶ λάτρις	2:9i
τόπον ἐκ τόπου καὶ οἰκίαν ἐξ	2:9j

οἰκίας
προσδεχομένη τὸν ἥλιον πότε   2:9k
δύσεται
ἵνα ἀναπαύσωμαι τῶν μόχθων   2:9*l*
μου καὶ τῶν *ὀδυνῶν* αἵ με νῦν
συνέχουσιν
And I am a wanderer and a
slave from place to place and
house to house,
waiting anxiously for the sun
to set,
that I might have rest from my
pains and toils which beset me.

Job's wife argues that her husband is not the only one who has suffered. In
7:2a, he complains that his suffering is like that of a slave (θεράπων) who
longs for the shade. In 2:9i, she reminds him that she also is like a slave
(λάτρις), who longs for the sun to set that she might have rest from her
troubles. Furthermore, in 30:16b, Job in his final speech says:

ἔχουσιν δέ με ἡμέραι *ὀδυνῶν*   30:16b   יאחזוני ימי עני
And days of pain seize me.   Days of affliction have seized
                                                me.

If days of pain have "seized" Job, his wife insists that μόχθων *and* ὀδυνῶν
have seized her. Her suffering is, therefore, worse than his.

ἀλλὰ εἰπόν τι ῥῆμα εἰς κύριον   2:9m   ברך אלהים ומת
καὶ τελεύτα
But say some word to the Lord   Bless (curse) God and die.
and die.

This is obviously a paraphrase of the Hebrew and, as in 2:9b, is rather
loose.

In conclusion, the general source of this "midrash" is to be found
within the sayings of the Book of Job itself. Job's wife becomes the distaff
adversary who reviles Job for his stubborn hope in the face of evident
futility and who insists that she is as much afflicted by the whole situation
as he. Words that appear elsewhere in the LXX but only here in Job are
προβαίνειν, καρτερεῖν, μόχθων, αἴθριος, δύειν. Words in 2:9 which appear
only in one or two other places in Job are: σκωλήκων (2), προσδέχεσθαι
(3), μνημόσυνον (1), κοπιᾶν (2), περιέρχεσθαι (1). As mentioned at the
beginning, vocabulary count is not a conclusive way to determine authorship. This vocabulary, even so, deserves consideration. The occurrence of
eight words in this addition not appearing elsewhere in Job seems to point

to a hand later than that of the translator. The fact that several of the above comparisons rest on the presupposition of an existing G-Job lends further credence to the theory of a later editor.

The insertion of the transitional time clause in 2:9 before εἶπεν αὐτῷ ἡ γυνὴ αὐτοῦ and ἀλλὰ before the last clause in 2:9e could be evidence either of a unified composition by the original translator or of a smoothing out of the text by the composer of these lines. If it was written by a later hand, as it probably was, the composer must have taken considerable liberty with the old Greek text lying before him to provide smooth transitional phrases for his inserted verse. In any event, the practice of reaching to other passages, so extensively carried on in the rest of Job, is in evidence here as well.

§14. Job 2:10c

εἰ τὰ ἀγαθὰ ἐδεξάμεθα ἐκ χειρὸς 2:10c	את הטוב נקבל מאת
κυρίου τὰ κακὰ οὐχ ὑποίσομεν	האלהים ואת הרע
οὐχ ὑποίσομεν	לא נקבל
If we have received good things from the hand of the Lord, should we not accept evil things?	We have received good things from God; should we not receive the evil?

The addition of ἐκ χειρός poses a problem for those who feel the translator is constantly concerned about anthropomorphisms, for he has not simply translated such a phrase as מיד יהוה but has supplied it. Gerleman gives one example of a paraphrastic translation of ידו as an indication of "dogmatic misgivings in the translator."[66] Actually, there are some seventeen times in Job when the Hebrew speaks of the hand of God. Three of these fall under asterisks, leaving fourteen translated by the old Greek. *Ten* of these fourteen are translated literally by the Greek. Gerleman defends his position by saying: "In less concrete contexts, on the other hand, the translator renders 'the hand of God' without paraphrasing *e.g.* in 2,5."[67] Gerleman apparently looks upon this addition in 2:10 with incredulity, for he says: "Sometimes the translator himself actually introduces such a faded metaphor into the text without any equivalent in the original *e.g.* in 2,10."[68]

The weight of the evidence points quite conclusively to the fact that the translator is not at all offended by this metaphor. Furthermore, its occurrence elsewhere in Scripture in a similar passage may have led to its inclusion in 2:10.

---

[66] Gerleman, *Studies in the LXX*, 58-59.

[67] Ibid. See H. Orlinsky ("Studies in the Septuagint of Job," *HUCA* 30 [1959] 163-167) for a detailed refutation of this type of argument.

[68] Gerleman, *Studies in the LXX*, 59.

ὅτι ἐπλήσθη ἡ ταπείνωσις αὐτῆς	Isa 40:2b	כי מלאה צבאה
λέλυται αὐτῆς ἡ ἁμαρτία	Isa 40:2c	כי נרצה עונה
ὅτι ἐδέξατο ἐκ χειρὸς κυρίου διπλᾶ τὰ ἁμαρτήματα αὐτῆς	Isa 40:2d	כי לקחה מיד יהוה כפלים בכל חטאתיה

Because her humiliation is completed, her sin has been put away; because she has received from the Lord's hand double for her sinful acts.

Because her servitude is completed, her iniquity has been pardoned; indeed she has received from Yahweh's hand double for all her sins.

This is the only other place in the LXX that speaks of receiving from the hand of the Lord. Jerusalem has received double punishment for her sins מיד יהוה, ἐκ χειρὸς κυρίου. Isa 40:1 also contains the exhortation נחמו נחמו עמי. In the prologue, though Job has not been punished for his sins, he has suffered physical calamities. Furthermore, his friends come to comfort him (לנחמו) in 2:11. All this may remind the translator of Isa 40:2. He then translates האלהים as κυρίου and inserts ἐκ χειρός. Both good and bad things come to Job from the hand of the Lord, just as the punishment upon Jerusalem was from his hand.

§15. Job 2:11

ἀκούσαντες δὲ οἱ τρεῖς φίλοι αὐτοῦ τὰ κακὰ πάντα τὰ ἐπελθόντα αὐτῷ	2:11a	וישמעו שלשת רעי איוב את כל הרעה הזאת הבאה עליו
παρεγένοντο ἕκαστος ἐκ τῆς ἰδίας χώρας πρὸς αὐτόν	2:11b	ויבאו איש ממקמו

And when his three friends heard of all the evil that had come upon him, they came to him, each one from his own country.

And the three friends of Job heard all this misfortune that had come upon him, and each came from his own place.

This verse was related along with 42:11 to 1:22 where harmonization was discussed relating to συμβεβηκότα.

ἤκουσαν δὲ πάντες οἱ αδελφοὶ αὐτοῦ καὶ αἱ ἀδελφαὶ αὐτοῦ πάντα τὰ συμβεβηκότα αὐτῷ καὶ ἦλθον πρὸς αὐτόν	42:11a 42:11b	ויבאו אליו כל אחיו וכל אחיתיו
ἐπὶ πᾶσιν οἷς ἐπήγαγεν αὐτῷ ὁ κύριος	42:11e	על כל הרעה אשר הביא יהוה עליו

And all his brothers and sis-
tes heard all the things that
had happened to him, and they
came to him . . . at all the
things that the Lord had
brought upon him.

And all his brothers and sis-
ters came to him . . . about
all the evil that Yahweh had
brought upon him.

Because a certain amount of harmonization is taking place between 1:22;
2:10, 11, and 42:11, הזאת is untranslated in 2:11a because it is absent in
42:11e. The πρὸς αὐτόν is added in 2:11b to agree wth 42:11b.

§16. Job 3:7, 8, 9

ἀλλὰ ἡ νὺξ ἐκείνη εἴη ὀδύνη	3:7a	הנה הלילה ההוא יהי גלמוד
καὶ μὴ ἔλθοι ἐπ᾽ αὐτὴν εὐφρο- σύνη μηδὲ χαρμονή	3:7b	אל תבא רננה בו
ἀλλὰ καταράσαιτο αὐτὴν ὁ καταρώμενος τὴν ἡμέραν ἐκείνην	3:8a	יקבהו אררי יום
ὁ μέλλων τὸ μέγα κῆτος χειρώ- σασθαι	3:8b	העתידים ערר לויתן
σκοτωθείη τὰ ἄστρα τῆς νυκτὸς ἐκείνης	3:9a	יחשכו כוכבי נשפו
ὑπομείναι καὶ εἰς φωτισμὸν μὴ ἔλθοι	3:9b	יקו לאור ואין
καὶ μὴ ἴδοι ἑωσφόρον ἀνατέλ- λοντα	3:9c	ואל יראה בעפעפי שחר

But may that night be pain, and
may no happiness or rejoicing
come on it; but may he who
curses that day curse it, he who
is ready to attack the great fish.
May the stars of that night be
darkened; may it wait, but not
come into light, and may it not
see the morning star arise.

Behold, may that night be bar-
ren; may no rejoicing come in
it. May those who curse the day
curse it, those who are prepared
to stir up Leviathan. May the
stars of its dawn be darkened;
may it wait for light but have
none, and may it not see the
eyelids of the dawn.

In 3:7b, רננה is translated twice, once as εὐφροσύνη and once as
χαρμονή. In 20:5, the same two Greek words translate רננה and שמחה.
The lexical choice at 20:5 may have been influenced by 3:7b. It is of further
interest to note that these Greek words often appear together.

συνεψήσθη χαρμοσύνη καὶ εὐφροσύνη ἐκ τῆς Μωαβ- είτιδος	Jer 48:33a (LXX 31:33a)	ונאספה שמחה וגיל מכרמל ומארץ מואב

Rejoicing and happiness have been swept out of Moab.

Rejoicing and exultation have been taken away from the fruitful field, the land of Moab.

φωνὴ εὐφροσύνης καὶ φωνὴ χαρμοσύνης
The sound of rejoicing and the sound of happiness.

Jer 33:11a (LXX 40:11a)

קול ששון וקול שמחה

The sound of exultation and the sound of rejoicing.

The occurrence of these same two Greek words together, even though the Hebrew behind them differs in each case, has probably influenced the translator to expand the single Hebrew word into this relatively common pair.[69] G-Job says now: "May neither happiness nor rejoicing come on that night," thus emphasizing the utter desolation of "that night."

In 3:8a, ἐκείνην is supplied from 3:7a. Since the night is qualified with a demonstrative in 3:7a, the translator wants the day to be so qualified in 3:8a. The result does not make sense, for the line now speaks of those who curse *that* day (i.e., of Job's birth) rather than of those who curse the day (any day).[70] Another interesting parallel that might possibly have influenced the G-translator of Job is Isa 27:1.

τῇ ἡμέρᾳ ἐκείνῃ ἐπάξει ὁ θεὸς τὴν μάχαιραν τὴν ἁγίαν καὶ τὴν μεγάλην καὶ τὴν ἰσχυρὰν ἐπὶ τὸν δράκοντα ὄφιν φεύγοντα ἐπὶ τὸν δράκοντα ὄφιν σκολιόν ἀνελεῖ τὸν δράκοντα
In that day, God will bring his holy, great, and strong sword upon the dragon, the fleeing serpent; upon the dragon, the crooked serpent; and he will destroy the dragon.

Isa 27:1

ביום ההוא יפקד יהוה
בחרבו הקשה והגדולה
והחזקה
על לויתן נחש ברח
ועל לויתן נחש עקלתון
והרג את התנין אשר בים

In that day, Yahweh will punish with his hard, great, and strong sword, Leviathan, the fleeing serpent, and Leviathan, the crooked serpent; and he will kill the sea creature that is in the sea.

The significance of "day" is, of course, different in Isaiah and in Job, but perhaps the presence of לויתן reminded the translator of Job of this passage and had some bearing on his choice of ἐκείνην.

The translation of לויתן in 3:8b is τὸ μέγα κῆτος. The other five occurrences of this word are translated in the LXX by δράκων (Isa

[69] The pair shows up also in Bar 2:23; 4:23.
[70] See M. H. Pope (*Job* [3d ed.; AB 15; Garden City, N.Y.: Doubleday, 1973] 30) for a discussion on the preference of יֹם over יום.

27:1[twice]; Ps 74:14; 104:26; Job 40:25). All kinds of creatures occur in the Book of Job and are variously translated, though most often by δράκων.[71] Elsewhere τὸ μέγα κῆτος is found only in Gen 1:21 and Jonah 2:1.

καὶ ἐποίησεν ὁ θεὸς τὰ κήτη τὰ μεγάλα	Gen 1:21a	ויברא אלהים את התנינם הגדלים
And God made the great fish.		And God made the great sea creatures.

καὶ προσέταξεν κύριος κήτει μεγάλῳ καταπιεῖν τὸν ᾿Ιωνᾶν	Jonah 2:1	וימן יהוה דג גדול לבלע את יונה
And the Lord commanded a great fish to swallow Jonah.		And Yahweh appointed a great fish to swallow Jonah.

The G-translator may have wanted more than δράκων for לויתן and dipped into Genesis and Jonah to find a word that would give him the largest sea animal possible.[72]

The Hebrew נשפו of 3:9a is translated with τῆς νυκτὸς ἐκείνης. Since the verb נשף means "to blow," and נֶשֶׁף refers to a time of breezes, it can be either dawn or dusk.[73] It is usually translated in the LXX with πρωΐ, σκότος, ἄωρος, or μεσονύκτιον; נשף could, therefore, legitimately be translated νυκτός,[74] but the choice of νυκτός and the expanded ἐκείνης has come under the influence of νὺξ ἐκείνη / νυκτὸς ἐκείνης in 3:7a, 9a.[75] In 3:9b, μὴ ἔλθοι has probably been influenced by 3:4c, μηδὲ ἔλθοι εἰς αὐτὴν φέγγος, "May light not come into it."

The translation of 3:9c is very interesting. Elsewhere עפעפים is translated by βλέφαρα (eyelids) eight of ten times. The two places where it is not so treated are Job 41:10 and here.

οἱ δὲ ὀφθαλμοὶ αὐτοῦ εἶδος ἑωσφόρου	41:10b	ועיניו כעפעפי שחר
And his eyes are (as) the appearance of the morning star.		And his eyes as the eyelids of the dawn.

῾Εωσφόρος occurs only seven times in the LXX and translates שחר only four times, three of which are in Job. The combination, ἑωσφόρον ἀνατέλλοντα, occurs only once outside of this passage—in the well-known poem of Isaiah 14.

---

[71] פתן, אפעה, כפיר, תנין, תנים, נחש, רהב.

[72] See N. K. Kiessling, "Antecedents of the Medieval Dragon in Sacred History," *JBL* 89 (1970) 167-177.

[73] See the standard lexicons.

[74] E. König (*Das Buch Hiob* [Gütersloh: Bertelsmann, 1929] 63) says: "Richtig also gibt LXX τὰ ἄστρα τῆς νυκτὸς ἐκείνης . . . ."

[75] So Orlinsky, "Studies in the Septuagint," *HUCA* 29 (1958) 252.

πῶς ἐξέπεσεν ἐκ τοῦ	Isa 14:12a	איך נפלת משמים
οὐρανοῦ ὁ ἑωσφόρος ὁ πρωὶ		הילל בן שחר
ἀνατέλλων		

How the early rising morning star has fallen from heaven.

How you have fallen from heaven, O morning star, son of dawn.

The appearance of these words together (ἑωσφόρος-ἀνατέλλων) as a paraphrastic rendering in both Isaiah and Job is too unusual to be circumstantial. The G-translator of Job has chosen ἑωσφόρος to render שחר on the basis of Isa 14:12 in spite of the fact that there הילל lies behind it. He follows through in the other two Job passages in which שחר occurs (38:12; 41:10).

§ 17. Job 3:10

| ὅτι οὐ συνέκλεισεν πύλας | 3:10a | כי לא סגר דלתי בטני |
| γαστρὸς μητρός μου | | |

Because it did not shut the doors of my mother's womb.

Because it did not shut the doors of my womb.

| καὶ εἶπεν αὐτὸς γυμνὸς | 1:21a | ויאמר ערם יצתי |
| ἐξῆλθον ἐκ κοιλίας μητρός μου | | מבטן אמי |

And he said, "I myself came forth naked from my mother's womb."

And he said, "Naked I came from my mother's womb."

The G-translator may be supplying μητρός in 3:10a simply to provide a needed specification of the owner of the בטן, but the precedent in 1:21a has surely encouraged him.

§ 18. Job 3:16

| ἢ ὥσπερ ἔκτρωμα ἐκπορευό- | 3:16a | או כנפל טמון לא אהיה |
| μενον ἐκ μήτρας μητρός | | |

Or as a stillbirth coming from the mother's womb?

Or why was I not as a hidden stillborn child?

Orlinsky lists this phrase as an example of the technique of changing negative constructions into positive. He insists that לא אהיה has been translated, but in a positive fashion.[76] Beer tries to get ἐκπορευόμενον out of מצא from טמון and assumes the rest to be an addition as μητρός was added in 3:10. Dhorme refers to it as a paraphrase.[77] These scholars have

---

[76] Ibid., 238.
[77] Beer, Der Text, 19; Dhorme, Book of Job, 33.

missed an obvious case of anaphoric translation. It was only after this discussion was worked up for my doctoral dissertation that T. Muraoka published an article arriving at the same conclusion.[78] This embellishment was taken verbatim from Num 12:12a.

μὴ γένηται ὡσεὶ ἴσον	Num 12:12a	אל נא תהי כמת
θανάτῳ ὡσεὶ ἔκτρωμα ἐκπορ-		אשר בצאתו
ευόμενον ἐκ μήτρας μητρός		מרחם אמו
Let her not become as a dead		Let her not be as a dead
thing, as a stillbirth coming		thing, which, when it comes
from the mother's womb.		from its mother's womb. . . .

Miriam has contracted leprosy because of her rebellion against Moses. Aaron implores Moses to intercede on her behalf lest she become as a stillborn child. Job wishes that he had been stillborn, and the G-translator fills out the image from Num 12:12a. In the process he ignores some of the Hebrew.

§ 19. Job 3:17a

ἐκεῖ ἀσεβεῖς ἐξέκαυσαν θυμὸν	3:17a	שם רשעים חדלו רגז
ὀργῆς		
There the ungodly burst forth		There the wicked stop agitating.
in fierce anger.		

Codex A reads ἔπαυσαν for B's ἐξέκαυσαν and thus follows the MT. Dhorme says: "For חדלו G has ἐξέκαυσαν (Sah., Syro-hex., Eth.), but G (A) ἔπαυσαν. Jerome and Aug. *deposuerunt* prove that the original reading was ἐξέπαυσαν = חדלו."[79] Ἐκπαύειν does not occur in the LXX, but παύειν is used for חדל at least five times outside of this passage (Gen 11:8; Exod 9:29, 33, 34; Isa 1:16). Lee-Brenton, in an effort to follow ἐξέκαυσαν and still agree with the MT, translates: "There the ungodly have burnt out the fury of rage."[80] This is what חדלו calls for, but ἐκκαίειν, almost without exception, means "to kindle, to break forth." This is especially true when referring to God's anger as in Deut 29:19; 32:22; 2 Sam 24:1 (KR); 2 Kgs 22:13, 17 (KR); Ps 2:12; Jer 4:4. Orlinsky sets out three arguments against the originality of ἐξέπαυσαν: (1) ἐκπαύειν does not occur in the entire LXX; (2) חדל is not equated with παύειν or any of its equivalents in Job; and (3) there is not a trace of ἐξέπαυσαν in any manuscript. Yet, since

[78]T. Muraoka, "Literary Device in the Septuagint," 29-30. See Heater, "A Septuagint Translation Technique," 103.
[79]Dhorme, *Book of Job*, 36.
[80]Lee-Brenton, *The Septuagint Version of the Old Testament*, 667.

the meaning of "burned up" or "out" cannot be established, he feels the emmendation must still be made to ἐξέπαυσαν.[81]

There are at least ten passages in the LXX where ὀργή and θυμός appear together (Isa 7:4; 9:18; 13:13; 30:27; 42:25; Jer 4:26; 30:24; 49:37; Ezek 25:14; Dan 8:6 [old Greek]). In at least eight of these occurrences, there are two Hebrew words lying behind the two Greek words. The precise arrangement of these words in Job 3:17a appears in Isa 9:18 and 13:13.

διὰ θυμὸν ὀργῆς κυρίου συγ- κέκαυται ἡ γῆ ὅλη	Isa 9:18a	בעברת יהוה צבאות נעתם ארץ
καὶ ἔσται ὁ λαὸς ὡς ὑπὸ πυρὸς κατακεκαυμένος	Isa 9:18b	ויהי העם כמאכלת אש

Because of the fierce anger of the Lord the whole land is burned up, and the people will be as if burned by fire.

At the wrath of Yahweh of hosts the land will reel,[82] and the people are as fuel for the fire.

καὶ ἡ γῆ σεισθήσεται ἐκ τῶν θεμελίων αὐτῆς διὰ θυμὸν ὀργῆς κυρίου σαβαώθ τῇ ἡμέρᾳ	Isa 13:13b	ותרעש הארץ ממקומה בעברת יהוה צבאות וביום חרון אפו

And the earth will be shaken from its foundations, because of the fierce anger of the Lord of hosts in the day. . . .

And the earth will be shaken from its place, through the wrath of Yahweh of hosts, and in the day of his burning anger.

As G[B] now stands (3:17a), it does not fit the context at all. On the contrary, it says the opposite of the Hebrew. In spite of this, B probably still has priority over A, for the translator, once he has settled on θυμὸν ὀργῆς as a translation of רגז, ignores the verb חדלו and supplies from the many OT references the verb ἐκκαίειν. Ἐκκαίειν is, therefore, original.

§20. Job 3:20

ἵνα τί γὰρ δέδοται τοῖς ἐν πικρίᾳ φῶς	3:20a	למה יתן לעמל אור
ζωὴ δὲ ταῖς ἐν ὀδύναις ψυχαῖς	3:20b	וחיים למרי נפש

For why is light given to those in bitterness, or life to those souls in griefs?

Why is light given to the toiler, or life to the bitter in spirit?

---

[81]Orlinsky, "Studies in the Septuagint," *HUCA* 33 (1962) 125-126.
[82]For a discussion of this *hapax legomenon*, see W. F. Moran, "The Putative Root ʿtm in Is. 9:18," *CBQ* 12 (1950) 153-154.

There are three occurrences of some form of מר נפש in Job: במר
נפש (7:11); במר נפש (10:1); בנפש מרה (21:25). These are translated
πικρίαν ψυχῆς (7:11); πικρίᾳ ψυχῆς (10:1); πικρίας ψυχῆς (21:25). In each
of the above references, מר refers to a quality of spirt, whereas in 3:20b,
מרי is personal, "to those bitter ones of spirit."[83] In 3:20a, the translator
has chosen πικρία for עמל and, therefore, wants a different word for מרי
in 3:20b. There is one other place in the LXX where the same choice is
made and which may have influenced the translation in 3:20b.

	Isa 38:15b	
καὶ ἀφείλατό μου τὴν ὀδύνην τῆς ψυχῆς		אדדה כל שנותי על מר נפשי
And he has taken away the sorrow of my soul.		I shall walk slowly[84] all my years because of the bitterness of my soul.

This is Hezekiah's psalm, which strikes a similar chord to that of Job 3. If
the G-translator of Job is thinking of this verse and, therefore, uses the
same word (ὀδύνην/ὀδύναις) in 3:20b, it would indicate that he was
working from LXX-Isaiah.

§21. Job 3:21-23

οἳ ὁμείρονται τοῦ θανάτου καὶ οὐ τυγχάνουσιν	3:21a	המחכים למות ואיננו
ἀνορύσσοντες ὥσπερ θησαυρούς	3:21b	ויחפרהו ממטמונים
περιχαρεῖς δὲ ἐγένοντο ἐὰν κατατύχωσιν	3:22	השמחים אלי גיל ישישו כי ימצאו קבר
θάνατος ἀνδρὶ ἀνάπαυμα	3:23a	לגבר אשר דרכו נסתרה
συνέκλεισεν γὰρ ὁ θεὸς κατ᾽ αὐτοῦ	3:23b	ויסך אלוה בעדו
Those who long for death do not even find it; digging for it as for treasures, they would be very happy if they should find it. Death is rest to (such) a man, for God has shut him in.		They long for death, but it does not come and dig for it more than for hidden treasures; they rejoice exceedingly and are happy when they find the grave. These are men whose path is hidden, and men whom God has hedged in.

[83]E. Kautzsch (ed., *Gesenius' Hebrew Grammar* [rev. A. E. Cowley; Oxford: Clarendon Press, 1909] 419) discusses this genitive relationship.
[84]No effort is being made to deal with the difficult אדדה or to interpret the colon.

Τυγχάνουσιν is added in 3:21a, Dhorme says, to explain ואיננו,[85] but it was brought in from 3:22 where κατατύχωσιν occurs as a translation of ימצאו.[86] Θάνατος in 3:23a surely reflects קבר from 3:22.[87] 'Ανάπαυμα (3:23a) is difficult. The translator is obviously paraphrasing,[88] but it is not easy to see the connection between the ideas of G and Hebrew. Isa 40:27 has:

ἀπεκρύβη ἡ ὁδός μου ἀπὸ Isa 40:27b τοῦ θεοῦ My way is hidden from God.	נסתרה דרכי מיהוה My way is hidden from Yah- weh.

But this has the sense of "God does not know what I am doing" and, hence, is not the same thought as in 3:23a. The answer may lie in Job 21:13.

συνετέλεσαν δὲ ἐν ἀγαθοῖς τὸν 21:13a βίον αὐτῶν ἐν δὲ *ἀναπαύσει* ἄδου ἐκοιμή- 21:13b θησαν And they finish their life in prosperity and lie down in the rest of Hades.	יבלו בטוב ימיהם וברגע שאול יחתו They finish their days in pros- perity and peacefully go down to Sheol.

Since the G-translator has set up a new thought in 3:23a by pulling in a noun from the preceding line, he needs to provide a complement. "Whose way is hidden" hardly provides that service, and so he brings in ἀνάπαυμα from 21:13b where it legitimately translates רגע. The "rest of Sheol" is, therefore, used as the equivalent of θάνατος in 3:23a, and in reality the Hebrew אשר דרכו נסתרה has been ignored.

§22. Job 4:19

τοὺς δὲ κατοικοῦντας οἰκίας 4:19a πηλίνας ἐξ ὧν καὶ αὐτοὶ ἐκ τοῦ αὐτοῦ 4:19b πηλοῦ ἐσμεν And those dwelling in clay houses, of whom we also are from the same clay.	אף שכני בתי חמר אשר בעפר יסודם How much more the dwellers in clay houses, whose founda- tion is in the dust.

---

[85] Dhorme, *Book of Job*, 38.
[86] See the discussion at 17:1 for a reference to Bel and the Dragon.
[87] So Beer, *Der Text*, 21; and Dhorme, *Book of Job*, 39.
[88] So Dhorme, *Book of Job*, 39.

Dhorme observes that the Hebrew of the second colon "is ill under-stood by G."[89] It would appear, however, that the G-translator has indeed understood the Hebrew but has taken the opportunity to give it an interpretative paraphrase or amplification based on other passages in the book.

μνήσθητι ὅτι *πηλόν* με ἔπλασας Remember that you made me clay.	10:9a	זכר נא כי כחמר עשיתני Remember that you made me as clay.
ἤγησαι δέ με ἴσα *πηλῷ* ἐν γῇ καὶ *σποδῷ* μου ἡ μερίς And you consider me as clay, and my portion is in earth and ashes.	30:19a 30:19b	הרני לחמר ואתמשל כעפר ואפר He has thrown me into the clay, and I am like dust and ashes.
ἐκ *πηλοῦ* διήρτισαι σὺ ὡς καὶ ἐγώ ἐκ τοῦ αὐτοῦ διηρτίσμεθα You are formed from the clay as I also am. We are formed from the same clay.	33:6a 33:6b	הן אני כפיך לאל מחמר קרצתי גם אני Look, I am toward God as you are; I too was formed from the clay.[90]

The clause in 4:19b is a "midrash" on "whose foundation is in the dust." The catalyst for this is 33:6, but it has also been influenced by 10:9a and 30:19. The G-translator cannot resist the temptation to comment on the common relationship of mankind.[91]

§23. Job 4:21

ἐνεφύσησεν γὰρ αὐτοῖς καὶ ἐξηράνθησαν ἀπώλοντο παρὰ τὸ μὴ ἔχειν αὐτοὺς σοφίαν For he blows on them, and they wither up. They perish be- cause they are not wise.	4:21a 4:21b	הלא נסע יתרם בם ימותו ולא בחכמה Is not their tent cord loosened within them? They die without wisdom.

Dhorme has already noted that 4:21a was taken over from Isa 40:24b.[92] The Hebrew of 4:21a has not been translated.

---

[89]Ibid., 53.
[90]See §106 for a discussion of this translation.
[91]For similar sentiment placed in the mouth of Solomon, see Wis 7:1-3.
[92]Dhorme, *Book of Job*, 55. Beer (*Der Text*, 28) also takes note of this borrowing and lists other who do.

ἔπνευσεν ἐπ' αὐτοὺς καὶ   Isa 40:24b   וגם נשף בהם ויבשו
ἐξηράνθησαν
He blows upon them, and   When he blows upon them,
they wither up.   they wither up.

The contexts of Job 4 and Isaiah 40 are similar. The fallible, transient
nature of humanity in contrast to that of God is being set forth. There does
not seem to be any logical reason beyond this similarity of contexts to
explain this insertion. Ἐξηράνθησαν may reflect ימותו of 4:21b, in spite of
the fact that it is translated ἀπώλοντο in its own place. It is possible that
the translator has taken the metaphor of the removal of a tent cord as a
good opportunity to expound further on the sovereignty of God over man's
life, and has brought in Isa 40:24b. For unknown reasons, the G-translator
has chosen ἐνεφύσησεν over ἔπνευσεν of Isaiah. It is possible that he had
Gen 2:7b in mind: καὶ ἐνεφύσησεν εἰς τὸ πρόσωπον αὐτοῦ πνοὴν ζωῆς.
Thus the same god who can breathe life into man, can blow it out of him
again.

§24. Job 6:21a

ἀτὰρ δὲ καὶ ὑμεῖς ἐπέβητέ μοι   6:21a   [כי עתה הייתם לא [לי
ἀνελεημόνως
But you also have come against   This is what you have now be-
me unmercifully.   come to me.

This is a difficult verse. Gray and Dhorme are somewhat typical
when they change כי to כן and לא (לו)[93] to לי to read: "So are ye now
become unto me" (Gray),[94] or "*Thus* have you been on this occasion for
me" (Dhorme).[95] Orlinsky assumes ἐπέβητε to be a corruption of ἀπέβητε,
which is the normal translation of היה ל in Job, in spite of the fact that
there is no manuscript evidence for it.[96] 30:21a may have some bearing on
the Greek of this verse.

ἐπέβησαν[97] δέ μοι ἀνελεημόνως   30:21a   תהפך לאכזר לי
And they have come against   You have become cruel to me.
me unmercifully.

---

[93]For the full data on the kĕtîb/qĕrēʾ, see J. B. De Rossi, *Variae lectiones Veteris
Testamenti* (Parmae: Ex Regio Typographeo, 1788) 4. 106-107.
[94]Gray, *Book of Job*, Pt. I, 65.
[95]Dhorme, *Book of Job*, 89. So Beer, *BHK*, 1112.
[96]Orlinsky, "Studies in the Septuagint," *HUCA* 29 (1958) 266; 33 (1962) 130; 36 (1965) 39.
[97]Ἐπέβης (ℵ); ἀπέβησαν (A). Ἐπέβης is surely correct here, since old Greek of 30:20a is
in the second person. The KR insert in 30:20b has third person plural, which has caused the
ἐπέβησαν of B.

In 6:21a, G must have read the *kĕtîb* לא rather than the *qĕrē* לו, which he then read לאכזר following 30:21a.[98] If so, this is a case of reaching forward in the Hebrew for help in translating an admittedly difficult passage. 30:21a provided the word needed to fill the lacuna in 6:21a so that both passages are rendered in the same way.[99]

§25. Job 6:25

ἀλλ' ὡς ἔοικεν φαῦλα ἀληθινοῦ ῥήματα	6:25a	מה נמרצו אמרי ישר
οὐ γὰρ παρ' ὑμῶν ἰσχὺν αἰτοῦμαι	6:25b	ומה יוכיח הוכח מכם
But as it seems, the words of a just man are worthless, for I do not ask strength from you.		How pleasant (1. נמלצו) are honest words, but what does your argument prove?

The versions all had problems with this verse as do modern exegetes.[100] Skehan says:

> The related case in Jb 6,25a has more often been identified for the contrived alliteration that it is; in the Hebrew, מה נמרצו אמרי ישר. Mostly *m*'s and *r*'s, that is, with its lone *aleph* and the two sibilants. The subject given it requires that the verb be read in the sense of *niml^eṣû*, with *resh* substituted for its *lamed*: "How agreeable are honest words!"[101]

'Aληθινοῦ ῥήματα in 6:25a was derived from אמרי ישר, but the rest of the colon cannot be considered a paraphrase, since it does not deal with either the Hebrew words or Hebrew sense. It has been imported from 6:3b.

ἀλλ' ὡς ἔοικεν τὰ ῥήματά μού ἐστιν φαῦλα	6:3b	על כן דברי לעו
But as it seems, my words are worthless.		Therefore, my words have been rash.

On the whole, G of 6:3b can be considered only a loose paraphrase of the Hebrew. The similarity of contexts with 6:25a, the obscurity of נמרצו, and the presence of "words" have led the translator to bring 6:3b into 6:25a.[102] G of 6:25b is not following the Hebrew at all. Dhorme has noted that

---

[98]Contra König (*Das Buch Hiob*, 96), who argues: "Das ἀνελεημόνως der LXX lässt sich als Ergänzung aus dem Kontext verstehen und setzt nicht אכזר als Text voraus. . . ." See Kissane (*The Book of Job*, 39): "The Greek suggests that the final word 'not' is a mistake for or an abbreviation of the word 'cruel,' which suits the theme of the rest of the strophe."

[99]'Aνελεήμονες also appears in 19:13c.

[100]See Dhorme (*Book of Job*, 91-92) for a survey.

[101]P. W. Skehan, "Second Thoughts on Job 6,16 and 6,25," *CBQ* 31 (1969) 211.

[102]Ziegler ("Der textkritische Wert," 291) has noted this.

ἰσχὺν presupposes הכח for הוכח, but he is mistaken again in calling the rest of the colon a paraphrase.[103] G was influenced by 6:22b.

ἢ τῆς παρ' ὑμῶν ἰσχύος ἐπι-δέομαι	6:22b	ומכחכם שחדו בעדי
Or do I beg strength from you?		Or from your wealth, "Give a gift in my behalf?"

G is, no doubt, reading הכח for הוכח (6:25b), but the translator has gone to an earlier verse that also had כח and brought much of the translation into 6:25b. The lexical choice of αἰτοῦμαι over ἐπιδέομαι was simply for variety.

§26. Job 7:2a

ἢ ὥσπερ θεράπων δεδοικὼς τὸν κύριον αὐτοῦ καὶ τετευχὼς σκιᾶς	7:2a	כעבד ישאף צל
Or as a servant fearing his master and finding only shadows.		Like a servant longing for the shadow.

This addition has come from 3:19b,[104] which has:

καὶ θεράπων [οὐ][105] δεδοικὼς τὸν κύριον αὐτοῦ	3:19b	ועבד חפשי מאדניו
And the servant (not) fearing his master.		And the servant is free from his master.

The state of the departed dead, says Job in 3:19, is far better than that of the living. There even the slave no longer fears his master. Job's living state, on the contrary, is like that of a slave who fears his master. The presence of עבד in both contexts has prompted this anaphoric insertion.

§27. Job 7:4c

πλήρης δὲ γίνομαι ὀδυνῶν ἀπὸ ἑσπέρας ἕως πρωί	7:4c	ושבעתי נדדים עדי נשף
And I am full of pains from evening until morning.		I am full of restlessness until the dawn.

---

[103]Dhorme, *Book of Job*, 91-92.
[104]So Beer, *Der Text*, 44.
[105]Orlinsky ("Studies in the Septuagint," *HUCA* 33 [1962] 127) is surely right in supposing that οὐ before δεδοικὼς (preserved in Ethiopic, א^c.b, 13 cursives and Cyril) has dropped out accidentally. The habit of the G-translator in Job of reversing negative and positive statements supports Orlinsky's opinion.

This verse should be compared with 3:9a where נשפו, treated as νυκτὸς ἐκείνης, is discussed. Dhorme has already noted a similarity of ideas between 7:4 and Deut 28:67,[106] a passage which promises suffering for disobedience.

τὸ πρωὶ ἐρεῖς πῶς ἂν γένοιτο ἑσπέρα	Deut 28:67a	בבקר תאמר מי יתן ערב
καὶ τὸ ἑσπέρας ἐρεῖς πῶς ἂν γένοιτο πρωί	Deut 28:67b	ובערב תאמר מי יתן בקר
At dawn you will say, "Would it were evening," and at evening you will say, "Would it were dawn."		In the morning you will say, "Would it were evening," and in the evening you will say, "Would it were morning."

However, the addition ἀπὸ ἑσπέρας in 7:4c has probably come from Exod 27:21a (Lev 24:3 is parallel). The instruction there is for the lighting of the lamp in the tabernacle.

ἐν τῇ σκηνῇ τοῦ μαρτυρίου ἔξωθεν τοῦ καταπετάσματος τοῦ ἐπὶ τῆς διαθήκης καύσει αὐτὸ Ἀαρὼν καὶ οἱ υἱοὶ αὐτοῦ ἀφ' ἑσπέρας ἕως πρωὶ ἐναντίον κυρίου	Exod 27:21a	באהל מועד מחוץ לפרכת אשר על העדת יערך אתו אהרן ובניו מערב עד בקר לפני יהוה
In the tent of witness, outside the veil that is before the covenant, Aaron and his sons will burn it from evening until morning, before the Lord.		In the tent of meeting, outside the veil that is before the witness, Aaron and his sons will maintain it from evening until morning, before Yahweh.

The identical phraseology occurs also at Num 9:21 to describe the cloud that was to guide Israel.

καὶ ἔσται ὅταν γένηται ἡ νεφέλη ἀφ' ἑσπέρας ἕως πρωί	Num 9:21a	ויש אשר יהיה הענן מערב עד בקר
And it will be when the cloud remains from evening until morning. . . .		And it will be when the cloud remains from evening until morning. . . .

---

[106]Dhorme (*Book of Job*, 99) relates Deut 28:67 to Job 7:4abc.

If πρωί stands for נשף in 7:4c, it is the only place in the LXX where it does. It is possible that נשף (evening breezes) was taken as night (as in 3:9), and then the amplification was made from these Pentateuchal passages. The only point of similarity between 7:4, Exod 27:21a, and Num 9:21a is the time element, but this is sufficient to motivate the G-translator of Job to bring in this phrase.

§28. Job 8:19a

ὅτι καταστροφὴ ἀσεβοῦς τοι- αύτη Because such is the destruction of the wicked.	8:19a	הן הוא משוש דרכו Behold, that is the rejoicing[107] of his way.

G of this colon was derived from 8:13b, but the concept of the "overthrow of the wicked" occurs several places in the book.

ἐλπὶς γὰρ ἀσεβοῦς ἀπολεῖται For the hope of the wicked will perish.	8:13b	ותקות חנף תאבד And the hope of the wicked will perish.
πᾶς ὁ βίος ἀσεβοῦς ἐν φροντίδι	15:20a	כל ימי רשע הוא מתחולל
ἥξει αὐτοῦ ἡ καταστροφή All the life of the wicked is spent in worry. His overthrow will come.	15:21c	שודד יבואנו The wicked man suffers all his days. The spoiler comes upon him.
ἔργα δὲ ἀσεβῶν οὐκ ἐφορᾷ οὐ μὴν δὲ ἀλλὰ καὶ ἀσεβῶν λύχνος σβεσθήσεται ἐπελεύσεται δὲ αὐτοῖς ἡ κατα- στροφή He does not regard the works of the wicked; nevertheless, the lamp of the wicked will be ex- tinguished, and destruction will come upon them.	21:16b 21:17a 21:17b	עצת רשעים רחקה מני כמה נר רשעים ידעך ויבא עלימו אידם The counsel of the wicked is far from me. How often is the lamp of the wicked extin- guished, or does destruction come upon them?
οὐ μὴν δὲ ἀλλὰ εἴησαν οἱ ἐχθροί μου ὥσπερ ἡ κατα- στροφὴ τῶν ἀσεβῶν	27:7a	יהי כרשע איבי

---

[107]This meaning does not fit the context, and משוש obviously gave the G-translator problems as it does contemporary exegetes; but since it has no direct bearing on the Greek text, the word will not be discussed here.

καὶ οἱ ἐπ᾽ ἐμὲ ἐπανιστανό-   27:7b   ומתקוממי כעול
μενοι ὥσπερ ἡ ἀπώλεια τῶν
παρανόμων
καὶ τίς γάρ ἐστιν ἐλπὶς ἀσεβεῖ   27:8a   כי מה תקות חנף
ὅτι ἐπέχει   כי יבצע

On the contrary, let my ene-   Let my enemy be as the wicked
mies be as the overthrow of   and my adversary as the un-
the wicked and my adversaries   righteous. For what is the hope
as the destruction of lawless   of the ungodly when he is cut
men. For what hope is there   off.
for the ungodly, that he should
hold to it.

'Ασεβοῦς (8:19a) has come from 8:13b,[108] but καταστροφή/הפכה is
virtually a technical term for the overthrow of Sodom and Gomorrah.[109]
The translator went to the Sodom and Gomorrah story because of ἀσεβής
(רשע) in 27:7a and Gen 18:23, 25. He then took καταστροφή from LXX-
Gen 19:29b (καὶ ἐξαπέστειλεν τὸν Λὼτ ἐκ μέσου τῆς καταστροφῆς ἐν τῷ
καταστρέψαι κύριον τὰς πόλεις).[110] Job uses καταστροφή four times as
noted in the above texts; ἀσεβής is mentioned in each of the passages. The
G-translator cannot say ἀσεβής without καταστροφή.[111] It is also possible
that he read משואה for משוש in 8:19a.[112] Additional discussion will be
provided at 27:7.

§29. Job 8:21a

ἀληθινῶν δὲ στόμα ἐμπλήσει   8:21a   עד ימלה שחוק פיך
γέλωτος
But he will fill the mouth of   He will yet (1. עד) fill your
the just with laughter.   mouth with laughter.

Job 8:21-22 contains second person singular suffixes in the Hebrew,
but the G-translator has shifted to third person plural to provide a
matching contrast with the preceding verses. This necessitates providing a
positive subject for both verses (ἀληθινῶν), which contrasts with ἀσεβοῦς

[108]So Dhorme, Book of Job, 123.
[109]For the allusion to Sodom and Gomorrah, see Isa 1:7 (כמהפכת), 9; Amos 4:11
(הפכתי/כמהפכת); Amos 4:11 has κατέστρεψεν for כמהפכת.
[110]Wis 10:6 makes the same allusions to this event using ἀσεβῶν but not καταστροφή.
[111]Cf. LXX-Prov 1:10, 18, 27, 31-32, but G-Job has enough material within his book
without going elsewhere.
[112]See A. Guillaume (Studies in the Book of Job [ed. J. MacDonald; Supplement II to the
Annual of Leeds University Oriental Society; Leiden: Brill, 1968] 87), who defends משוש
from the Arabic with the sense of "confused," "confounded." See the commentaries for other
suggestions.

of 8:19, 20, 22. The choice of ἀληθινός resulted from the continual attribution of this adjective to Job. The prologue has it three times (1:1; 1:8; 2:3). Eliphaz argues in 4:7 that the pure (καθαρός) and just (ἀληθινοί) do not perish. Ἀληθινός translates יָשָׁר in Job at 1:8; 2:3; 4:7; 6:25; 8:6, and possibly 1:1. Job argues in 6:25a:

ἀλλ᾽ ὡς ἔοικεν φαῦλα ἀληθινοῦ ῥήματα	6:25a	מה נמרצו אמרי ישר
But as it seems, the words of a just man are worthless.		How pleasant (1. נמלצו) are honest words.

Bildad in 8:6a lashes out at Job with these words:

εἰ καθαρὸς εἶ καὶ ἀληθινός δεήσεως ἐπακούσεταί σου	8:6a	אם זך וישר אתה כי עתה יעיר עליך
If you are pure and just, he will hear your prayer.		If you are pure and just, surely now he will arouse himself for you.

In light of this general practice, the translator has chosen the word ἀληθινῶν in 8:21a to provide a subject for his generalization.

§30. Job 9:26

ἦ καὶ ἔστιν ναυσὶν ἴχνος ὁδοῦ ἦ ἀετοῦ πετομένου ζητοῦντος βοράν	9:26a 9:26b	חלפו עם אניות אבה כנשר יטוש עלי אכל
Or further, is there a trace of the path of ships or of a flying eagle seeking prey?		They pass as reed boats like an eagle swooping upon its prey.

Gray says that אבה was misunderstood by the ancients.[113] The presence of two *hapax legomena* (יטוש and אבה) has prompted the translator to go to a familiar passage in Prov 30:19 for help.

ἴχνη ἀετοῦ πετομένου	Prov 30:19a	דרך הנשר בשמים
καὶ ὁδοὺς ὄφεως ἐπὶ πέτρας	30:19b	דרך נחש עלי צור
καὶ τρίβους νηὸς ποντοπορούσης	30:19c	דרך אניה בלב ים
καὶ ὁδοὺς ἀνδρὸς ἐν νεότητι	30:19d	ודרך גבר בעלמה
The trace of a flying eagle, and the ways of a snake on a		The way of an eagle in the sky, the way of a snake on a rock,

[113]Gray, *Book of Job*, Pt. II, 59; so also Dhorme, *Book of Job*, 141. See De Rossi (*Variae lectiones*, 4. 109) for the Hebrew variant איבה appearing in several MSS.

| rock, and the paths of a sail-
ing boat, and the ways of a
man in youth. | the way of a boat in the open
sea, and the way of a man
with a maiden. |

The LXX of Prov 30:19 has taken דרך in a concrete sense as it relates to an eagle, snake, boat, and a man. They have broken up the monotony of the repetitious Hebrew דרך with a variety of words (ἴχνη, ὁδούς, τρίβους). The nexus words between the Proverbs and Job passages are נשר (ἀετοῦ) and אניה (νηός). Ἴχνος is taken from the first colon of Prov 30:19 and applied to both eagle and boats in Job 9:26. Ὁδοῦ is taken from 30:19b, d, and πετομένου, a paraphrase of בשמים in Prov 30:19a, is now brought to Job 9:26b. יטוש is a *hapax legomenon* that gave the G-translator problems.[114] Consequently, he selected the verbal action for the eagle from Prov 30:19a (πετομένου). He then paraphrased עלי אכל with ζητοῦντος βοράν.[115]

§31. Job 9:33b

| καὶ διακούων ἀνὰ μέσον
ἀμφοτέρων | 9:33b | ישת ידו על שנינו |
| And one to hear (the case)
between both of us. | | That he might lay his hand
upon us both. |

| διακούετε ἀνὰ μέσον τῶν
ἀδελφῶν ὑμῶν | Deut 1:16b | שמע בין אחיכם |
| Hear (the cases) between
your brothers. | | Hear (the cases) between
your brothers. |

Deut 1:16b is the only other place in the LXX where διακούειν appears. Moses here admonishes the judges to adjudicate between the brothers. The G-translator of Job has this Pentateuchal backdrop from which to paraphrase the Hebrew in terms readily familiar to his readers.

§32. Job 10:13

| ταῦτα ἔχων ἐν σεαυτῷ οἶδα
ὅτι πάντα δύνασαι | 10:13a | ואלה צפנת בלבבך |
| ἀδυνατεῖ δέ σοι οὐθέν | 10:13b | ידעתי כי זאת עמך |

---

[114]Kennicott (*Vetus Testamentum Hebraicum*, 2. 487) shows one MS reading ישוט, a verb that appears at 1:7 and 2:2.

[115]So Beer, *Der Text*, 60. יטוש is probably a corruption of יעיט, what birds of prey normally do to their victims (used metaphorically of people in 1 Sam 14:32, qĕrēʾ, and 15:19). G probably saw the text as it now stands in MT.

Since you have these things in youself, I know that you can do all things; for nothing is impossible with you.

And you have hidden these things in your heart; I know that this is in your plan.

οἶδα ὅτι πάντα δύνασαι	42:2a	ידעת[^116] כי כל תוכל
ἀδυνατεῖ δέ σοι οὐθέν	42:2b	ולא יבצר ממך מזמה

I know that you can do all things, for nothing is impossible with you.

I know that you can do all things, and no purpose of yours can be frustrated.

Both the second half of 10:13a and all of 10:13b come from 42:2.[^117] G of 42:2b reads מאומה for מזמה to produce the word οὐθέν.[^118] In both contexts, Job is addressing God. The Hebrew "I know that this is in your plan" leaves a little ambiguity, which the G-translator removes by importing 42:2a-b to replace 10:13b entirely except for כי ידעתי. ידעתי provides the literary link with chap. 42. There is no way of knowing how the mechanics of this interpolation were carried out. G is the same in both verses. It may be that the G-translator went to 42:2, translated the Hebrew to bring it into 10:13, and afterward brought that translation from 10:13 to 42:2. The only definite conclusion is that the passages were in some way being translated together. Gard attributes G of 10:13 to a desire on the part of the translator to avoid the thought of God having evil thoughts against Job, but the entire chapter in *Greek* precludes such a possibility.[^119] Beer missed this anaphoric insertion and assumed a double translation (paraphrase) of the Hebrew.[^120]

§33. Job 11:2

ὁ τὰ πολλὰ λέγων καὶ ἀντα-κούσεται	11:2a	הרב דברים לא יענה
ἢ καὶ ὁ εὔλαλος οἴεται εἶναι δίκαιος	11:2b	ואם איש שפתים יצדק
εὐλογημένος γεννητὸς γυναικὸς ὀλιγόβιος	11:2c	
μὴ πολὺς ἐν ῥήμασιν γίνου	11:3a	בדיך מתים יחרישו
οὐ γάρ ἐστιν ὁ ἀντικρινόμενός σοι	11:3b	ותלעג ואין מכלם

[^116]: *Qĕrēʾ*: ידעתי.
[^117]: So Dhorme, *Book of Job*, 151.
[^118]: Ibid., 645.
[^119]: Gard, *Exegetical Method*, 6-7. He apparently was not even aware of the identical Greek in 42:2. See also Orlinsky ("Studies in the Septuagint," *HUCA* 32 [1961] 249-268) for a refutation of the idea that G tries to protect God from various charges.
[^120]: Beer, *Der Text*, 64.

He who speaks much should listen in turn, or does the talkative man indeed consider himself to be right? Blessed is woman's short-lived offspring. Do not be verbose, for there is no one to respond to you.

Should not the man of many words be answered, or must the talkative man be considered right? At your babblings shall mortals keep silent, or when you mock should no one reprove?

βροτὸς γὰρ γεννητὸς γυναικὸς	14:1a	אדם ילוד אשה
ὀλιγόβιος καὶ πλήρης ὀργῆς	14:1b	קצר ימים ושבע רגז

For the mortal offspring of woman is short-lived and full of wrath.

Man, born of woman, is few of days and full of trouble.

G of 11:2c was borrowed from 14:1.[121] It would appear that G was reading ברוך for בדיך (11:3a) to arrive at εὐλογημένος.[122] מתים was treated as γεννητὸς γυναικός, which prompted the translator to bring in 14:1 to fill out the colon. He may also have read יחרישו as יחישו, which reminded him of ὀλιγόβιος in 14:1b.[123] ותלעג was then expanded to G of 11:3a probably on the basis of 11:2a,[124] and 11:3b then paraphrases ואין מכלם.

§34. Job 11:10

ἐὰν δὲ καταστρέψῃ τὰ πάντα	11:10a	אם יחלף ויסגיר
τίς ἐρεῖ αὐτῷ τί ἐποίησας	11:10b	ויקהיל ומי ישיבנו

But if he overthrows all things, who will say to him, "What have you done?"

If he pass through,[125] or imprison, or call to judgment, who can stop him?

The Hebrew is difficult and has prompted the translator to go to 9:12 for help.

ἐὰν ἀπαλλάξῃ τίς ἀποστρέψει	9:12a	הן יחתף מי ישיבנו
ἢ τίς ἐρεῖ αὐτῷ τί ἐποίησας	9:12b	מי יאמר אליו מה תעשה

If he should take away, who will turn him back; or who will say to him, "What have you done?"

If he seizes (me), who can stop him? Who can say to him, "What are you doing?"

---

[121]So Dhorme, *Book of Job*, 157.
[122]Ibid.
[123]Cf. the presence of חיש in a similar context at Ps 90:10 (P. W. Skehan called this to my attention).
[124]So Dhorme, *Book of Job*, 157.
[125]יחלף is strange in this context; see the commentaries for emendations.

G may be reading יחלף in 11:10a as some sort of overturning and so has καταστρέψῃ.[126] Verse 10b is brought in whole cloth from 9:12b,[127] probably under the influence of ישיבנו, which appears at both places.[128]

§35. Job 11:12b

βροτὸς δὲ γεννητὸς γυναικὸς	11:12b	ועיר פרא אדם יולד
ἴσα ὄνῳ ἐρημίτῃ		
And the mortal offspring of woman is like a wild ass.		And as a wild ass's colt is born a man.

The Hebrew of this verse has given commentators great difficulties in both ancient and modern times. Dhorme explains the unusual Greek of 11:12a as a Greek corruption, since there is no resemblance whatever to the Hebrew.[129] However, 11:12b is based on 14:1a as was 11:2c (cf. §33 above). אדם יולד are the anchor words for the addition. This has become virtually a stock phrase in G-Job.

§36. Job 11:15

οὕτως γὰρ ἀναλάμψει σου τὸ πρόσωπον ὥσπερ ὕδωρ καθαρόν	11:15a	כי אז תשא פניך ממום
ἐκδύσῃ δὲ ῥύπον καὶ οὐ μὴ φοβηθῇς	11:15b	והיית מצק ולא תירא
For thus your face will shine again as clean water, and you will put away filth and not fear.		Surely then you may lift up your face blamelessly; you may be firm and unafraid.

Orlinsky maintains that the phrase ὥσπερ ὕδωρ καθαρόν treats ממום as כמים,[130] but he adds: "The term 'pure' was added because 'like (ordinary) water' was pointless in the context, and to accord with ἐκδύσῃ δὲ ῥύπον 'you shall divest yourself of impurity' for והיית מצק in the parallel stich."[131] However, it may also have been influenced by Num 5:17a.

καὶ λήμψεται ὁ ἱερεὺς ὕδωρ	Num 5:17a	ולקח הכהן מים
καθαρὸν ζῶν ἐν ἀγγίῳ ὀστρακίνῳ		קדשים בכלי חרש

---

[126]Dhorme (Book of Job, 161) says that יחלף is omitted and יסגיר is being read ימגר.
[127]So Beer, Der Text, 69.
[128]For this phrase elsewhere, see Eccl 8:4; Wis 12:12.
[129]Dhorme, Book of Job, 163.
[130]Orlinsky, "Studies in the Septuagint," HUCA 29 (1958) 250.
[131]Ibid., 267.

And the priest shall take clean running water in an earthen vessel.	And the priest shall take holy water in an earthen vessel.

It is possible that ἀναλάμψει (11:15a) is a G corruption of ἀναλήμψεις.[132] This would certainly agree with תשא. Holmes and Parsons give no evidence for this variant, but it could have happened very early, and all MSS containing ἀναλήμψεις could have disappeared. If ἀναλήμψεις be correct for 11:15a, the verse would be tied in even more closely to Num 5:17a. As the priest in Num 5:17 takes (λήμψεται) pure running water (ὕδωρ καθαρὸν ζῶν), so Job, says Zophar, could lift up toward God a clear countenance (נשא פנים = ἀναλήμψει πρόσωπον)[133] as clear water reflects the sky.[134]

᾿Εκδύσῃ δὲ ῥύπον is considered a paraphrase by Dhorme based on an interpretation of מצק of "melted down," "purified in the crucible."[135] It is more probable that it was influenced by 9:31.

ἱκανῶς ἐν ῥύπῳ με ἔβαψας	9:31a	אז בשחת תטבלני
ἐβδελύξατο δέ με ἡ στολή	9:31b	ותעבוני שלמותי
But you have completely dipped me in filth, and my garment has abhorred me.		Yet you would plunge me into a pit, and my garments would abhor me.

There is another passage that at least pictures this idea of filthy garments, if it has not influenced the present Job passage.

ἀφέλετε τὰ ἱμάτια τὰ ῥυπαρὰ ἀπ᾿ αὐτοῦ	Zech 3:4b	הסירו הבגדים הצאים מעליו
Remove the filthy garments from him.		Remove the filthy garments from him.

Job has complained in G 9:31 that God had so completely dipped him into the filth that his own garment could not stand him. Zophar now responds (11:15) by saying that if Job would repent, he could lift up his face toward God as clear water and put off the filth.

§37. Job 11:16b

ὥσπερ κῦμα παρελθὸν καὶ οὐ πτοηθήσῃ	11:16b	כמים עברו תזכר

---

[132]᾿Αναλαμβάνειν appears seven times in Job translating נשא four times. ᾿Αναλάμπειν occurs only here in Job and only five times in the LXX.

[133]Contrast Gen 4:6b καὶ ἵνα τί συνέπεσεν τὸ πρόσωπόν σου.

[134]Numbers 5 was used by the G-translator also at 31:11. A. A. Di Lella called my attention to the connection of Num 5:17 with 11:15.

[135]Dhorme, Book of Job, 164-165.

As a wave that has passed by,
and you will not be terrified.

You will remember it as waters
that have passed by.

ἢ ὥσπερ κῦμα παρῆλθόν με   6:15b   כאפיק נחלים יעברו
Or as a wave, they passed me
by.

As the flow in the wadies that
runs dry.

The transient nature of Job's friends is described in 6:15; 11:16 teaches
that if Job would repent he would forget the troubles of the past. The
similarity of ideas prompted the harmony of images. Κῦμα is used in
11:16b for מים as it was used in 6:15b for אפיק נחלים.[136]

§38. Job 11:20

σωτηρία δὲ αὐτοὺς ἀπολείψει   11:20a   ועיני רשעים תכלינה
ἡ γὰρ ἐλπὶς αὐτῶν ἀπώλεια   11:20b   ומנוס אבד מנהם
ὀφθαλμοὶ δὲ ἀσεβῶν   11:20c   ותקותם מפח נפש
τακήσονται

And deliverance will leave
them, for their hope is destruction, and the eyes of the ungodly will waste away.

And the eyes of the wicked will
fail; escape will be cut off from
them, and their hope will be
death.[137]

G 11:20a is equivalent to Hebrew 11:20b; G 11:20b is parallel to
Hebrew 11:20c. G 11:20c is a translation of Hebrew 11:20a.[138] The source
of ἡ ἐλπὶς αὐτῶν is תקותם, but the rest of the colon has been borrowed
from 8:13b.

ἐλπὶς γὰρ ἀσεβοῦς ἀπολεῖται   8:13b   ותקות חנף תאבד
For the hope of the ungodly
will perish.

And the hope of the ungodly
will perish.

The presence of אבד in 11:20b, though paraphrased as ἀπολείψει (11:20a),
along with תקותם (11:20c) probably caused the G-translator to go to 8:13b
for the colon in G 11:20b.[139]

§39. Job 13:25

ἢ ὡς φύλλον κινούμενον ὑπὸ   13:25a   העלה נדף תערוץ
ἀνέμου εὐλαβηθήσῃ

---

[136]So Dhorme, *Book of Job*, 165.
[137]Lit.: "The breathing out of the soul."
[138]So Beer, *Der Text*, 70. The change in order may have come about to create a more
logical sequence of events: deliverance leaves them, hope is destruction, and finally, the eyes
waste away.
[139]For further discussion of 8:13, see §66.

ἢ ὡς χόρτῳ φερομένῳ ὑπὸ
πνεύματος ἀντίκεισαί μοι

13:25b

ואת קש יבש תרדף

Or why are you disturbed at
me as at a leaf driven by the
wind; and why do you set yourself against me as against grass
carried along by the breeze?

Will you frighten the wind-
driven leaf, or pursue the dry
straw?

G has added words to make the imagery more precise, but there are
literary precedents for his lexical choices.

καὶ ὡς χνοῦς φερόμενος
And as chaff carried along.

Isa 29:5b

וכמץ עבר

Like flying stubble.

καὶ διέσπειρα αὐτοὺς ὡς
φρύγανα φερόμενα ἀπὸ
ἀνέμου εἰς ἔρημον

Jer 13:24

ואפיצם כקש עובר
לרוח מדבר

And I scattered them as
sticks carried by[140] the wind
into the desert.

And I shall scatter them like
straw driven by the wind of
the desert.

Lev 26:36 uses the expression φύλλου φερομένου. Wis 5:14a has ὅτι ἐλπὶς
ἀσεβοῦς ὡς φερόμενος χνοῦς ὑπὸ ἀνέμου, which reflects G 11:20b and
13:25. This may be less a case of direct borrowing than a choice of words
common to the Alexandrian Jews of that day, but the other references may
have influenced the translator's thinking.

§40. Job 14:2a

ἢ ὥσπερ ἄνθος ἀνθῆσαν ἐξ-
έπεσεν

14:2a

כציץ יצא וימל

Or he falls like a flower that
has bloomed.

Like a flower, he springs up
and withers.

The presence of ἐξέπεσεν for וימל has led some to emend the text to
יבל.[141] It is more likely that Isa 40:7 has influenced G.[142]

ἐξηράνθη ὁ χόρτος καὶ τὸ
ἄνθος ἐξέπεσεν

Isa 40:7

יבש חציר נבל ציץ

The grass withers and the
blossom falls.

The grass withers and the
flower wilts.

---

[140]Reading ὑπό with אAQ.
[141]Beer, BHK, 1120; so also Gray, Book of Job, Pt. II, 88.
[142]So Dhorme, Book of Job, 195.

§41. Job 14:5a

ἐὰν καὶ μία ἡμέρα ὁ βίος αὐτοῦ ἐπὶ τῆς γῆς	14:5a	אם חרוצים ימיו
Even if his life is but one day on the earth.		If his days are determined.
πότερον οὐχὶ πειρατήριόν ἐστιν ὁ βίος ἀνθρώπου ἐπὶ τῆς γῆς	7:1a	הלא צבא לאנוש על [143] ארץ
καὶ ὥσπερ μισθίου αὐθημερινοῦ ἡ ζωὴ αὐτοῦ	7:1b	וכימי שכיר ימיו
But is not a man's life on earth a trial and his life as that of a hireling by the day?		Does not man have forced labor upon the earth; are not his days as the days of a hireling?

The G addition has come from 7:1a.[144] The point of departure was ימיו found in 14:5a and 7:1b. The rest of 7:1a has been tailored to fit the translator's need in 14:5a.

§42. Job 15:30

οὐδὲ μὴ ἐκφύγῃ τὸ σκότος	15:30a	לא יסור מני חשך
τὸν βλαστὸν αὐτοῦ μαράναι ἄνεμος	15:30b	ינקתו תיבש שלהבת
ἐκπέσοι δὲ αὐτοῦ τὸ ἄνθος	15:30c	ויסור ברוח פיו
Nor will he escape the darkness. May the wind wither his shoot, and may his blossom fall.		He will not escape the darkness. The flame will wither his shoot, and his blossoms (l. פרחו) will be blown away by the wind.

There has been much effort to emend the Hebrew text to maintain the plant figure in the third colon. Beer suggests, on the basis of G, וישור for ויסור in 15:30c (נשר is a later Hebrew word).[145] He gives an alternate reading of ויסער as in Hos 13:3. On the basis of αὐτοῦ τὸ ἄνθος (15:30c), he suggests that פיו be read פרחו or פריו. Gray follows the same pattern.[146] Dhorme adopts פרחו and ויסער and reads "And his blossom will be swept

---

[143]Qěrēʾ: עלי.

[144]So Dhorme, *Book of Job*, 196.

[145]Beer, *BHK*, 1122. Gray (*Book of Job*, Pt. II, 101) says that this word does not exist, but it is in Jastrow and modern Hebrew dictionaries. As Beer states, [neo-hebr], it does not appear in biblical Hebrew.

[146]Gray, *Book of Job*, Pt. II, 101.

away by the wind."[147] The emendation of this text, however, should not be based on G since the G-translator probably saw the same Hebrew as in the MT. He has continued the plant metaphor but on the basis of the precedent in 14:2a, which has already been discussed (§40).

ἢ ὥσπερ ἄνθος ἀνθῆσαν ἐξέπεσεν	14:2a	כציץ יצא וימל
Or he falls like a flower that has bloomed.		Like a flower, he springs up and withers.
καὶ τὸ ἄνθος ἐξέπεσεν	Isa 40:7b	נבל ציץ
And the blossom falls.		And the flower wilts.
ἐκπέσοι δὲ ὡς ἄνθος ἐλαίας	15:33b	וישלך כזית נצתו
Let him fall as the olive blossom.		And he will cast off his blossom like an olive tree.

Dhorme feels that 15:30c may have been influenced by 15:33b.[148] It is probable that there has been a cumulative influence beginning with 14:2a affected by Isa 40:7, which in turn affected 15:30c and 15:33b. The translator has imported 15:30c to provide a parallel to 15:30b.[149]

§43. Job 15:35

ἐν γαστρὶ δὲ λήμψεται ὀδύνας	15:35a	הרה עמל וילד און
ἀποβήσεται δὲ αὐτῷ κενά	15:35b	
ἡ δὲ κοιλία αὐτοῦ ὑποίσει δόλον	15:35c	ובטנם תכין מרמה
And he will conceive sorrows, and his destiny will be emptiness, and his stomach will bring forth deceit.		They conceive malice and bring forth emptiness, and their stomach prepares deceit.
κενὰ γὰρ ἀποβήσεται αὐτῷ	15:31b	כי שוא תהיה תמורתו
For his destiny will be emptiness.		Because his recompense will be emptiness.

The G addition in 15:35b has come from 15:31b[150] almost intact, where G has translated only the first three words of the Hebrew. Ἀποβαίνεσθαι is a favorite word of the G-translator of Job (some seventeen occurrences).

---

[147]Dhorme, *Book of Job*, 223.

[148]Ibid.

[149]See Gard (*Exegetical Method*, 36) for his discussion of 15:30c as an antianthropomorphism.

[150]So Dhorme, *Book of Job*, 226. Beer (*Der Text*, 99) assumes it to be from וילד און.

Orlinsky, after an extensive discussion of the word, says it should be included among the *Lieblingswörter* used by the translator.[151] The colon in 15:35b will show up also at 34:20 where it will be discussed further.[152] The translator sees in this statement an answer to Job's hope expressed in 13:16a. Job there feels that his defense before God will result in vindication.

καὶ τοῦτό μοι ἀποβήσεται εἰς 13:16a   גם הוא לי לישועה
σωτηρίαν
And this will result in my de-   This will be my deliverance.
liverance.

However, Eliphaz argues in 15:31b, 35b that the ungodly man can only expect emptiness.

§44. Job 16:16a

ἡ γαστήρ μου συγκέκαυται ἀπὸ 16:16a   פני חמרמרה מני בכי
κλαυθμοῦ
My belly is burned out from   My face is flushed from weep-
weeping.   ing.

The translator could have been reading בטני for פני, which he frequently translated γαστήρ, but as Dhorme has already observed, he was influenced by Lam 1:20; 2:11.[153]

ἡ κοιλία μου ἐταράχθη   Lam 1:20b   מעי חמרמרו
My stomach is troubled.   All within me is in ferment.

ἐταράχθη ἡ καρδία μου   Lam 2:11b   חמרמרו מעי
My heart is troubled.   All within me is in ferment.

All three contexts are concerned with weeping, and these are the only occurrences of חמר in the *pĕʿalʿal*.[154] Apparently the translator felt on the basis of the Lamentation passages that something inside one, rather than one's face, should be in ferment. Hence the translation ἡ γαστήρ.

§45. Job 17:1

ὀλέκομαι πνεύματι φερόμενος   17:1a   רוחי חבלה ימי
δέομαι δὲ ταφῆς καὶ οὐ τυγχάνω   17:1b   נזעכו קברים לי

---

[151]Orlinsky, "Studies in the Septuagint," *HUCA* 33 (1962) 132.
[152]Cf. also Wis 2:3a, οὗ σβεσθέντος τέφρα ἀποβήσεται τὸ σῶμα.
[153]Dhorme, *Book of Job*, 238.
[154]Kautzsch, *Gesenius' Hebrew Grammar*, 152.

I perish, carried off by the wind; I pray for the grave but find it not.	My spirit is broken, (the lamp of) my days is extinguished, the grave awaits me.

Job's complaint in chap. 17 takes the G-translator to chap. 13, where Job accuses God of unfairly attacking him.

ἢ ὡς χόρτῳ φερομένῳ ὑπὸ πνεύματος ἀντίκεισαί μοι	13:25b	ואת קש יבש תרדף
And why do you set yourself against me as against grass carried along by the breeze?		Or pursue the dry straw.

רוחי is taken by G in a hostile sense: "The spirit (wind) that attacks me" (an idea that fits 13:25), because the translator got ὀλέκομαι. . . (17:1a) from רוּחִי חֻבָּלָה יָמַי. Ὀλέκειν is used in a similar context at 10:16b πάλιν γὰρ μεταβαλὼν δεινῶς με ὀλέκεις, "and again, you have changed and are frightfully destroying me." Φερομένῳ ὑπὸ πνεύματος was interpolated into 13:25 as discussed above (§39). Now in 17:1a רוחי, taken as the destroying spirit/wind, has prompted the borrowing of the phrase from 13:25b.

G has read the three words in 17:1b as a unit. He apparently treated זעך as זעק = צעק to get δέομαι.[155] Now, with the idea of praying for something, and with קברים לי in the Hebrew, the translator goes to 3:21a for help in translating the colon.

οἱ ὁμείρονται τοῦ θανάτου καὶ οὐ τυγχάνουσιν	3:21a	המחכים למות ואיננו
Those who long for death do not even find it.		They long for death, but it does not come.

Ὁμείρονται here parallels δέομαι in 17:1b, and θανάτου is equivalent to ταφῆς in 17:1b. In LXX-Bel and the Dragon is another passage that is similar.

καὶ ἐνεβάλοσαν τὸν Δανιὴλ οἱ ὄχλοι εἰς ἐκεῖνον τὸν λάκκον ἵνα καταβρωθῇ καὶ μηδὲ ταφῆς τύχῃ	Bel 32b
And the crowd threw Daniel into that pit that he might be eaten and not have a grave.	

---

[155]Cf. צעקה in Sir 4:6; 32:17, 20 (δέησις, ἱκετία, δέησις).

The reinterpretation of 17:1, along the lines of chap. 13 and chap. 10, has led the translator to 13:25b and 3:21a for help with his Greek.[156] His interpretation was based on a misunderstanding of the structure of the Hebrew; he made two cola from three.

§46. Job 18:4

κέχρηταί σοι ὀργή	18:4a	טרף נפשו באפו
τί γὰρ ἐὰν σὺ ἀποθάνῃς ἀοίκητος ἡ ὑπ' οὐρανόν	18:4b	הלמענך תעזב ארץ
ἢ καταστραφήσεται ὄρη ἐκ θεμελίων	18:4c	ויעתק צור ממקמו

Anger has possessed you! For what if you should die? Would the earth become uninhabited, or the mountains be overthrown from their foundations?

You who tear yourself in your anger, will the earth be abandoned for your sake, or the rock moved from its place?

The treatment of טרף נפשו is prompted by 16:9.[157]

ὀργῇ χρησάμενος κατέβαλέν με	16:9a	אפו טרף וישטמני

Having dealt with me in anger, he threw me down.

He has torn me in his anger and has been my enemy.

16:9a was in turn influenced by 10:17b.

ὀργῇ δὲ μεγάλῃ μοι ἐχρήσω	10:17b	ותרב כעשך עמדי

You have dealt with me in great anger.

You increase your anger toward me.

The same pattern is followed in 19:11a.

δεινῶς δέ μοι ὀργῇ ἐχρήσατο	19:11a	ויחר עלי אפו

And he has dealt with me fearfully in anger.

And his anger he has kindled against me.

The translation of 18:4c was prompted by inner Greek harmonization of G-Job. The verse underlying 18:4c is 9:5-6a.

ὁ παλαιῶν ὄρη καὶ[158] οὐκ οἴδασιν	9:5a	המעתיק הרים ולא ידעו
ὁ καταστρέφων αὐτὰ ὀργῇ	9:5b	אשר הפכם באפו

---

[156]Ziegler ("Der textkritische Wert," 290) has taken note of the relation between 3:21 and 17:1.

[157]So Dhorme, *Book of Job*, 259.

[158]καὶ = B[ab] A𝔑.

ὁ σείων τὴν ὑπ' οὐρανὸν ἐκ 9:6a המרגיז ארץ ממקומה
θεμελίων
οἱ δὲ στῦλοι αὐτῆς σαλεύονται 9:6b ועמודיה יתפלצון

Who makes the mountains old, and (men) do not know it; who overturns them in anger and shakes the earth from its foundations; and its pillars are shaken.

He removes mountains, and (men) do not know it; he overturns them in his wrath; he shakes the earth from its place, and its pillars shudder.

A similar passage occurs in 14:18b, which was not translated in old Greek.

But as a mountain falls and 14:18a ואולם הר נופל יבול
erodes away; and the rock is 14:18b וצור יעתק ממקמו
removed from its place.

The common elements in 9:5-6a and 18:4 are עתק and מקום. "Mountain(s)" appears in 14:18a and 9:5a; ארץ is also found in 9:6a and 18:4b. In the OT καταστρέφειν translates עתק only in Job 18:4c. Παλαιοῦν translates עתק the other four times it appears in Job. Orlinsky fails to note this harmonization when he says:

Duhm and Ball miss the point when they propose ממסודיו in place of M. It need not be assumed that our translator had in mind Isa. 13:13 ממקומו (ותרעש הארץ) / ἐκ τῶν θεμελίων when working on our passages (on the reasonable assumption that Isaiah was translated into Greek prior to Job); the context provided sufficient ground for equating θεμέλιον rather than the usual τόπος, or the like, with מקום. Contrast 38.12 (השחר מקמו) ידעת where the context justified G's τὴν ἑαυτοῦ τάξιν "its own position."[159]

The similar imagery and vocabulary prompted the translator to harmonize 18:4c with 9:5-6a. One subject is chosen (ὄρη), צור is dropped, two verbs are merged (עתק and הפך), and the translation for the latter is employed for the former, against the internal pattern of G-Job. 'Εκ θεμελίων is used for ממקמו in 9:6a and 18:4c.

§47. Job 19:3

γνῶτε μόνον ὅτι ὁ κύριος 19:3a זה עשר פעמים תכלימוני
ἐποίησέ με οὕτως
καταλαλεῖτέ μου 19:3b

Know only that the Lord has treated me in this way. You speak against me.

These ten times you have insulted me.

---

[159]Orlinsky, "Studies in the Septuagint," *HUCA* 29 (1958) 250.

The MT, at least, is quite clear and needed no assistance from another passage. The G-translator, however, read עשה זה זה as עשה זה זה;[160] פעמים, now without a qualifying number, has apparently been obscured with μόνον. He then supplied a subject and verb from 19:6a. The Hebrew verb תכלימוני was translated with καταλαλεῖτέ μου in 19:3b.

γνῶτε οὖν ὅτι ὁ κύριός ἐστιν ὁ ταράξας	19:6a	דעו אפו כי אלוה עותני
Know then that it is the Lord who has troubled me.		Know, therefore, that God has wronged me.

§48. Job 19:4c-d

G has a gloss here of two cola, which probably in part come from 15:3.[161]

λαλῆσαι ῥήματα ἃ οὐκ ἔδει τὰ δὲ ῥήματά μου πλανᾶται καὶ οὐκ ἐπὶ καιροῦ	19:4c 19:4d	
To speak words that were not fitting; and my words were wrong and not proper.		
ἐλέγχων ἐν ῥήμασιν οἷς οὐ δεῖ	15:3a	הוכח בדבר לא יסכון
Reasoning with words that are not fitting.		Should he argue with words of no value?

Job, in Hebrew 19:4a-b, makes a hypothetical statement about his error. Job, in G, seems to be admitting the error, and so the translator feels a compulsion to provide a statement of the content of the error, which he draws from 15:3. Eliphaz accuses Job in 15:3a of "arguing with words of no value." This error is now assumed by Job himself in G 19:4c. The second colon, 19:4d, has been created out of the context of 19:4a-c.

§49. Job 20:5a

εὐφροσύνη δὲ ἀσεβῶν πτῶμα ἐξαίσιον	20:5a	כי רננת רשעים מקרוב
For the rejoicing of the wicked is an extraordinary fall.		That the elation of the wicked is short-lived.

The interpretation of מקרוב with πτῶμα ἐξαίσιον comes from 18:12; 18:12 and 20:5a have in turn influenced 37:16b.

---

[160]So Dhorme, *Book of Job*, 270.
[161]Ibid., 271.

πτῶμα δὲ αὐτῷ ἡτοίμασται ἐξαίσιον	18:12	ואיד נכון לצלעו
But an extraordinary fall is prepared for him (the ungodly).		And destruction is ready at his side.

ἐξαίσια δὲ πτώματα πονηρῶν	37:16b	מפלאות תמים דעים
And extraordinary falls of the wicked.		The miraculous works of him who is perfect in knowledge.

In 18:12, πτῶμα ἐξαίσιον is a paraphrase of איד. In 37:16b, ἐξαίσια is equivalent to מפלאות (cf. Job 5:9 and 9:10); and πονηρῶν represents רעים (for דעים). Πτώματα has been supplied (perhaps reading מות) where תמים stands in the Hebrew but under the influence of 18:12 and 20:5a.

§50. Job 20:7

ὅταν γὰρ δοκῇ ἤδη κατεστη-ρίχθαι	20:7a	כגללו
τότε εἰς τέλος ἀπολεῖται	20:7b	לנצח יאבד
For just when he seems to be established (by outside sup-port), then he perishes forever.		Like his dung [fuel], he will perish forever.

20:7a is an expansion of כגללו, which Dhorme supposes to reflect בגדלו or כגדלו.[162] G, however, could have been interpreting כגללו as, "When he rolls (his responsibility) on to someone else." In any event, the phrase ὅταν δοκῇ ἤδη . . . occurs three times in Job in similar contexts.

ὅταν δοκῇ ἤδη εἰρηνεύειν	15:21b	בשלום שודד יבואנו
ἤξει αὐτοῦ ἡ καταστροφή	15:21c	
Just when he seems to be at peace, his destruction will come.		When at peace, the destroyer will come upon him.

Eliphaz is discussing the fate of the wicked man in chap. 15, and the same familiar debate is carried on in chap. 20 by Zophar. The third occurrence of ὅταν δοκῇ κ.τ.λ. is found in 20:22a.

ὅταν δὲ δοκῇ ἤδη πεπληρῶσθαι	20:22a	במלאות שפקו יצר לו
θλιβήσεται		
And when he seems to be fully satisfied, he will be brought into trouble.		In the fullness of his sufficiency, he will be brought into straits.

[162]Dhorme, *Book of Job*, 292.

Dhorme sees at 20:22a an effort of G to interpret שפק through Aramaic.[163] The fact is that these three passages, 20:7a, 22a, and 15:21b, are treated alike by the G-translator. In each case, he has established a protasis beginning with ὅταν, which describes a supposed good state of affairs for the wicked. Each of these is followed by an apodosis stating certain dire results. G has, therefore, harmonized the passages because of this similar message.

§51. Job 20:14a

καὶ οὐ μὴ δυνηθῇ βοηθῆσαι 20:14a (13a)   יחמל עליה ולא יעזבנה
ἑαυτῷ

And in no way will he be   If he keeps it and will not
able to help himself.   let it go.

The old Greek translates Hebrew v 10 and skips to 14a; however, 14a has no counterpart in the Hebrew of 14a. It is commonly assumed to be a paraphrase of 13a,[164] following the reading יעזרנה for יעזבנה. However, even if the translator was working from the Hebrew of 20:13a, he was probably influenced by 4:20b.

παρὰ τὸ μὴ δύνασθαι αὐτοὺς 4:20b   מבלי משים לנצח יאבדו
ἑαυτοῖς βοηθῆσαι ἀπώλοντο

They perish, because they are   With none regarding it, they
not able to help themselves.   perish forever.

This verse is also problematic. Dhorme argues that G has read מושיע for משים, a reading that he adopts as the original Hebrew.[165] Whatever the translator was doing at 4:20, the colon is now brought into 20:14a to complete the thought begun in v 10.[166]

§52. Job 20:24a

καὶ οὐ μὴ σωθῇ ἐκ χειρὸς 20:24a   יברח מנשק ברזל
σιδήρου

And he will in no way be saved   He will flee from the iron
from the power of the iron   weapon.
weapon.

---

[163]Ibid., 301.
[164]So Dhorme, *Book of Job*, 294; Beer, *Der Text*, 134.
[165]Dhorme, *Book of Job*, 54.
[166]Note that this cliché occurs also in Ep Jer 57b: οὔτε ἑαυτοῖς οὐ μὴ βοηθήσωσιν; Wis 13:16b: εἰδὼς ὅτι ἀδυνατεῖ ἑαυτῷ βοηθῆσαι.

There are two verse that have similar features.

ἐντέταλται γὰρ ἤδη εἰς χεῖρας σιδήρου	15:22b	רצפו הוא אלי חרב
For he has already been turned over to the power of the iron weapon.		And he feels marked for the sword.[167]
ἐν πολέμῳ δὲ ἐκ χειρὸς σιδήρου λύσει σε	5:20b	ובמלחמה מידי חרב
And in war, he will deliver you from the power of the iron weapon.		And in war, from the power of the sword.

Orlinsky considers the presence of χεῖρας in 15:22b only a Hebraism introduced into G,[168] but Dhorme is more probably correct in seeing in it a reminiscence of 5:20b.[169] It is also of interest that σιδήρου has an exact equivalent (ברזל) only at 20:24a. The other two passages have חרב. It would appear, therefore, that the translator has related all three passages and possibly anticipated the ברזל of 20:24a in 5:20b and 15:22b. Of course, σίδηρος means "iron weapon, sword," in all three citations.

§53. Job 21:22a; 22:2

πότερον οὐχὶ ὁ κύριός ἐστιν ὁ διδάσκων σύνεσιν καὶ ἐπι- στήμην	21:22a	הלאל ילמד דעת
But is it not the Lord who teaches understanding and knowledge?		Can anyone teach God know- ledge?
πότερον οὐχὶ ὁ κύριός ἐστιν ὁ διδάσκων σύνεσιν καὶ ἐπι- στήμην	22:2	הלאל יסכן גבר
But is it not the Lord who teaches understanding and knowledge?		Can a man be profitable to God?

G has read הלאל as הלא אל (whether accidentally or by design) in both these places. The translator then followed 21:22a in 22:2 simply because he did not understand the root סכן.[170] Σύνεσιν καὶ ἐπιστήμην for

---

[167] See Dhorme (*Book of Job*, 217) for this translation.

[168] Orlinsky, "Studies in the Septuagint," *HUCA* 30 (1959) 157-158.

[169] Dhorme, *Book of Job*, 217.

[170] See the discussion at 34:9.

דעת is said by Dhorme to be double translation.[171] It is more likely that the expansion is based on other verses.

ἐν πολλῷ χρόνῳ σοφία	12:12a	בישישים חכמה
ἐν δὲ πολλῷ βίῳ ἐπιστήμη	12:12b	וארך ימים תבונה
παρ' αὐτῷ σοφία καὶ δύναμις	12:13a	עמו חכמה וגבורה
αὐτῷ βουλὴ καὶ σύνεσις	12:13b	לו עצה ותבונה

In much time is wisdom, and in long life is knowledge. With him are wisdom and power; with him are counsel and understanding.

With old age is wisdom, and with length of days understanding. With him are wisdom and might. To him belong counsel and understanding.

In spite of the fact that דעת does not appear in 12:12-13, these verses may have had some bearing on the translation of דעת in 21:22a. A more cogent possibility occurs at Job 34:35.

| Ἰὼβ δὲ οὐκ ἐν συνέσει ἐλάλησεν | 34:35a | איוב לא בדעת ידבר |
| τὰ ῥήματα αὐτοῦ οὐκ ἐν ἐπιστήμῃ | 34:35b | ודבריו לא בהשכיל |

But Job has not spoken with understanding, nor are his words (spoken) with knowledge.

Job speaks without knowledge, and his words are without understanding.

The charge against Job in 34:35 has been anticipated at 21:22a, and both things that Job lacks in 34:35 (σύνεσιν and ἐπιστήμην) are used here for דעת as things that originate with God.

§54. Job 22:4a

| ἢ λόγον σου ποιούμενος ἐλέγξει σε | 22:4a | המיראתך יכיחך |

Will he reprove you when he takes account of you?

Is it because of your piety that he rebukes you?

König writes: "Dass 4a nur wegen seiner scheinbaren Unmöglichkeit von LXX zu ἢ λόγον σου ποιούμενος ἐλέγξεις [sic] umgestaltet ist, ergibt sich daraus, dass sie 4b einfach genau wiedergibt."[172] Dhorme sees it as a paraphrase for מיראתך, which was interpreted as "from fear of you." He

---

[171] Dhorme, *Book of Job*, 318. Kennicott (*Vetus Testamentum Hebraicum*, 2. 500) lists one MS with דעת for גבר at 22:2.

[172] König, *Das Buch Hiob*, 225.

then relates it to 9:32-33.[173] G makes better sense, however, if understood as the same scoffing question in Hebrew: "Will god reprove you when he takes account of you (your piety)?" The answer in both G and Hebrew is an emphatic "No!" God reproves Job because of the sins enumerated in the following verses, but the G-translator has used 14:3a to help him with this paraphrase.[174]

οὐχὶ καὶ τούτου λόγον ἐποιήσω	14:3a	אַף עַל זֶה פָּקַחְתָּ עֵינֶךָ
καὶ τοῦτον ἐποίησας εἰσελθεῖν ἐν κρίματι ἐνώπιόν σου	14:3b	וְאֹתִי תָבִיא בְמִשְׁפָּט עִמָּךְ
Is it not even of this one that you have taken account,[175] and brought him into judgment before you?		Upon such a one will you open your eye, and will you bring me into judgment before you?

G, in 14:3a, has interpreted the Hebrew, "Opening your eyes on such a one" correctly, as "taking account." Likewise, G has captured the general sense of the Hebrew of 22:4a, but 14:3a was brought in to assist in the translation.

§55. *Job 22:11a*

τὸ φῶς σοι σκότος ἀπέβη	22:11a	אוֹ חֹשֶׁךְ לֹא תִרְאֶה
Light has become darkness to you.		Or darkness, in which you cannot see.

Many emend the Hebrew to אוֹרְךָ חָשַׁךְ following G.[176] König wants to keep the MT, commenting: "'Das Licht ist dir in Finsternis übergegangen' (LXX) ist doch einer ihrer Erleichterungen, . . . sollte also nicht zur Änderung des Textes in 'Dein Licht wird dunkel, du siehst nicht mehr' . . . Anlass geben."[177] Eliphaz, in 22:11a, applies specifically to Job a statement made generally of the wicked in 18:5-6.

καὶ οὐκ ἀποβήσεται αὐτῶν ἡ φλόξ	18:5b	וְלֹא יִגַּהּ שְׁבִיב אִשּׁוֹ
τὸ φῶς αὐτοῦ σκότος ἐν διαίτῃ	18:6a	אוֹר חָשַׁךְ בְּאָהֳלוֹ
ὁ δὲ λύχνος αὐτῷ σβεσθήσεται	18:6b	וְנֵרוֹ עָלָיו יִדְעָךְ

---

[173]Dhorme, *Book of Job*, 327.

[174]I believe 14:3a is more relevant than Dhorme's 9:32-33.

[175]Ἐποιήσω is an aorist, middle, second person form. I do not understand Dhorme (*Book of Job*, 196): "The change from the second person to the first eliminates the anthropomorphism."

[176]Gray, *Book of Job*, Pt. II, 154; also *RSV*, *JB*, and *NEB*. *NAB* retains the MT reading. Kennicott (*Vetus Testamentum Hebraicum*, 2. 501) lists one MS for יֶחְשַׁךְ.

[177]König, *Das Buch Hiob*, 226.

And their flame will not continue. His light will become dark in his dwelling, and his lamp will be extinguished.	And the flame of his fire gives no light. The light in his tent becomes dark, and his lamp above him goes out.

G of 18:5-6 represents the Hebrew fairly well. The use of one of the translator's favorite words (ἀποβήσεται) in 18:5b and in 22:11a (ἀπέβη) and the presence of φῶς in both 18:6a and 22:11a indicate probable dependence of 22:11a on 18:5-6. G, therefore, is supplying φῶς from 18:6a and is not reading אור for או.

§56. Job 22:12

μὴ οὐχὶ ὁ τὰ ὑψηλὰ ναίων 22:12a ἐφορᾷ	הלא אלוה גבה שמים
τοὺς δὲ ὕβρει φερομένους ἐτα- 22:12b πείνωσεν	וראה ראש כוכבים כי רמו
Has not he who dwells on high seen? And has he not humbled the proud?	Is not God on high in the heavens? And look at the distant stars, how high they are.

G approximates the Hebrew of the first colon with the addition of וראה from 22:12b (read as וראה),[178] but the translation of 22:12b cannot be tied into the Hebrew. It has been influenced by other passages of Scripture.

πᾶν δὲ ὑβριστὴν ταπείνωσον 40:11b	וראה כל גאה והשפילהו
And humble every proud man.	And look upon every one who is proud and humble him.

The presence of the imperative וראה surely had some influence on the G-translator and, no doubt, was the reason for the influence of 40:11b on 22:12b. Two passages in Isaiah may also have affected the interpolation.

καὶ ἀπολῶ ὕβριν ἀνόμων καὶ Isa 13:11b ὕβριν ὑπερηφάνων ταπεινώσω	והשבתי גאון זדים וגאות עריצים אשפיל
And I shall destroy the pride of the lawless, and the pride of the arrogant I shall humble.	And I shall put an end to the pride of the arrogant, and the pride of tyrants I shall humble.
καὶ ταπεινώσει τὴν ὕβριν Isa 25:11b αὐτοῦ	והשפיל גאותו
And he will humble his pride.	And he will humble his pride.

---

[178] So Beer, *Der Text*, 146.

All three of these passages, but particularly Job 40:11b, have influenced G of 22:12b.[179]

§57. Job 22:21a

γενοῦ δὴ σκληρός ἐὰν ὑπομείνῃς	22:21a	הסכן נא עמו ושלם
Resist (him) now, if you can endure.		Come to terms now with him [God], and be at peace.

'Εὰν ὑπομείνῃς is probably reading אם תשלם.[180] The fact that the translator did not know what to do with the root סכן will be discussed at 34:9. The translator, in order to get help with הסכן, goes to 9:4b.

τίς σκληρὸς γενόμενος ἐναντίον αὐτοῦ ὑπέμεινεν	9:4b	מי הקשה אליו וישלם
Who ever resisted him and stayed alive?		Who ever withstood him without harm?

The meanings in the two contexts are opposite, but the presence of שלם in 22:21a and the difficult (for the translator) הסכן led him to 9:4b for a colon that has nothing to do with the Hebrew of 22:21a.[181]

§58. Job 22:25

ἔσται οὖν σου ὁ παντοκράτωρ βοηθὸς ἀπὸ ἐχθρῶν	22:25a	והיה שדי בצריך
καθαρὸν δὲ ἀποδώσει σε ὥσπερ ἀργύριον πεπυρωμένον	22:25b	וכסף תועפות לך
Therefore, the Almighty will be your help against your enemies, and he will present you pure as silver tried by the fire.		Then the Almighty will be your gold and your choice silver.

G is reading בצריך as if from the root צרר, but the expansion βοηθὸς ἀπὸ ἐχθρῶν is based on Deut 33:7d.

καὶ βοηθὸς ἐκ τῶν ἐχθρῶν ἔσῃ	Deut 33:7d	ועזר מצריו תהיה

---

[179] A similar situation is found in the Qumran Isaiah scroll (1QIsaᵃ). 1QIsaᵃ 40:26a has שאו מרום עיניכמה. Since 1QIsaᵃ 51:6a has שאו שמים עיניכמה, the scroll copyist has inserted וראו מי ברא את אלה from 40:26b and omitted 51:6b. The technique is similar to that practiced by the G-translator of Job.

[180] So Dhorme, *Book of Job*, 336.

[181] Beer (*Der Text*, 148) needlessly assumes a reading of הסכל נא אם תשלם. See also Ziegler ("Der textkritische Wert," 291), who links 9:4b and 22:21a.

And you will be a help against (his) enemies.	And you will be a help against his enemies.

As God is to be Judah's help against his enemies, so, says Eliphaz in G, God will be Job's help against his enemies.

The second colon is paraphrased, but probably with the help of another passage.

τὰ λόγια κυρίου λόγια ἁγνά	Ps 12:7a (LXX 11:7a)	אמרות יהוה אמרות טהרות
ἀργύριον πεπυρωμένον δοκίμιον τῇ γῇ	12:7b	כסף צרוף בעליל לארץ
κεκαθαρισμένον ἑπτα- πλασίως	12:7c	מזקק שבעתים
The oracles of the Lord are pure oracles; as purified silver, proved in a furnace of earth, purified sevenfold.		The promises of Yahweh are pure promises, silver purified in a furnace in the earth, refined sevenfold.

Beer is probably correct in assuming that the expansion became necessary in G 22:25a because of the failure to understand בצריך correctly.[182] G has also expanded תועפות with the help of Ps 12:7, again, because of a failure to comprehend it. The word appears only three times elsewhere and is paraphrased each time.[183]

§59. Job 22:28

Bildad's argument in chap. 8 has influenced this verse.

εὐξαμένου δέ σου πρὸς αὐτὸν εἰσακούσεταί σου	22:27a	תעתיר אליו וישמעך
δώσει δέ σοι ἀποδοῦναι τὰς εὐχάς	22:27b	ונדריך תשלם
ἀποκαταστήσει δέ σοι δίαιταν δικαιοσύνης	22:28a	ותגזר אומר ויקם לך
ἐπὶ δὲ ὁδοῖς σου ἔσται φέγγος	22:28b	ועל דרכיך נגה אור
When you pray to him, he will hear you and enable you to pay your vows. And he will restore to you a dwelling of righteousness, and a light will shine on your ways.		You will pray to him, and he will hear you, and you will pay your vows. When you make a decision, it will work out for you, and a light will shine on your ways.

---

[182]Beer, Der Text, 150.

[183]Num 23:22 and 24:8: δόξα; Ps 95:4: ὕψη.

εἰ καθαρὸς εἶ καὶ ἀληθινός	8:6a	אם זך וישר אתה
δεήσεως ἐπακούσεταί σου ἀπο-		כי עתה יעיר עליך
καταστήσει δέ σοι δίαιταν δικαι-	8:6b	ושלם נות צדקך
οσύνης		

If you are pure and just, he will hear your prayer and restore your dwelling of righteousness.

If you are pure and just, indeed now he will arouse himself for you and restore your just dwelling.

The Hebrew of 22:28a should not have presented any particular problem to the translator since it is clear. The two jussive verbs create a conditional sentence which is good Hebrew idiom.[184] Chap. 22 contains Eliphaz's argument that Job has in some way sinned but that if he will repent, God will restore him to his former state. His urging of Job to prayer in 22:27 leads the G-translator back to chap. 8, where Bildad makes essentially the same claim. In addition, the תשלם of 22:27b may have reminded him of the ושלם in 8:6b. Even though the sense is different, it is the last word before the clause in question. Consequently, 8:6b is brought into 22:28a in lieu of the Hebrew. Now there is a positive result to Job's prayer in both 8:6b and 22:28a.[185]

§60. Job 24:4a; 24:11b

There is the addition of one word in these two passages, and since the approach of the translator is the same, the verses will be presented together.

ἐξέκλιναν ἀδυνάτους ἐξ ὁδοῦ δικαίας	24:4a	יטו אביונים מדרך

They have turned aside the weak from the just way.

They turn aside the poor from the road.

ὁδὸν δὲ δικαίων οὐκ ᾔδεισαν	24:11b	יקבים דרכו ויצמאו

And they did not know the just way.

They tread out the wine presses, yet are thirsty.

ὁδὸν δὲ δικαιοσύνης οὐκ ᾔδεισαν	24:13b	לא הכירו דרכיו

And they did not know the righteous way.

They do not know its ways.

The Hebrew of chap. 24 is Job's complaint that tyrants are able to get off scot-free with the mistreatment of the poor. God simply does not bring

---

[184]P. Joüon, *Grammaire de l'Hébreu Biblique* (Rome: Institut Biblique Pontifical, 1923) 512.

[185]Beer (*Der Text*, 150) has noted the borrowing as have others.

them into account for their misdeeds. The addition of δικαίας (24:4a) and δικαίων (24:11b) is a homiletical reworking on the part of the G-translator. This is a case where J. de Waard's discussion of the implicitness of a word in the source language can hardly apply.[186] The addition could be called merely a homiletical gloss,[187] but there is a good precedent for it.

Ps 1:6 speaks of "the way of the just" (ὁδὸν δικαίων, דרך צדיקים). Ps 2:12 says: "And you will perish from the just way" (καὶ ἀπολεῖσθε ἐξ ὁδοῦ δικαίας, ותאבדו דרך). Prov 10:17 has: "Instruction keeps the right ways of life" (ὁδοὺς δικαίας ζωῆς φυλάσσει παιδεία, ארח לחיים שומר מוסר).[188] Closer to home is Job 24:11b: "And they did not know the just way." The Hebrew of 24:7-13 deals extensively with the suffering of the poor in which, says Job, God shows no interest. In G, this section is made to refer primarily to the oppressors. Part of the result is that 24:11b in Hebrew is ignored completely, and G of 24:13b is inserted (δικαίων is chosen over δικαιοσύνης, probably from 24:4a). Job 28:4 also figures in with "And those who kept forgetting the just way became weaker than mortal men" (οἱ δὲ ἐπιλανθανόμενοι ὁδὸν δικαίον ἠσθένησαν ἐκ βροτῶν, הנשכחים מני רגל דלו מאנוש נעו).

The "just way" of 24:4a (מדרך) becomes "they did not know the just way" in 24:11b (דרכו) and "they did not know the righteous way" in 24:13b (דרכיו). The לא הכירו of 24:13b has provided the οὐκ ἤδεισαν of v 11 and is translated twice in v 13. These verses (24:4, 11, 13) represent a progression in homiletical thought. Their interdependence is obvious, but they are also related to other wisdom literature.[189] It may also be that these passages represent a translation technique growing out of homiletical considerations that are antecedent to all of them.

§61. Job 24:6

ἀγρὸν πρὸ ὥρας οὐκ αὐτῶν ὄντα ἐθέρισαν	24:6a	בשדה בלילו יקצירו
ἀδύνατοι ἀμπελῶνας ἀσεβῶν ἀμισθὶ καὶ ἀσιτὶ ἠργάσαντο	24:6b	וכרם רשע ילקשו
They have harvested a field not theirs early in the day. Without pay or food, the weak work the vineyards of the wicked.		The mixed fodder (of cattle) they reap in the field, and they take away the late-ripe fruit from the vineyard of the rich.[190]

---

[186] De Waard, "Translation Techniques Used by the Greek Translators of Ruth," 503-506.

[187] Orlinsky ("Studies in the Septuagint," *HUCA* 29 [1958] 268) deals with it in the section devoted to explanatory additions.

[188] Δικαίας is omitted in Aℵᶜ; evidence of correction toward the Hebrew.

[189] Cf., e.g., Prov 12:26; 21:16; Bar 4:13; Wis 5:6, 7; 12:24 for moralizing on "the way."

[190] Driver's translation in Gray, *Book of Job*, Pt. I, 208.

ἡ τομὴ αὐτοῦ πρὸ ὥρας φθαρήσεται	15:32a	בלא יומו תמלא
καὶ ὁ ῥάδαμνος αὐτοῦ οὐ μὴ πυκάσῃ	15:32b	וכפתו לא רעננה
τρυγηθείη δὲ ὡς ὄμφαξ πρὸ ὥρας	15:33a	יחמס כגפן בסרו
ἐκπέσοι δὲ ὡς ἄνθος ἐλαίας	15:33b	וישלך כזית נצתו

His harvest will rot prematurely, and his branch will not flourish, and may he be "harvested" as an unripe grape prematurely, and may he "fall off" as an olive blossom.

[His stalk] will die before its time, and his branch will not flourish, and he will shake off his unripened fruit as a vine and cast off his blossom as an olive.

The text of 24:6a is a difficult, and commentators have approached it in a variety of ways. Driver, as can be seen from the translation, has left בלילו intact in spite of its problems.[191] Most have emended to בלילה.[192] NAB has transferred 24:6b to follow 24:11a to maintain the figure of wild, open fields in 24:1-6 and domestic work in 24:7-12. The *hapax legomenon* לקש is treated as "gleaning the late ripened fruit" by Driver,[193] but most take it as an equivalent to לקט.

Eliphaz, in chap. 15, is detailing the dire end of the wicked. He describes his fate under the metaphor of the plant kingdom in vv 30-34. The premature death of the wicked man is described in 15:32a with the clause בלא יומו תמלא (תמל?). G has properly handled בלא יומו with πρὸ ὥρας. These two words are then inserted at 15:33a where the idea of "premature" or "unripe" is implicit in בסרו, and where the "harvest" idea of τομή in 15:32a is carried on in the verb τρυγηθείη "may he be 'harvested.'" Πρὸ ὥρας may have been brought into 24:6a by connecting בלא יומו of 15:32a with בלילו of 24:6a, which was read בלי לו and translated οὐκ αὐτῶν ὄντα and also related to בלא יומו for πρὸ ὥρας.[194] Dhorme believes πρὸ ὥρας was added on the order of 15:33 since בלי לו does not account for all the consonants in בלא יומו.[195] This position is strengthened by the difference in nuance of πρὸ ὥρας in 24:6a, "early in the day," and in 15:32a, 33a, "premature." In addition, the G-translator may be reading בלילו the first time as בְּלָיִל or בְּלָיְלָה and treating it as "before dawn."

[191]Gray, *Book of Job*, Pt. II, 166.

[192]Beer, *BHK*, 1131.

[193]Gray, *Book of Job*, Pt. II, 166.

[194]Beer (*Der Text*, 159) says: "בלילו ist von G 2 mal übers. 1) πρὸ ὥρας (בלילו) 2) οὐκ αὐτῶν ὄντα (בלי לו)."

[195]Dhorme, *Book of Job*, 358.

The possibility still exists that the G-translator saw a connection between chaps. 15 and 24 since both passages are concerned with plants. Harvesting or gathering is also common to both G passages. In 24:6b, ἀδύνατοι has been supplied from 24:4a to provide a subject for לקש, which in turn is translated ἠργάσαντο.[196]

§62. Job 24:7

γυμνοὺς πολλοὺς ἐκοίμισαν ἄνευ ἱματίων	24:7a	ערום ילינו מבלי לבוש
ἀμφίασιν δὲ ψυχῆς αὐτῶν ἀφείλαντο	24:7b	ואין כסות בקרה

They have caused many naked to sleep without clothes, and the covering of their lives they have taken away.	They spend the night naked, without clothes, and there is no covering in the cold.

The addition involved here is ἀφείλαντο. The reading ψυχῆς is explained by Dhorme, who follows Merx, as an inner Greek corruption coming from ἐν ψύκει [sic].[197] Merx has the correct ἐν ψύχει according to Beer.[198] It must have been a visual error by an early copyist since the difference in accent between ψύχει and ψυχῆς would seem to rule out an auditory error. Orlinsky sums it up:

As suggested already by Merx (followed by Ball and Dhorme), G is a corruption of ἐν ψύχει, "in the cold." This is to be accepted not only because קרה=ψύχος in 37:9 (and elsewhere in the Septuagint), but because there is no reason why G should have paraphrased בקרה and by "of their soul" at that. It is very unlikely that G (mis)construed בקרה as from root יקר and that ψυχῆς in our passage therefore has the meaning "something precious, dear as the very life."[199]

In an effort to locate the source for this addition, it should be noted that the noun ἀμφίασις appears only in Job (22:6; 24:7; 38:9), and the verbal form ἀμφιάζειν appears only once outside Job. The translator has reached back to 22:6, where Eliphaz is accusing Job of the kind of things wicked men do.

ἠνεχύραζες δὲ τοὺς ἀδελφούς σου διὰ κενῆς	22:6a	כי תחבל אחיך חנם

---

[196]The G-translator has treated לקש as if a synonym of לקט, as do moderns; לקט does appear in one Hebrew MS according to De Rossi.

[197]Dhorme, Book of Job, 358-359. The same error is in the French edition.

[198]Beer, Der Text, 160.

[199]Orlinsky, "Studies in the Septuagint," HUCA 33 (1962) 146. See also Schleusner (Novus thesaurus, 5. 568) and Ziegler ("Der textkritische Wert," 292), who have noted this.

ἀμφίασιν δὲ γυμνῶν ἀφείλου   22:6b   ובגדי ערומים תפשיט

And you have taken pledges from your brothers for no reason, and the clothing of the naked you have taken away.

You have taken pledges of your brothers for no reason and have stripped off the clothes of the naked.

ἀλλὰ πεινώντων ἐστέρησας ψωμόν   22:7b   ומרעב תמנע לחם

But you have held back the morsel from the hungry.

And you have refused bread to the hungry.

G is following 22:6b, not only in the insertion of ἀφείλαντο, but in the lexical choice of ἀμφίασιν for כסות. The same kind of parallel is followed in 24:10.

γυμνοὺς δὲ ἐκοίμισαν ἀδίκως 24:10a ערום הלכו בלי לבוש
πεινώντων δὲ τὸν ψωμὸν 24:10b ורעבים נשאו עמר
ἀφείλαντο

They cause them to sleep naked unjustly and take away the morsel of the hungry.

They go naked without clothes, and, hungry, they carry the sheaves.

Eliphaz, in chap. 22, accuses Job of a number of misdeeds. Job replies in chaps. 23-24, claiming that it is wicked men who do those things, but that God does not judge them for it. The G-translator wants to harmonize these two chapters and, therefore, fills out 24:7b from 22:6b. Though all the elements are present in the G translation of 24:10b, it is not a proper translation of the Hebrew. This verse has also been affected by the treatment of 22:6 and 24:7.

§63. Job 24:14a

γνοὺς δὲ αὐτῶν τὰ ἔργα παρ- 24:14a (There is no comparable He-
έδωκεν αὐτοὺς εἰς σκότος   brew.)

And when he knew their works he handed them over to darkness.

This is a moralizing statement and is not a treatment of 14a at all. Vv 14-18a are absent in the old Greek, except for 14a, one colon, which is a summary of their contents. KR has apparently not noted this, with the result that he failed to translate 14a and inserted his lines the best he could. There is no statement comparable to this in the LXX except Job 34:25a.

ὁ γνωρίζων αὐτῶν τὰ ἔργα 34:25a לכן יכיר מעבדיהם

The one who knows their works.

Thus he takes note of their works.

It would appear that Job 34:25a has influenced the translator in his summarizing statement at 24:14a.[200]

§64. Job 24:19b

There are considerable textual problems in 24:17-20, and G has compounded that difficulty.

ἀγκαλίδα γὰρ ὀρφανῶν ἥρπασαν The sheaves of the orphans they have plundered.	24:19b	יגזלו מימי שלג שאול חטאו (The Hebrew cannot be translated.)
ἥρπασαν ὀρφανὸν ἀπὸ μαστοῦ They have snatched away the orphan from the breast.	24:9a	יגזלו משד יתום They snatch away the orphan from the breast.
πεινώντων δὲ τὸν ψωμὸν ἀφείλαντο They take away the morsel of the hungry.	24:10b	ורעבים נשאו עמר And, hungry, they carry the sheaf.

As Dhorme has already observed, the Hebrew יגזלו, in 24:19b, has caused the G-translator to go to 24:9a for ἥρπασαν ὀρφανόν.[201] It is possible, as Dhorme also suggests, that ἀγκαλίδα is a translation of עמר in 24:10b.[202] If Dhorme is correct, G resorted to the Hebrew of 24:10b, which he knew, even though he did not translate it literally (ἀγκαλίδα) in its own place, nor did he handle the colon correctly. He actually was influenced in his treatment of 24:10b by 22:6b and 24:7b (see §62). Now, however, he goes back to the *Hebrew* of 24:10b for assistance in 24:19b.

§65. Job 24:20

εἶτ' ἀνεμνήσθη αὐτοῦ ἡ ἁμαρτία	24:20a	(חטאו:) ישכחהו
ὥσπερ δὲ ὁμίχλη δρόσου ἀφανὴς ἐγένετο	24:20b	רחם מתקו רמה עוד לא יזכר
ἀποδοθείη δὲ αὐτῷ ἃ ἔπραξεν	24:20c	
συντριβείη δὲ πᾶς ἄδικος ἴσα ξύλῳ ἀνιάτῳ	24:20d	ותשבר כעץ עולה

---

[200] Dhorme (*Book of Job*, 362) has noted this. So also Beer (*Der Text*, 162-163), who lists others who have commented on it.

[201] Dhorme, *Book of Job*, 387-388.

[202] Ibid.

Then is his sin remembered, and he disappears as the mist of the dew. May the things he has done be requited him, and may every unjust person be smashed as rotten wood.

(The Hebrew is too problematic to attempt a translation, except for the last line.)

And wickedness will be smashed as wood.

ἀλλὰ *ἀποδιδοῖ* ἀνθρώπῳ καθὰ 34:11a
ποιεῖ ἕκαστος αὐτῶν
※ καὶ ἐν τρίβῳ ἀνδρὸς εὑρήσει 34:11b
αὐτόν ⸓

כי פעל אדם ישלם לו

וכארח איש ימצאנו

But may he render to a man in accordance with what each one does, and in a man's path he will find him.

For he will repay a man in accordance with his work, and he will deal with a man according to his ways.

It is most difficult to relate G of 24:20 to the Hebrew. Ἡ ἁμαρτία is from Hebrew 24:19b, but it is difficult to see how ישכחהו came to be ἀνεμνήσθη. It is possible that שכח is being read as an Aramaic verb "to find"; or it may be, on the other hand, that the translator has reversed the negative of לא יזכר so that 24:20b would say לו יזכר = ἀποδοθείη δὲ αὐτῷ. Another possibility is that ἀφανὴς ἐγένετο is a working of עוד לא יזכר. None of this can be determined with any assurance. In any event, the extra line in G, 24:20c, has been brought in from 34:11,[203] where both Hebrew cola are combined into one in G (as evidenced by the ἕκαστος for איש in 34:11b). The clause in 24:20c with varying words for works (ἁμαρτίας, ἔργα, ὁδούς, etc.) is a recurring thought found in Exod 20:5; Ps 62:13; Prov 24:12; Sir 11:26; Isa 65:7; 66:4; Jer 32:18. It is not a new idea to the translator, and the problematic Hebrew has given him sufficient reason to bring it in at this point.

This is now the second time in this chapter the translator has gone to chap. 34 for help in this textually difficult section. It may well be that he has reached into the Elihu speeches with their moral tone to provide some Greek for these sections of chap. 24, which are almost impossible in Hebrew.

§66. Job 27:7

οὐ μὴν δὲ ἀλλὰ εἴησαν οἱ 27:7a
ἐχθροί μου ὥσπερ ἡ κατα-
στροφὴ τῶν ἀσεβῶν

יהי כרשע איבי

---

[203]So Dhorme, *Book of Job*, 388.

καὶ οἱ ἐπ᾽ ἐμὲ ἐπανιστανό- 27:7b   ומתקוממי כעול
μενοι ὥσπερ ἡ ἀπώλεια τῶν
παρανόμων
On the contrary, let my enemies   Let my enemy be as the wicked,
be as the overthrow of the   and my adversary as the un-
wicked, and my adversaries as   righteous.
the destruction of lawless men.

The addition of καταστροφή and ἀπώλεια provides an explanation of what is implicit in כרשע and כעול. Job's fervent request in the Hebrew is not that the enemy be "as" the wicked but that his fate might be that of the wicked, and G has made this explicit.[204] The background for this addition, however, is part of Bildad's speech in 8:19 describing the lot of the wicked, which also influenced 11:20b. It is not a paraphrase, as Dhorme calls it,[205] but an expansion based on the earlier passages.

ὅτι καταστροφὴ ἀσεβοὺς τοι- 8:19a   הן הוא משוש דרכו
αύτη
Because such is the destruction   Behold, that is the rejoicing of
of the wicked.   his way.[206]

ἐλπὶς γὰρ ἀσεβοῦς ἀπολεῖται 8:13b   ותקות חנף תאבד
For the hope of the wicked   And the hope of the wicked
will perish.   will perish.

ἡ γὰρ ἐλπὶς αὐτῶν ἀπώλεια 11:20b   ותקותם מפח נפש
For their hope is destruction.   And their hope will be death.

καὶ τίς γάρ ἐστιν ἐλπὶς ἀσεβεῖ 27:8a כי מה תקות חנף כי יבצע
ὅτι ἐπέχει
For what hope is there for the For what is the hope of the
ungodly that he should hold   ungodly when he is cut off.
to it.

The presence of חנף (ἀσεβεῖ) and תקות (ἐλπίς) in 27:8a has reminded the translator of the parallel passages in 8:19a; 8:13b, and 11:20b. From these passages he has imported καταστροφή into 27:7a, and the verb ἀπολεῖται he has turned into a noun, ἀπώλεια.[207]

[204]This verse, at least, surely belongs to Job's speech. See Dhorme (*Book of Job*, 382), who agrees, and *NAB* which places it in Zophar's response.
[205]Dhorme, *Book of Job*, 382.
[206]I shall not deal with the problematic Hebrew here. See the commentaries for suggestions as well as my discussion above (§ 28)
[207]Orlinsky ("Studies in the Septuagint," *HUCA* 29 [1958] 267-268) compares the two passages but does not arrive at this conclusion. Ziegler ("Der textkritische Wert," 292) links 27:7 to 20:5, a good parallel but not as likely as 8:13b, 19a; 11:20b.

§67. Job 27:8b

πεποιθὼς ἐπὶ κύριον ἄρα σωθή-   27:8b   כי ישל אלוה נפשו
σεται

When he has put his trust in   When God requires (1. יִשְׁאַל)
the Lord, will he be saved?   his life.

No effort will be made here to deal with the very difficult Hebrew except to note that G seems to be taking it in the sense of prayer as some commentators suggest.[208] Dhorme suggests that G read יציל for ישל because of σωθήσεται,[209] but ישל was surely read in such a way as to provide πεποιθώς, and σωθήσεται does not have God for the subject. The apodosis, ἄρα σωθήσεται, was brought in possibly from LXX-Prov 29:25b, which contains a double translation of the Hebrew.

ὁ δὲ πεποιθὼς ἐπὶ κυρίῳ   Prov 29:25b   ובוטח ביהוה ישגב
εὐφρανθήσεται ὃς δὲ πέ-
ποιθεν ἐπὶ τῷ δεσπότῃ σω-
θήσεται

But the one who has trusted   But the one who trusts in
in the Lord will be made   Yahweh is safe.
glad. But whoever has trust-
ed in the Lord will be saved.

The only problem with relating Job 27:8b and Prov 29:25b is that the second line of LXX-Prov 29:25b might be later than the first line and, therefore, later than Job. P. W. Skehan thinks it is. He points out that δεσπότῃ for God is unique to this place in Proverbs.[210] Lagarde thinks both lines belong to the original translator.[211] In light of the possibility of recensional activity in Prov 29:25b, there can be no real assurance that it lies behind Job 27:8b, but the possibility exists.

§68. Job 27:10

μὴ ἔχει τινὰ παρρησίαν ἔναντι   27:10a   אם על שדי יתענג
αὐτοῦ

---

[208]E.g., Dhorme, *Book of Job*, 382.
[209]Ibid.
[210]P. W. Skehan, private communication.
[211]P. de Lagarde (*Anmerkungen zur griechischen Übersetzung der Proverbien* [Leipzig: G. C. Brockhaus, 1863) 90] says: "Doppelt da (Hitzig): beide übersetzungen vom ersten interpreten, der 25ᵃ einmal mit 24ᵇ verbunden hatte und denn den ganzen vers noch einmal übertrug. in חרדת אדם sah der mann *menschenfurcht* (gegensatz θεοσέβεια: vgl zu 7.2) und nahm diese für ἀσέβεια."

ἢ ὡς ἐπικαλεσαμένου αὐτοῦ 27:10b
εἰσακούσεται αὐτοῦ

יקרא אלוה בכל עת

He does not have any boldness before him, does he? Or when he calls on him, will he hear him?

Will he delight himself in the Almighty or call upon God continually?

εἶτα παρρησιασθήσῃ ἐναντίον 22:26a
κυρίου
ἀναβλέψας εἰς τὸν οὐρανὸν 22:26b
ἱλαρῶς
εὐξαμένου δὲ σου πρὸς αὐτὸν 22:27a
εἰσακούσεταί σου
δώσει δέ σοι ἀποδοῦναι τὰς 22:27b
εὐχάς

כי אז על שדי תתענג

ותשא אל אלוה פניך

תעתיר אליו וישמעך

ונדריך תשלם

Then you will be bold before the Lord when you look up to heaven cheerfully. And when you pray to him, he will hear you and enable you to pay your vows.

Because then you will delight yourself in the Almighty, and you will lift up your face to God. You will pray to him, and he will hear you, and your vows you will fulfill.

Most commentators have missed the connection between chap. 27 and chap. 22, but the relationship is especially obvious in this problematic section on the prayers of the unjust. Chap. 22 is Eliphaz's admonition to Job to confess to God his sinful condition so that God might look with favor on him. He accuses Job of certain misdeeds (22:6-11) and tells him what he must do to get right with God (22:21-25). The verses under discussion (22:26-27) give the promised results of Job's confession.

The G-translator has taken note of the similarity between these two chapters and particularly between 22:26-27 and 27:7-10. Dhorme is probably correct in saying that "Job here repeats, in order to challenge them, the words of Eliphaz in 22:26a." He argues further that Job is showing the inconsistency of the three friends in asking him to pray (22:21-30) and at the same time saying he is a wicked man (22:1-20), which by their own definition means he is an enemy of God and, therefore, cannot be heard.[212] The emendation suggested by Beer would be more plausible in light of this connection. In 27:10b, he suggests יעתר לו for בכל עת; תעתיר אליו appears in 22:27.[213] But this emendation is not justified in light of the established patterns of borrowing in G. Having seen the relationship between chaps. 22 and 27, the translator presents them in stark contrast.

---

[212]Dhorme, *Book of Job*, 384.
[213]Beer, *BHK*, 1134.

Eliphaz tells Job that if he would repent, "then you would have boldness (παρρησιασθήσῃ, translating the *hitpaᶜēl* of עגג) before the Lord" (22:26a). Job retorts in 27:10a: "Such a person (the godless) doesn't have boldness (παρρησίαν, יתענג) before (the Lord), does he?"

Thus, 27:10b departs from the MT not because of textual problems, but because the translator is following chap. 22. In 22:27a, תעתיר אליו corresponds to יקרא אלוה in 27:10b. The former is translated εὐξαμένου δέ σου πρὸς αὐτόν; the latter ἐπικαλεσαμένου αὐτοῦ. Then the translator brings in the phrase εἰσακούσεταί σου from 22:27a and ignores בכל עת of 27:10b.[214]

§69. Job 27:18

ἀπέβη δὲ ὁ οἶκος αὐτοῦ ὥσπερ σῆτες	27:18a	בנה כעש ביתו
καὶ ὥσπερ ἀράχνη	27:18b	וכסכה עשה נצר
But his house will disappear as a moth's (house) or as a spider's (web).		He builds his house like the moth's or like a hut a vine watcher erects.

There is a passage similar to this in chap. 8.

ἀράχνη δὲ αὐτοῦ ἀποβήσεται ἡ σκηνή	8:14b	ובית עכביש מבטחו
But his tent will disappear as a spider's web.		But his trust is a spider's web.

The context of 27:18 describes the vapidity of the wicked man's ill-gotten gain; 8:14 is Bildad's presentation of what happens to one who forgets God. G has supplied the verb ἀποβήσεται in 8:14b to complete better the metaphor of the spider's web.

Driver feels that the correct reading is כעכביש as in 8:14 (without the כ). The present G text, he says, retains both the original reading כעש and the correction.[215] Beer believes it to be a double translation explained by the fluctuation between כעש and כעכביש.[216] Dhorme also says it is a double translation.[217] Schleusner says: "Verba ὥσπερ ἀράχνη huc delata statuit non tam ex VIII, 14. quam ex alia versione graeca, cuius auctor in priore huius versiculi membro pro כָּעָשׁ legerit כָּעֲכָבִישׁ."[218] But all the

---

[214]Ziegler ("Der textkritische Wert," 286) links the εἰσακούσεται phrase of 27:10b through "vertical dittography" with 27:9a.

[215]Gray, *Book of Job*, Pt. II, 187.

[216]Beer, *Der Text*, 175.

[217]Dhorme, *Book of Job*, 395.

[218]Schleusner, *Novus thesaurus*, 1. 426.

arguments to the contrary, ὥσπερ ἀράχνη is really trying to do something with the second colon and is to be related in some way to כסכה.[219] It would appear that the G-translator is trying to keep the same figure for both cola. Since the contexts of 8:14 and 27:18 are similar, he has probably drawn on 8:14 for both ἀράχνη and ἀπέβη.

§70. Job 28:4b

οἱ δὲ ἐπιλανθανόμενοι ὁδὸν 28:4b δικαίαν	הנשכחים מני רגל
And those forgetting the just way.	Forgotten by the foot(?).

There are two problems in G of this textually difficult Hebrew. The first one concerns ὁδόν for מני רגל. Driver suggests that G is reading מעגל.[220] There is quite a distance between מני רגל and מעגל, but the G-translator was probably struggling with this passage as do moderns, and ὁδός does translate מעגל in Isa 59:8, a passage reminiscent of Job 24:11 in G.[221] The addition of δικαίαν has already been discussed in §60. After the G-translator rendered מני רגל as ὁδόν, he added δικαίαν as a moralizing adjective as he did in other passages.[222]

§71. Job 28:11

ἔδειξεν δὲ ἑαυτοῦ δύναμιν εἰς φῶς 28:11b	ותעלמה יצא אור
He brings his power to light.	And he brings its hidden things to light.

Zophar, in chap. 11, tries to get Job to admit his abject position in relation to God and wishes that God would declare the secrets of wisdom to Job so that he would repent.

εἶτα ἀναγγελεῖ σοι δύναμιν σοφίας 11:6a	ויגד לך תעלמות חכמה
Then he will declare to you the power of wisdom.	And he will declare to you the secrets of wisdom.

[219]Schleusner points out in the discussion just quoted: "Mihi vero LXX pro more suo alia imagine usi esse videntur ad indicandam *rem, quae subito transit ac perit,* quae notio latet in *aranea* pariter, ad *halitu oris.* --סֻכָּה, *tugurium.* . . . Mihi vero vocem סֻכָּה de *reti araneae* s. *araneo,* quod commode *tugurium* et *domus araneae* dici potest, accepisse videntur."

[220]Gray, *Book of Job,* Pt. II, 193.

[221]Beer (*Der Text,* 178) quotes Voigt for this reading, who also connects it with Isa 26:7 and 59:8.

[222]See the discussion in §60.

The Hebrew תעלמה occurs in only one other place, where it is correctly translated κρύφια (Ps 44:22; LXX 43:22). As a verb עלם occurs in Job three times and is translated πεπηγώς (6:16),[223] λέληθεν (28:21), and κρύπτων (42:3). The translator obviously knows the meaning of "hidden" or "secret" for עלם, but he appears to be also relating it to עֶלֶם, which has the sense of virility.[224] In any event, having chosen δύναμιν as the equivalent of תעלמה in 11:6, he carries it on in 28:11, where the two wisdom contexts prompt harmonization in translation.

§72. Job 29:12

In this case, a word was read differently, and its resultant translation was affected by other passages.

διέσωσα γὰρ πτωχὸν ἐκ χειρὸς δυνάστου	29:12a	כי אמלט עני משוע
καὶ ὀρφανῷ ᾧ οὐκ ἦν βοηθὸς ἐβοήθησα	29:12b	ויתום ולא עזר לו
For I have delivered the poor from the hand of the mighty, and the orphan, who had no help, I helped.		For I delivered the poor who was crying out and the orphan and the one who had no help.
ὅτι ἐρρύσατο πτωχὸν ἐκ χειρὸς δυνάστου	Ps 72:12a (LXX 71:12a)	כי יציל אביון משוע
καὶ πένητα ᾧ οὐχ ὑπῆρχεν βοηθός	72:12b (LXX 71:12b)	ועני ואין עזר לו
Because he delivered the poor from the hand of the mighty and the needy who had no help.		Because he delivers the poor when they are crying out and the humble when there is none to help him.
ἀδύνατος δὲ ἐξέλθοι ἐκ χειρὸς δυνάστου	Job 5:15b	ומיד חזק אביון
And may the weak escape from the hand of the mighty.		And (he saves) the poor from the hand of the mighty.
ἢ ἐκ χειρὸς δυναστῶν ῥύσασθαί με	Job 6:23b	ומיד עריצים תפדוני
Or deliver me from the hand of the mighty.		And redeem me from the hand of the oppressor.

---

[223] P. W. Skehan ("Second Thoughts on Job 6,16 and 6,25," 210-211) believes the writer of 6:16b intended יתערם ("heap up," then, "pack [of snow]") and has deliberately written יתעלם for alliterative purposes.

[224] Beer (*Der Text*, 180) says: "Zu δυν. vgl. עלם, עלים (targ.) = 'stark sein.'" See also Schleusner, *Novus thesaurus*, 2. 205.

The phrase ἐκ χειρὸς δυνάστου has a Hebrew base in 5:15b and 6:23b. There is probably some dependence on Ps 72:12, as Dhorme has noted,[225] including the choice of πτωχόν for עני (אביון in Ps 72:12). G is reading מִשׁוֹעַ ("from the noble, mighty one") in both Ps 72:12 and Job 29:12. 11QtgJob supports G with א]רו אנה שיזבת לעגא מן[, which has been translated "[C]ar moi, j'ai délivré le misérable (de la main) du [puissant."[226] The G-translator of Job has an example for שׁוֹעַ in this sense at 34:19, which he translates ἁδροῖς. The addition, or perhaps better, interpretation, of 29:12a has come about under the influence of Job 5:15b; 6:23b, and Ps 72:12a.

§73. Job 29:18

This verse has given rise to much discussion and speculation. What the G-translator does is somewhat unique and certainly different from what is usually attributed to him.

εἶπα δέ ἡ ἡλικία μου γηράσει	29:18a	ואמר עם קני אגוע
ὥσπερ στέλεχος φοίνικος πολὺν	29:18b	וכחול ארבה ימים
χρόνον βιώσω		
(This verse is not in old Greek.)	29:19a	שרשי פתוח אלי מים
	29:19a	וטל ילין בקצירי
And I said, "My age will ex-		And I said, "I shall die with
tend as the palm-tree. I shall		my nest, and as sand I shall
live for a long time."		multiply days; my root will be
		open to water, and dew will
		lodge in my branches."

The rendering of the Hebrew of 29:18 is quite difficult. All of the ancients had problems with it.[227] Moderns either translate "with my nest," that is, "among my progeny," or assume that the phoenix legend lies behind the line. Kissane emends קני to קנה and translates: "Like the reed shall I die."[228] Delitzsch translates the second colon: "and like the phoenix, have long life," assuming a corruption in G from φοίνιξ to στέλεχος φοίνικος.[229] Dhorme emends the text with the help of G to זקן אגוע: "I will die an old man."[230] To follow G, Dhorme must assume that γηράσει translates גוע and that ἡ ἡλικία comes from זקני.[231] The problem with this

---

[225]Dhorme, *Book of Job*, 423; so also Beer, *Der Text*, 187.

[226]J. P. van der Ploeg and A. S. van der Woude, *Le Targum de Job de la Grotte XI de Qumrân* (Leiden: Brill, 1971) 38-39.

[227]See Gray (*Book of Job*, Pt. II, 201-204) for a discussion.

[228]Kissane, *Book of Job*, 187.

[229]F. Delitzsch, *The Book of Job* (2 vols.; Grand Rapids: Eerdmans, 1949) 2. 127-132. So also Dillmann, *Hiob*, 252.

[230]Dhorme, *Book of Job*, 426.

[231]Schleusner (*Novus thesaurus*, 3. 23) relates ἡλικία and קן.

is that γηράσκειν translates זקן thirteen times, and never גוע. A better explanation for G of this passage is that it is an anaphoric translation based on chap. 14.

ἔστιν γὰρ δένδρῳ ἐλπίς	14:7a	כי יש לעץ תקוה
ἐὰν γὰρ ἐκκοπῇ ἔτι ἐπανθήσει	14:7b	אם יכרת ועוד יחליף
καὶ ὁ ῥάδαμνος αὐτοῦ οὐ μὴ ἐκλείπῃ	14:7c	וינקתו לא תחדל
ἐὰν γὰρ *γηράσῃ* ἐν γῇ ἡ ῥίζα αὐτοῦ	14:8a	אם יזקין בארץ שרשו
ἐν δὲ πέτρᾳ τελευτήσῃ τὸ στέλεχος αὐτοῦ	14:8b	ובעפר ימות גזעו
ἀπὸ ὀσμῆς ὕδατος ἀνθήσει	14:9a	מריח מים יפרח
ποιήσει δὲ θερισμὸν ὥσπερ νεόφυτον	14:9b	ועשה קציר כמו נטע

For there is hope for a tree. For if it should be cut down, it will yet blossom, and its branch will in no way fail. For if its root grows old in the ground, or its stump dies in the rocks, at the smell of water it blossoms and produces a crop like a young plant.

Because there is hope for a tree. If it is cut down, yet it will flourish anew, and its shoot will not cease. If its root grow old in the ground, or its stump die in the dust, at the smell of water, it will flourish and produce a branch like a young plant.

In chap. 14, Job is presenting the frailty of humanity; he contrasts that frailty with the virility of a tree in vv 7-9. Job's metaphor in 29:19 of his root opening up to the water and dew lodging in his branches connects these two passages. Chap. 14 speaks of the continuation of life for a tree (in contrast to a human being), while chap. 29 expresses Job's nostalgia for the old life which would have resulted in lengthened years. The translator had problems with the Hebrew of the first colon in 29:18—much as his latter day counterparts—and used chap. 14 to assist in the translation. The fact that G does not translate v 19 does not alter the fact that it formed part of the link in the translator's mind with chap. 14. The comparison of the two verses follows:

14:8a	אם יזקין בארץ שרשו
29:18a	ואמר עם קני
14:8a	ἐὰν γὰρ γηράσῃ ἐν γῇ ἡ ῥίζα αὐτοῦ
29:18a	εἶπα δὲ ἡ ἡλικία μου γηράσει

Dhorme is correct in assuming that G read a ו with קני, but the form was probably יזקין and was translated γηράσει not ἡλικία.[232] The question

―――――――――

[232]Dhorme, *Book of Job*, 426.

then arises as to the source of ἡ ἡλικία. The answer is that it is supplied to match the subject (ἡ ῥίζα αὐτοῦ) in 14:8. An alternative is that both words paraphrase יקין.

The second colon has a similar point of contact:

14:8b	ובעפר ימות גזעו
29:18b	אגוע וכחול ארבה ימים
14:8b	ἐν δὲ πέτρᾳ τελευτήσῃ τὸ στέλεχος αὐτοῦ
29:18b	ὥσπερ στέλεχος φοίνικος πολὺν χρόνον βιώσω

Στέλεχος in 14:8 means simply the stump or trunk of the tree. The translator relates the גזע of 14:8 with אגוע of 29:18.[233] An objection may be raised that ὥσπερ should be translating the כ on כחול and, therefore, should stand between στέλεχος and φοίνικος; but in view of the fact that the translator is rearranging the material, and that στέλεχος φοίνικος as a unit means simply "palm tree," the objection is not conclusive. G, of course, is reading נחל for חול to arrive at φοίνικος (palm tree).

Since G has made no attempt to deal with קני as nest, the question of whether the phoenix legend lies behind the Hebrew of Job 29:18 is unaffected by G.[234] The conjecture of Delitzsch, Dillmann, and others that φοίνιξ was original and has been corrupted to στέλεχος φοίνικος cannot be accepted, particularly when these two words appear together in three other places in the LXX.[235]

§ 74. Job 29:22b

This passage has been influenced by 3:22b because of the Hebrew metaphor.

περιχαρεῖς δὲ ἐγίνοντο ὁπόταν αὐτοῖς ἐλάλουν 29:22b	ועלימו תטף מלתי
And they were very happy when I was speaking to them.	And upon them my speech dripped.
περιχαρεῖς δὲ ἐγένοντο ἐὰν κατα-τύχωσιν 3:22b	ישישו כי ימצאו קבר
And they would be very happy should they find it.	They rejoice when they reach the grave.

The contexts of these two passages are different, and the Hebrew is different, so the normal reasons for harmonization do not exist. The

---

[233] Beer (Der Text, 187) cites Bickell as suggesting עם גזע נחל.

[234] For a link between the Hebrew and Ugaritic, see M. Dahood, "Nest and Phoenix in Job 29,18," Bib 48 (1967) 542-544.

[235] With this Gray (Book of Job, Pt. II, 203) agrees.

G-translator may have thought that ועלימו תטף מלתי would not be intelligible to his Greek readers.[236] Schleusner feels that G has simply provided the sense of the Hebrew.[237] Dhorme says:

> G περιχαρεῖς δὲ ἐγίνοντο ὁπόταν αὐτοῖς ἐλάλουν paraphrases the 2nd hemistich and interprets תטף in the sense of "to please," "to be agreeable,"; cf. Syr. ܚܡܐܡ "was pleasing" and Targ. תשפר "was agreeable." Vulg. *stillabat* preserves the true meaning.[238]

G, however, along with Syriac and Targum, may have associated נטף with נפת (cf. Cant 4:11 and Prov 5:3) and then paraphrased with the same stock phrase of his own that he uses for the morbid rejoicing of 3:22.[239]

§75. Job 30:5

This chapter has much paraphrasing, which could explain G of 30:5, but it may have been affected by other passages.

	30:5a	מן גו יגרשו
ἐπανέστησάν μοι κλέπται	30:5b	יריעו עלימו כגנב
Thieves have risen up against me.		They were driven from among men (1. גוי). (People) shout at them as at a thief.
δίκαιος δὲ ἐπὶ παρανόμῳ ἐπανασταίη	17:8b	ונקי על חנף יתערר
May the just rise up against the transgressor.		And the innocent are aroused against the impious.

G 30:5a has apparently read something like יעורו עלי כמו גנב. That עור and רוע can be confused is illustrated by Ps 60:10 and 108:10, where רוע means "to triumph over"; and Ps 65:14, where it means "to shout," or "to sing." On the other hand, עור in Job 31:29 means "to exult," but it normally means "to arouse oneself."

Job in chap. 30 declares that the state to which he has fallen is such that insignificant people are now mocking him. G reduces thirteen cola to

---

[236] The Hebrew idiom is common enough with נטף in the *hipᶜîl*, though it is used without מלה or its equivalent דבר (Ezek 21:2, 7; Amos 7:16; Mic 2:6, 11). Liddell-Scott (*A Greek-English Lexicon*, 1632) do not give a comparable Greek idiom in their examples of στάζειν.

[237] Schleusner (*Novus thesaurus*, 4. 323) comments: "*summopere laetor.* נטף, *stillo*, *destillo.* Job XXIX, 22. Ita nempe putarunt quoad sensum explicanda esse, quae in hebr. de *stillante* aut de *fluente oratione* dicta sunt."

[238] Dhorme, *Book of Job*, 421.

[239] I am indebted to P. W. Skehan for the contents of this paragraph. The only other place in the LXX where περιχαρεῖς occurs is 3 Macc 5:44. Cf. also Job 31:29: εἰ δὲ καὶ ἐπιχαρὴς ἐγενόμην.

eight; 30:5a is not translated, and 30:5b is made to refer to Job, not his new adversaries. The translator was either *reading* יעורו in his *Vorlage* or was simply reminded of יתערר in 17:8b, where Job requests that the just rise up against the transgressor. He translates there the *hitpôlēl* of עור as ἐπαναστείη. Now, says Job, the reverse of what should be exists: "Thieves rise against me." Ἐπανιστάναι is used only in these two places and Daniel for עור.[240]

§ 76. *Job 30:6*

ὧν οἱ οἶκοι αὐτῶν ἦσαν	30:6a	בערוץ נחלים לשכן
τρῶγλαι πετρῶν	30:6b	חרי עפר וכפים
Whose homes were rock caves.		To dwell on the sides of the wadies, in caves of the ground and rocks.

G has combined the cola. Οἱ οἶκοι αὐτῶν comes from לשכן in 30:6a, while τρῶγλαι πετρῶν translates חרי . . . כפים. Though all this Greek can be accounted for by the Hebrew, it is possible that passages from Isaiah have influenced it.

καὶ ἐλεύσονται πάντες	Isa 7:19a	ובאו ונחו כלם
ἐν ταῖς φάραγξι τῆς χώρας	7:19b	בנחלי הבתות
καὶ ἐν ταῖς τρώγλαις τῶν πετρῶν	7:19c	ובנקיקי הסלעים
And all will enter the gullies of the land and in caves of the rocks.		And all of them will come and light in the steep wadies and in the cracks of the rocks.

εἰσενέγκαντες εἰς τὰ σπήλαια	Isa 2:19a	ובאו במערות צרים
καὶ εἰς τὰς σχισμὰς τῶν πετρῶν καὶ εἰς τὰς τρώγλας τῆς γῆς	2:19b	ובמחלות עפר
Having brought (them) into caverns and into the cracks of the rocks and into caves of earth.		And they will come into rock caves and holes in the ground.

The presence of נחל (7:19b) and עפר (2:19b) in addition to G τρώγλαις (7:19c), τρώγλας (2:19b), and πετρῶν has influenced the G-translator to summarize the contents of 30:6 as he has. Both passages in Isaiah are of a

---

[240]Both LXX and "Θ" used it at 11:2.

judgmental character, whereas Job 30 is simply presenting the pitiful state of those who are mocking Job; but the similar phraseology has probably assisted the G-translator in summarizing the two cola before him at Job 30:6.

§77. Job 30:14

It is difficult to relate G of 30:13-14 to the Hebrew. The G-translator probably had as many problems with the text as scholars today.

ἐξέδυσαν γὰρ μου τὴν στολήν	30:13b	להותי יעילו לא עזר למו
βέλεσιν αὐτοῦ κατηκόντισέν με	30:14a	כפרץ רחב יאתיו
For they have stripped off my garment. He has shot his arrows at me.		To destroy me, they come up (l. יעלו) with none to restrain (l. לא עצר). As through a wide breach they come.
ἀνοίξας γὰρ φαρέτραν αὐτοῦ ἐκάκωσέν με	30:11a	כי יתרו פתח ויענני
For he has opened his quiver and afflicted me.		Because he has loosened his bow-string and afflicted me.

Στολήν in 30:13b is probably derived from יעילו,[241] but there is nothing in the Hebrew to account for ἐξέδυσαν, which has been supplied to match the noun. In 30:14a is the strange statement about "shooting arrows." Beer suggests the possibility that the translator was reading בחץ אותי רבה,[242] but this attributes too much imagination to the translator. The original translation omitted 11b-13a, which was subsequently provided by KR. The G-translator has simply chosen to ignore the Hebrew of 13b-14a and to create an entirely new line to match his translation of 11a. G reads now (11a, 13b, 14a): "For he has opened his quiver[243] and afflicted me. For they have stripped off my garment. He has shot his arrows at me." This is harmonizing in a different sense. The words of another passage have not been brought in, but the concept of earlier verses has been linked with the verse, and words have been supplied to bring it into a harmonizing whole.

§78. Job 31:11

θυμὸς γὰρ ὀργῆς ἀκατάσχετος[244]	31:11a	כי הוא זמה
τὸ μιᾶναι ἀνδρὸς γυναῖκα	31:11b	והיא עון פלילים

[241] Dhorme, *Book of Job*, 438.
[242] Beer, *Der Text*, 194.
[243] יתר is translated φαρέτραν in Ps 11:2.
[244] Cf. Prov 6:34; 27:4.

For the defilement of a man's wife would result in unchecked rage of anger.	For that would be immoral conduct and iniquity worthy of judgment.

Dhorme has already noted that τὸ μιᾶναι ἀνδρὸς γυναῖκα is an explanation of זמה based on Num 5:11-31.[245] That passage gives instuction in the case of suspected adultery. One verse, in particular, is similar to Job 31:11b.

εἰ δὲ σὺ παραβέβηκας ὑπ'	Num 5:20	ואת כי שטית תחת
ἀνδρὸς οὖσα ἢ μεμίανσαι		אישך וכי נטמאת
And if you have transgressed, being under your husband, or have been defiled . . .		And if you have turned aside while under your husband and defiled yourself . . .

There is a passage in Ezekiel which bears on this same issue.[246]

καὶ τὴν γυναῖκα τοῦ πλησίον	Ezek 18:6b	ואת אשת רעהו לא טמא
αὐτοῦ οὐ μὴ μιάνῃ		
And in no wise defile the wife of his neighbor.		And he does not defile the wife of his neighbor.

It would appear that, as at 1:5, the translator feels a need to expand G so as to bring in the pertinent Levitical legislation involving the issue at hand, in this case, adultery.

§79. Job 31:23a

φόβος γὰρ κυρίου (om. B) συν-	31:23a	כי פחד אלי איד אל
έσχεν με		
For the fear of the Lord constrained me.		For a calamity of God is a terror to me.

The Hebrew is somewhat ambiguous. NAB has emended to כי פחד אל עלי. Beer emends to פחד אל עצרני and refers to G,[247] but G can be accounted for as an anaphoric translation from 3:24.

δακρύω δὲ ἐγὼ συνεχόμενος	3:24b	ויתכו כמים שאגתי
φόβῳ		
And I weep being gripped with fear.		And my groanings are poured out like water.

---

[245] Dhorme, Book of Job, 454.

[246] Ezek 33:26 contains: ואיש את אשת רעהו טמאתם, but there is recensional activity in LXX for this verse (e.g., איש = ἀνήρ not ἕκαστος).

[247] Beer, BHK, 1139.

The translator has paraphrased 3:24b and even anticipated 3:25a, but in 31:23a the difficult Hebrew forces him to reach into chap. 3 for help with a result similar to that attained by the emendation of *NAB*.[248]

§80. Job 31:29b

καὶ εἶπεν ἡ καρδία μου εὖγε 31:29b
And my heart said, "Aha!"

והתעררתי כי מצאו רע
And exulted because calamity met him.

Beer says that G translated freely according to the sense.[249] Dhorme agrees but points out that the translator followed Ps 35:25.[250]

μὴ εἴπαισαν ἐν καρδίαις   Ps 35:25a
αὐτῶν εὖγε εὖγε τῇ ψυχῇ   (LXX 34:25a)
ἡμῶν
Let them not say in their hearts, "Aha, aha, (it is pleasing) to our soul."

אל יאמרו בלבם האח
נפשנו
Let them not say in their heart, "Aha, our soul."

Job claims that he has never rejoiced at the fall of his enemy nor said in his heart, "Aha!" The translator goes to Ps 35:25 where the Psalmist entreats God not to let his enemies do that very thing, and he brings that Greek text into Job 31:29b.

§81. Job 32:1a

ἡσύχασαν δὲ καὶ *οἱ τρεῖς φίλοι* 32:1a
αὐτοῦ ἔτι ἀντειπεῖν Ἰώβ
But his three friends also ceased to speak further against Job.

וישבתו שלשת האנשים האלה
מענות את איוב
And these three men ceased responding to Job.

ἀκούσαντες δὲ *οἱ τρεῖς φίλοι* 2:11a
αὐτοῦ
And when his three friends heard . . . .

וישמעו שלשת רעי איוב
. . . .
And Job's three friends heard . . . .

This reference to the three men is brought by G into harmony with the prose introduction at 2:11 by calling them "friends."[251] The same

---

[248]Orlinsky ("Studies in the Septuagint," *HUCA* 32 [1961] 241) says: "Unless the Hebrew *Vorlage* differed from our received text, anthropopathism went beyond the translator's call of duty."

[249]Beer, *Der Text*, 202.

[250]Dhorme, *Book of Job*, 463. Kissane (*Book of Job*, 208) makes a similar comparison in the Hebrew with Proverbs.

[251]So Dhorme, *Book of Job*, 472.

interest in harmony will be brought to bear on the epilogue. Orlinsky rightly faults Beer for assuming that G had read שלשת רעיו on the basis that G is merely explaining who these men are,[252] but it is harmonistic as well as explanatory.

§82. Job 32:13

D. N. Freedman has presented the view that the speeches of Elihu were composed to be inserted at appropriate places to rebut Job's argument.[253] Whether that was the designed purpose, the Elihu speeches do indeed pick up threads of thought from the previous discourse and deal with them. The translator has followed this pattern and, in the case of 32:13, has gone beyond the Hebrew.

ἵνα μὴ εἴπητε εὕρομεν σοφίαν κυρίῳ προσθέμενοι	32:13a	פן תאמרו מצאנו חכמה אל ידפנו לא איש
Lest you say, "We have found wisdom, having joined ourselves to the Lord."		Lest you say, "We have found wisdom; God will rout him, not man."

Job makes a remark in 13:9b against his friends which in G is far different from the Hebrew.

εἰ γὰρ τὰ τάντα ποιοῦντες προστεθήσεσθε αὐτῷ	13:9b	אם כהתל באנוש תהתלו בו
For if, while doing everything, you join yourself to him.		Or will you trifle with him as one trifles with a man?

There is no way of knowing how the G-translator of 13:9b managed to get what he did from the Hebrew, but the results now influence 32:13a. Lee-Brenton translates G of 32:13a: "Lest ye should say, We have found that we have added wisdom to the Lord."[254] However, it would be better to see the main clause as "We have found wisdom," since this much appears in the Hebrew. Κυρίῳ comes from אל in the second colon, but προσθέμενοι, though it may be the result of reading יספנו for ידפנו, is probably from 13:9b.[255] These two Greek words (κυρίῳ προσθέμενοι), then, should be translated as a modifying phrase: "We have found wisdom, having joined ourselves to the Lord."[256] In other words, Elihu warns them in G against

---

[252]Orlinsky, "Studies in the Septuagint," *HUCA* 29 (1958) 251.

[253]D. N. Freedman, "The Elihu Speeches in the Book of Job," *HTR* 61 (1968) 51-59.

[254]Lee-Brenton, *The Septuagint Version of the Old Testament*, 689.

[255]G may have read תתלוו for תהתלו in 13:9b. Προστιθέναι is used for לוה in the *nip῾al* at Num 18:2, 4 and Esth 9:27. In later Hebrew it occurs in the *hitpa῾ēl* with this sense.

[256]Lee-Brenton is not consistent in his translation of 13:9b and 32:13a.

saying: "We have come to see Job from God's viewpoint, namely, that he is just."

§83. Job 32:22a

To make the discussion easy to follow, 32:21 will be given first.

ἄνθρωπον γὰρ οὐ μὴ αἰσχυνθῶ	32:21a	אל נא אשא פני איש
ἀλλὰ μὴν οὐδὲ βροτὸν οὐ μὴ ἐντραπῶ	32:21b	ואל אדם לא אכנה
οὐ γὰρ ἐπίσταμαι θαυμάσαι πρόσωπα	32:22a	כי לא ידעתי אכנה
εἰ δὲ μή καὶ ἐμὲ σῆτες ἔδονται	32:22b	כמעט ישאני עשני

For I am not embarrassed before any person nor ashamed before a mortal. For I do not know how to respect persons. If I should, even the moths would eat me.

I shall not be partial to anyone, nor shall I give titles to man. Because I do not know how to give titles. (If I did), my maker would quickly take me away.

The translator has paraphrased אשא פני in 32:21a with αἰσχυνθῶ and אכנה with ἐντραπῶ. Yet when he comes to אכנה in 32:22a, he has θαυμάσαι πρόσωπα, which, as Dhorme notes,[257] is reminiscent of 32:21a אשא פני. As in 32:13, the translator is linking up the Elihu speeches with Job's previous statements. Job says in 13:10b:

εἰ δὲ καὶ κρυφῇ πρόσωπα θαυμάσεσθε	13:10b	אם בסתר פנים תשאון

But if also in secret you respect persons . . . .

If in secret you respect persons . . . .

Job insinuates that his three friends are really the ones who are partial in their dealings with people. Now Elihu makes it quite clear in both Hebrew and Greek that he is not a respecter of persons. In the process, the translator brings in the rendering of 13:10b.[258]

Dhorme and Beer state that εἰ δὲ μή καὶ ἐμὲ σῆτες ἔδονται (32:22b) has come about through reading עשים for עשני.[259] There is a verse in

---

[257]Dhorme, Book of Job, 485.

[258]Orlinsky ("Studies in the Septuagint," HUCA 30 [1959] 160) has missed this point entirely. See his full discussion of the LXX treatment of נשא פנים in "The Textual Criticism of the Old Testament," The Bible and the Ancient Near East (ed. G. E. Wright; Garden City, N.Y.: Doubleday, 1965) 154-155.

[259]Dhorme, Book of Job, 485; Beer, Der Text, 208. In biblical Hebrew עש is always a collective and should be the form read here by G rather than עשים.

Isaiah, however, where this metaphor is used, and it may well have influenced G of 32:22b.

ἰδοὺ πάντες ὑμεῖς ὡς ἱμάτιον παλαιωθήσεσθε	Isa 50:9c	הן כלם כבגד יבלו
καὶ σὴς καταφάγεται ὑμᾶς	50:9d	עש יאכלם
Behold, all of you will become old as a garment, and moths will eat you.		Behold, all of them will waste away as a garment. Moths will eat them.

There are also passages in the LXX of Isa 51:8 and Mic 7:4 that contain the metaphor of the moth eating people as if they were cloth. These three passages, and particularly Isa 50:9, may have inspired the translator of Job 32:22b, with the word עשני as the point of departure.[260]

§84. Job 33:3

καθαρά μου ἡ καρδία ῥήμασιν	33:3a	ישר לבי אמרי
σύνεσις δὲ χειλέων μου καθαρὰ νοήσει	33:3b	ודעת שפתי ברור מללו
My heart will be (shown to be) pure by (my) words, and the discernment of my lips will perceive purity.		My speech declares the uprightness of my heart, and my lips speak knowledge sincerely.

Καθαρά, in 33:3a, may be paraphrasing ישר; but if so, this is the only place in the LXX where καθαρός is used for יָשָׁר or יָשָׁר. It is more likely that Ps 24:4 lies behind it.[261]

ἀθῷος χερσὶν καὶ καθαρὸς τῇ καρδίᾳ	Ps 24:4a (LXX 23:4a)	נקי כפים ובר לבב
Pure of hands and clean in heart.		Innocent hands and pure heart.

In the Psalm passage, the person who has innocent hands and a pure heart is permitted to ascend the mountain of the Lord. Elihu argues in Job 33:3a that he is capable of refuting Job because "my heart is pure when I speak." Καθαρός translates בר in Ps 24:4a, as it translates ברור in 33:3b. In 33:3b ברור has provided the translation of ישר with καθαρός in 33:3a, but this was influenced by the use of בר in Ps 24:4a.

---

[260]I am indebted to A. A. Di Lella for noticing this anaphoric translation.
[261]Cf. KR of Job 22:30 for similar Greek. The Hebrew, ימלט אי נקי ונמלט בבר כפיך may have influenced the G-translator at 33:3a.

§85. Job 33:4

πνοὴ δὲ παντοκράτορος ἡ δι- 33:4b δάσκουσά με The breath of the Almighty has taught me.	ונשמת שדי תחיני The breath of the Almighty gives me life.
πνοὴ δὲ παντοκράτορός ἐστιν 32:8b ἡ διδάσκουσα And the breath of the Almighty is the one teaching.	ונשמת שדי תבינם And the breath of the Almighty gives them understanding.

The phrase, "The breath of the Almighty," has caused the translator to
dip into the beginning of Elihu's speech (32:8) to complete the sentence.
Dhorme thinks that G is reading תחוני as does Beer.[262] Orlinsky argues for
the originality of תחוני and connects it with 32:8 for the parallel concept as
an argument for its priority over תחיני.[263] In light of the general practice of
the translator, Orlinsky cannot speak with any assurance even though he
may well be right. The most cogent argument is that the translator
harmonized 33:4b and 32:8b.

§86. Job 33:5

ἐὰν δύνῃ δός μοι ἀπόκρισιν 33:5a πρὸς ταῦτα ὑπόμεινον στῆθι κατ᾽ ἐμὲ καὶ 33:5b ἐγὼ κατὰ σέ If you are able, give me an answer to these things. Wait, stand against me, and I shall stand against you.	אם תוכל השיבני ערכה לפני התיצבה If you are able, answer me. Set out your case before me and stand forth.

Elihu had waited (ὑπόμεινον), according to 32:4a, to give an answer
(ἀπόκρισιν) to Job. Now in 33:5b, he challenges Job to give an answer to
these things, if possible. "Wait," he says, "stand against me, and I shall
stand against you." This poses Job and Elihu as the two adversaries, not
simply by the content of the remarks but by the very choice of words.

§87. Job 33:21

ἕως ἂν σαπῶσιν αὐτοῦ αἱ σάρκες 33:21a	יכל בשרו מראי

---

[262]Dhorme, *Book of Job*, 489; Beer, *Der Text*, 209.
[263]Orlinsky, "Studies in the Septuagint," *HUCA* 36 (1965) 46-47.

καὶ ἀποδείξῃ τὰ ὀστᾶ αὐτοῦ 33:21b   ושפי עצמותיו לא ראו
κενά

Until his flesh be decayed and   His flesh rots so that it cannot
his bones become exposed.[264]   be seen, and his bones, which
    were not seen, stick out.

    G may be paraphrasing, but the similarity of wording in 19:20 points
to an anaphoric translation.

ἐν δέρματί μου ἐσάπησαν αἱ 19:20a   בעורי ובבשרי דבקה עצמי
σάρκες μου
τὰ δὲ ὀστᾶ μου ἐν ὀδοῦσιν 19:20b   ואתמלטה בעור שני
ἔχεται

My flesh rotted in my skin,   My bones cling to my skin and
and my bones are held in (my)   my flesh, and I have escaped
teeth.   by the skin of my teeth.

'Εσάπησαν in 19:20a is reading רקבה for דבקה.[265] The presence of ὀστᾶ
and σάρκες in 19:20 has influenced the translator to bring in σαπῶσιν at
33:21a. Now, the flesh is said to "rot" in both verses.

§88. Job 33:22-27

    G of Eliphaz's speech in chap. 22, as already discussed (§59) was
affected by Bildad's in chap. 8. Both speeches contain admonitory words
and stated benefits if those words are heeded. Now Elihu has picked up the
baton.

> We left the sick man on the brink of the grave (v. 22). It is then that divine
> intervention takes place. Between man and God is found an intermediary whose
> function is to protect man and to shield him from divine anger; such a one is
> Michael in Dn 12:1.[266]

    The G-translator has taken great liberties with the text and has
imported material from other places.

ἤγγισεν δὲ εἰς θάνατον ἡ ψυχὴ 33:22a   ותקרב לשחת נפשו
αὐτοῦ
ἡ δὲ[267] ζωὴ αὐτοῦ ἐν ᾅδῃ 33:22b   וחיתו לממתים
ἐὰν ὦσιν χίλιοι ἄγγελοι θανα- 33:23a   אם יש עליו מלאך
τηφόροι

---

[264]Literally, "And he show his bones bare."
[265]So Dhorme (Book of Job, 279) and Beer (Der Text, 120).
[266]Dhorme, Book of Job, 501.
[267]ἤδε ἡ in B; ἡ δὲ in B^b ℵAC.

εἰς αὐτῶν οὐ μὴ τρώσῃ αὐτόν	33:23b	מליץ אחד מני אלף
ἐὰν νοήσῃ τῇ καρδίᾳ ἐπιστρα- φῆναι πρὸς κύριον	33:23c	
ἀναγγείλῃ δὲ ἀνθρώπῳ τὴν ἑαυτοῦ μέμψιν	33:23d	להגיד לאדם ישרו
τὴν δὲ ἄνοιαν αὐτοῦ δείξῃ	33:23e	
ἀνθέξεται τοῦ μὴ πεσεῖν εἰς θάνατον	33:24a	ויחננו ויאמר פדעהו מרדת שחת
ἀνανεώσει δὲ αὐτοῦ τὸ σῶμα ὥσπερ ἀλοιφὴν ἐπὶ τοίχου	33:24b	מצאתי כפר
τὰ δὲ ὀστᾶ αὐτοῦ ἐμπλήσει μυελοῦ	33:24c	
ἀπαλυνεῖ δὲ αὐτοῦ τὰς σάρκας ὥσπερ νηπίου	33:25a	רטפש בשרו מנער
ἀποκαταστήσει δὲ αὐτὸν ἀνδρω- θέντα ἐν ἀνθρώποις	33:25b	ישוב לימי עלומיו
εὐξάμενος δὲ πρὸς κύριον καὶ δεκτὰ αὐτῷ ἔσται	33:26a	יעתר אל אלוה וירצהו
εἰσελεύσεται δὲ προσώπῳ ἱλαρῷ σὺν ἐξηγορίᾳ	33:26b	וירא פניו בתרועה
ἀποδώσει δὲ ἀνθρώποις δικαιο- σύνην	33:26c	וישב לאנוש צדקתו

And his soul draws near to death, and his life is in Hades. Though there should be a thousand messengers of death, not one of them would dispatch him: if he should purpose in his heart to turn to the Lord and declare to man his fault and show his folly, he (the Lord) will support him so that he will not perish in death and will renew his body as plaster on a wall, and he will fill his bones with marrow. And he will soften his flesh as a baby's and will restore him among men in full strength. And when he prays to the Lord, his prayer

And his soul draws near the pit, and his life to the place[268] of the dead. If then there be for him an angel, a mediator, one in a thousand, to tell of the man's uprightness, and (if) he has pity on him and says, "Deliver him from going down to the pit; I have found a ransom (for him)." Then his flesh will become fresher than (in his) youth; he will be again as in the days of his youthful vigor. He will pray to God, and he (God) will favor him. He will see his (God's) face with rejoicing, and he will restore to man his righteousness.[269]

---

[268]Reading למו מתים (NAB) or למקום מתים (Dhorme, Book of Job, 500).

[269]This Hebrew colon is being translated as it is and where it is since this is what G did. See Dhorme (Book of Job, 501) and NAB, who place it after 33:23d, and Gray (Book of Job, Pt. II, 251), who leaves it where it is by following the emendation of וישב to ויספר or ויבשר.

will be received, and he will
enter with a joyful face, with
a confession. And he will render to men (their) due.

The first major departure in G comes with the treatment of מלאך
(33:23a). G translated מלאך with χίλιοι ἄγγελοι θανατηφόροι by reaching
into 33:23b for אלף. Θανατηφόροι seems to be a rendering of לממתים at
the end of 33:22b, which has been translated once as ᾅδῃ.[270] G then says,
"Not *one* of them would dispatch him," if he should repent (33:23b). "One"
is taken from אחד in 33:23b, but the rest of the colon is contrived with the
help of other passages.

The word τιτρώσκειν[271] appears seven times in Job; only two have a
Hebrew equivalent. The first occurrence is at 6:9a.

ἀρξάμενος ὁ κύριος *τρωσάτω* με 6:9a	ויאל אלוה וידכאני
Let the Lord begin to dispatch me.	Even that God would decide to crush me.

Here τρωσάτω is the equivalent of דכא. Job is asking that God "finish the
job" of killing him.[272] The concept in G of God killing man will become a
midrash in the rest of the book. Job complains at G 16:6c:

ἐὰν δὲ καὶ σιωπήσω τί ἔλαττον *τρωθήσομαι* 16:6c	ואחדלה מה מני יהלך
And even if I should be silent, shall I be (mortally) wounded any less?	And if I cease, it (my pain) will not depart from me.

At 20:24b, Zophar says that God will pierce the wicked man with a bronze
bow. There is also a Hebrew equivalent here.

τρῶσαι αὐτὸν τόξον χάλκειον 20:24b	תחלפהו קשת נחושה
Let the bronze bow kill him.	The bronze bow will pierce him through.

36:14b contains Elihu's statement of the results of impious acts. G reads the
Hebrew differently (קְדֵשִׁים for קְדֹשִׁים),[273] and adds τιτρωσκομένη to
continue the midrash.

---

[270]So Dhorme, *Book of Job*, 500.

[271]Τιτρώσκειν in classical Greek means to injure, wound or harm in some way. It also
means to inflict a death wound (Liddell-Scott, *Greek-English Lexicon*, 1799). In Num 31:19,
τετρωμένου is a translation of חלל, which there means "corpse." In Job, therefore, the
meaning is probably to wound mortally or kill.

[272]This in spite of G 6:9b "But let him not utterly destroy me."

[273]Job 5:1 has קְדֹשִׁים, which is translated ἀγγέλων ἁγίων.

ἀποθάνοι τοίνυν ἐν νεότητι   36:14a   תמת בנער נפשם
ἡ ψυχὴ αὐτῶν
ἡ δὲ ζωὴ αὐτῶν τιτρωσκομένη   36:14b   וחיתם בקדשים
ὑπὸ ἀγγέλων

Therefore, may their soul die   They expire in youth, and their
in youth and their life be de-   life ends among temple prosti-
stroyed by angels.   tutes.[274]

The same thought continues at 36:25b.

ὅσοι τιτρωσκόμενοί εἰσιν   36:25b(24b)[275]   אשר שררו אנשים
βροτοί

However many mortals are   Of which men have sung.
killed.

The only place τιτρώσκειν is not applied to man is 41:20 where it refers to
Leviathan. Thus, when εἰς αὐτῶν οὐ μὴ τρώσῃ αὐτόν appears at 33:23b, it
is only a square in the mosaic begun at 6:9a and continued in the other five
passages.

     The second point of departure is the addition of the repentance line
(33:23c). This expansion is supplied by G with the assistance of 22:22-23.[276]

ἔκλαβε[277] δὲ ἐκ στόματος αὐτου   22:22a   קח נא מפיו תורה
ἐξηγορίαν
καὶ ἀνάλαβε τὰ ῥήματα αὐτοῦ   22:22b   ושים אמריו בלבבך
ἐν καρδίᾳ σου
ἐὰν δὲ ἐπιστραφῇς καὶ ταπει-   22:23a   אם תשוב עד שדי תבנה
νώσῃς σεαυτὸν ἔναντι κυρίου
πόρρω ἐποίησας ἀπὸ διαίτης   22:23b   תרחיק עולה מאהלך
σου ἄδικον

But receive from his mouth   Receive instruction from his
confession, and lay up his   mouth, and lay up his words
words in your heart. And if   in your heart. If you return
you turn and humble yourself   to the Almighty, you will be
before the Lord, you will have   restored. If you put iniquity
put unrighteousness far from   far from your tent. . . .
your dwelling.

---

[274]See Gray (Book of Job, Pt. I, 311) for a defense of this translation.

[275]Old Greek (24a, 25b) was working only with Hebrew 24a,b. See further, §101.

[276]Gray (Book of Job, Pt. II, 249) simply notes that G has an addition at this point. Beer
(Der Text, 212) refers to it as a paraphrase. Dhorme (Book of Job, 500-501) says that 33:23c is
a combination of 22:22b and 22:23a.

[277]Following A rather than B (ἔκβαλε).

Eliphaz, in chap. 22, is instructing Job in the way of spiritual success. The points of contact between chaps. 22 and 33 are ἐν καρδίᾳ σου (22:22b) and τῇ καρδίᾳ (33:23c); ἐπιστραφῇς . . . ἔναντι κυρίου (22:23a) and ἐπιστραφῆναι πρὸς κύριον (33:23c).[278]

G next (33:23d) translates the Hebrew להגיד לאדם and paraphrases ישרו with its opposite, μέμψιν.[279] The first Hebrew word in 33:24a (ויחננו) is treated in G 33:23e as from חוה in the *pi⁽ᶜ⁾ēl* (δείξῃ), and a colon, parallel to 33:23d, is created to complete it. The subject of להגיד (33:23d) is the angel, but since the G-translator has turned him into a hostile character,[280] the man (33:23b) is now made the subject of ἀναγγείλῃ and δείξῃ. Commentators do not agree on the identity of the subject of the Hebrew apodosis in 33:24-26. Gray feels it is the interpreting angel who is speaking to an angel of death, and he quotes Dillmann as favoring God for the subject.[281] G, however, very clearly makes the Lord, mentioned in 33:23c, the subject throughout the apodosis. God is actually resisting the angel by supporting the man, and thus preventing him from going down to the pit.[282] Through the ויאמר of 33:24a, the translator has gone to 2 Sam 24:16 and 1 Chr 21:15 where the Lord stops the plague by speaking to the angel (ויאמר למלאך). This allows him to have the intervention of the Lord at this point.

The remainder of 33:24a has been colored by the Hebrew of 33:28a פדה נפשי מעבר בשחת, which is otherwise untranslated in old Greek. פדעהו (33:24a) is read פדהו, and then the rest of 33:24a is translated. The Hebrew parallels are מרדת שחת (33:24a); מעבר בשחת (33:28a).

The first word in 33:24b, ἀνανεώσει, was developed from רטפש in 33:25a in conjunction with ישוב in 33:25b (both Hebrew words are translated a second time in 33:25a-b). The rest of the colon was constructed by reading כפר with the sense of "cover, coat, pitch" (Gen 6:14) rather than as "ransom."[283] מצאתי was read as עצמותיו as in 33:21b to provide σῶμα (33:24b) and τὰ ὀστᾶ (33:24c). G has now established a healthy opposite of the punished man in 33:21.

ἕως ἂν σαπῶσιν αὐτοῦ αἱ σάρκες	33:21a	יכל בשרו מראי
καὶ ἀποδείξῃ τὰ ὀστᾶ αὐτοῦ κενά	33:21b	ושפי עצמותיו לא ראו

[278]Cf. also ἐξηγορίαν of 22:22a discussed below with 33:26b.

[279]Dhorme (*Book of Job*, 501) says G has connected ישרו with יסר, "to criticize, reproach, correct." But see the discussion of 24:20 in §65, where G apparently renders by opposites. On the use of μέμψιν in G-Job, see 33:10a.

[280]Cf. Isa 54:16 and 2 Sam 24:16 for the motif of a destroying angel.

[281]Gray, *Book of Job*, Pt. I, 291.

[282]Ἀνθέξεται should be read as a middle of ἀντέχειν in the sense of "supporting" as in 1 Thess 5:14 (ἀντέχεσθε τῶν ἀσθενῶν).

[283]So Dhorme, *Book of Job*, 502.

| Until his flesh be decayed, and his bones become exposed.[284] | His flesh wastes away so that it cannot be seen, and his bones, once invisible, protrude. |

The rotting flesh (33:21a) will become a renewed body (33:24b). The exposed (κενά) bones (33:21b) will become bones (σῶμα, עצמותיו) covered with flesh (ἀλοιφήν) (33:24b) and bones (τὰ ὀστᾶ) filled with marrow (33:24c). There are also Hebrew antecedents of 33:24-25. 20:11a (not in old Greek) has עצמותיו מלאו עלומו "(Though) his bones are full of his youthful vigor"; and 21:24b ומח עצמתיו ישקה, "And the marrow of his bones is fresh." G for this last verse has μυελὸς δὲ αὐτοῦ διαχεῖται, "He is full of marrow."[285] G has created a chiastic structure with these four lines.

> 24b   a generalization about renewing the body like plaster on a wall (bones and flesh)
> 24c   a specific statement about filling the bones with marrow
> 25a   a specific statement about softening the flesh
> 25b   a generalization about being restored among men in full strength

The Hebrew of 33:25a-b is generally followed by G, but it should be added that ἀποκαταστήσει (33:25b) shows up also in 22:28a, and ἀποδώσει (33:26c) has the echoing expressions δώσει and ἀποδοῦναι in 22:27b.

δώσει δέ σοι ἀποδοῦναι τὰς εὐχάς	22:27b	ונדריך תשלם
ἀποκαταστήσει δέ σοι δίαιταν δικαιοσύνης	22:28a	ותגזר אומר ויקם לך
And he will enable you to pay your vows, and he will restore to you a dwelling of righteousness.		And you will pay your vows, and when you make a decision, it will work out for you.

In 33:26b וירא פניו בתרועה is translated εἰσελεύσεται δὲ προσώπῳ ἱλαρῷ σὺν ἐξηγορίᾳ. Orlinsky follows Schleusner in explaining εἰσελεύσεται as an interpretation of seeing God's face rather than a Hebrew variant יבא.[286] Ἱλαρῶς was provided at 22:26b to complete the imagery of the forgiven man coming to God. The same word is now imported here.[287]

---

[284]Literally, "And he show his bones bare."

[285]Literally, "And his marrow is poured out (throughout his body)."

[286]Orlinsky, "Studies in the Septuagint," HUCA 30 (1959) 160-161; see Job 13:16b for similar Greek.

[287]Bℵ* have ἱλαρῷ (33:26b) as opposed to καθαρῷ in ℵ[c.a] (postea restit ἱλ.) AC. An argument could be made that the reading in Bℵ* was brought into harmony with 22:26b; but it could as easily be original, since harmonization is common to A but not to B. Holmes and Parsons (Vetus Testamentum Graecum, 3, ad loc.) list 22 MSS as having καθαρῷ in 33:26b.

ἀναβλέψας εἰς τὸν οὐρανὸν 22:26b
ἱλαρῶς

ותשא אל אלוה פניך

When you look up to heaven
cheerfully.

And you will lift up your face
to God.

G has also in 33:26b the word ἐξηγορία, which appears in the LXX
only here and at 22:22a (the texts are presented above). There are thirteen
occurrences of ἐξαγορεύειν, ten of which translated ידה.[288] Ἐξηγορία,
then, is surely reading תודה for תורה in 22:22a. It makes better sense to
receive "instruction" (תורה) from God's mouth than "confession" (תודה),
but G has read the latter. Σὺν ἐξηγορίᾳ in 33:26b stands for בתרועה,[289] but
it is there under the influence of 22:22a.[290]

§89. Job 34:2a

The introductory remarks in 34:2a have been influenced by 33:31a.

ἀκούσατέ μου σοφοί 34:2a
ἐπιστάμενοι ἐνωτίζεσθε τὸ 34:2b
καλόν[291]

34:4b

שמעו חכמים מלי
וידעים האזינו לי

נדעה בינינו מה טוב

Hear me, O wise ones. O knowing ones, listen to the good.

Hear, O wise ones, my words,
and listen to me, you who
know. Let us learn among us
what is good.

ἐνωτίζου Ἰώβ καὶ ἄκουέ μου 33:31a
Listen, O Job, and hear me.

הקשב איוב שמע לי

Pay attention, O Job; listen
to me.

Only the pronoun on מלי in 34:2a is translated (μου) in harmony with
33:31a. It might be argued that מלי is paraphrased in 34:2b with τὸ καλόν
(if τὸ καλόν is even original). The objects in the two cola would then be
reversed. However, G has omitted 34:3-4 except for טוב in 34:4b, which is
brought into 34:2b.[292] If this is the correct accounting for τὸ καλόν,
it is probable that 33:31a has influenced 34:2a in the treatment of מלי.

---

[288] Lev 5:5; 16:21; 26:40; Num 5:7; 1 Kgs 8:31; Ezra 10:1 (Aא); Neh 1:6; 9:2-3; Job 31:34;
Ps 32:5; Bar 1:14; Dan (Θ) 9:20.

[289] תרועה appears some 35 times in the OT and is translated in a variety of ways but never
by ἐξηγορία.

[290] I am indebted to P. W. Skehan for many suggestions in this section.

[291] τὸ καλόν אc.aAC; B omits the words.

[292] Dhorme (Book of Job, 509) agrees; he thinks the cola were dropped out by homoeoteleuton.

§90. Job 34:6, 8

ἐψεύσατο δὲ τῷ κρίματί μου	34:6a	על משפטי אכזב
	34:6b	אנוש חצי בלי פשע
He acted falsely in condemning me.		I am counted a liar (*nipᶜal*) in spite of my right. My wound from the arrow is incurable, though I am sinless.
(34:6b is not in old Greek.)		
οὐχ ἁμαρτὼν οὐδὲ ἀσεβήσας	34:8a	
Even though I am not sinning nor have acted wickedly.		(For the Hebrew, see the discussion below.)

Old Greek has not translated 34:7a-b, but the Greek phrase now in 34:8a is really a development of בלי פשע in Hebrew 34:6b and is out of place in 34:8a. The KR insertion failed to note or has ignored this fact, with the resultant separation of 34:6a and 6b by three new literal lines. Dhorme says:

> At the beginning of v. 8 we find οὐχ ἁμαρτὼν οὐδὲ ἀσεβήσας which is a remnant of the translation of v. 6b in G. In fact, οὐχ ἁμαρτὼν corresponds to בלי פשע as in 33:9, and οὐδὲ ἀσεβήσας comes from a second reading with רשע instead of פשע (cf. G ἀσεβεῖν for the verb רשע in 10:2, 7, 15).[293]

In 10:7a, Job says that God knows full well that he has not committed iniquity.

οἶδας γὰρ ὅτι οὐκ ἠσέβησα	10:7a	על דעתך כי לא ארשע
For you know that I have not committed iniquity.		Although you know that I am not wicked.

In 33:9a, Elihu quotes Job's protestations of innocence with the phrase:

διότι λέγεις καθαρός εἰμι οὐχ ἁμαρτὼν	33:9a	זך אני בלי פשע
Because you say, "I am pure, I have not sinned."		I am pure and without transgression.

With these two passages containing Job's complaint before him, the translator now works with 34:6b, supplying οὐχ ἁμαρτὼν from 33:9a and ἀσεβήσας from 10:7a. G of 34:6a-b (8a) is especially interesting in light of all the effort to prove that the translator has set out to remove ideas derogatory to God. G now says bluntly: "He acted falsely in condemning me, even though I am not sinning nor have acted wickedly."[294]

---

[293] Ibid., 511.

[294] Even Lee-Brenton (*The Septuagint Version of the Old Testament*, 690) softens this in translation to "erred" with a footnote containing "lied."

§91. Job 34:9

μὴ γὰρ εἴπῃς ὅτι οὐκ ἔσται ἐπισκοπὴ ἀνδρός	34:9a	כי אמר לא יסכן גבר
καὶ ἐπισκοπὴ αὐτῷ παρὰ κυρίου	34:9b	ברצתו עם אלהים
For you should not say, "Man will not have a visitation," when there will be a visitation on him from the Lord.		Because he has said, "A man does not profit from pleasing God."
ἐπισκοπὴ δὲ κυρίου ὑπερεῖδέν με	6:14b	ויראת שדי יעזוב
And the Lord's care of me has ceased.[295]		Though he forsakes the fear of the Almighty.[296]
ὅτε ὁ θεὸς ἐπισκοπὴν ἐποιεῖτο τοῦ οἴκου μου	29:4b	בסוד אלוה עלי אהלי
When God protected my house.		When God protected (1. בסוך) my tent.

Job, in G 6:14b, laments that God has ceased to be concerned for him. Ἐπισκοπή here is apparently the result of reading a noun form of ראה for יראת,[297] and, therefore, something about "oversight," "protection," or "guidance" should be the meaning of G. Again in 29:4b, Job expresses nostalgia for the days when God provided protection (סוך) for his tent. God's "oversight" no longer exists. Now Elihu vehemently denounces Job in G for making such a charge.[298] The G-translator has formed an entirely different sentence, at least in part, because he did not understand the verb יסכן. סכן appears six times in Job,[299] and nowhere is it translated correctly. This includes even 15:3a where the parallel line has יועיל and is translated ὄφελος. Consequently, at 34:9a, G is taking a stab at the line by means of antecedent verses; 34:9a is a negative statement about ἐπισκοπή. Job is not to say that God does not "oversee" a man. Then in 34:9b, the translator turns it into a positive assertion. "Indeed, there will be a visitation on him from the Lord."[300] ברצתו (34:9b) has been ignored in the creation of these two cola. G has turned Job's scoffing question into an absolute negation and then has had Elihu repudiate it in the rest of the chapter.

[295] Literally, "And the visitation of the Lord has disregarded me."
[296] See Dhorme (*Book of Job*, 85) for a discussion of the various ways commentators have handled 6:14b.
[297] So Dhorme, *Book of Job*, 84.
[298] The meaning of ἐπισκοπή in 34:9 has more of a judgmental nuance (cf. 34:11), but G even so is relating it to the earlier verses.
[299] 15:3; 22:2 twice; 22:21; 34:9; 35:3.
[300] Ziegler ("Der textkritische Wert," 287) lists the two occurences of ἐπισκοπή in 34:9 as an example of "vertical dittography."

§92. *Job 34:10, 12*

μή μοι εἴη ἔναντι κυρίου ἀσε-βῆσαι	34:10b	חללה לאל מרשע
καὶ ἔναντι *παντοκράτορος* *ταράξαι τὸ δίκαιον*	34:10c	ושדי מעול

Far be it from me to sin before the Lord, or to disturb justice before the Almighty.

Far be it from God to do wickedness, and from the Almighty to practice iniquity.

οἴη δὲ τὸν κύριον ἄτοπα ποιήσειν	34:12a	אף אמנם אל לא ירשיע
ἢ ὁ *παντοκράτωρ ταράξει κρίσιν*	34:12b	ושדי לא יעות משפט

And do you think the Lord will do wrong, or that the Almighty will disturb[301] judgment?

Truly, God does not practice wickedness, nor does the Almighty pervert justice.

The phrase ταράξαι τὸ δίκαιον, in 34:10c, is not dealing with מעול at all but is supplied under the influence of 34:12b and other passages where ταράσσειν is used for עות. There is an "inner Job" treatment of the word עות. Nowhere else is it translated (poorly) by ταράσσειν, as it is three times in Job (8:3; 19:6; 34:12).

γνῶτε οὖν ὅτι ὁ κύριός ἐστιν ὁ *ταράξας*	19:6a	דעו אפו כי אלוה עותני

Know then that it is the Lord who has troubled me.

Know, therefore, that God has wronged me.

μὴ ὁ κύριος *ἀδικήσει κρίνων*	8:3a	האל יעות משפט
ἢ ὁ τὰ πάντα ποιήσας *ταράξει* *τὸ δίκαιον*	8:3b	ואם שדי יעות צדק

Will the Lord be unjust when he judges; or will he who made all things disturb justice?

Does God pervert judgment, or does the Almighty pervert justice?

G of 34:10c, ταράξαι τὸ δίκαιον, is similar to 8:3b.[302] In addition, 34:12b has משפט as in 8:3a and שדי as in 8:3b. The presence of שדי in 34:10c has induced the translator to ignore מעול and to interpolate the last three words of 8:3b partly under the influence of 34:12b and 19:6a. It should be pointed out as well that G has made Elihu the subject of the

---

[301]Ταράσσειν is not the best translation of עות. It can have the meaning of "throw into disorder (an army)," which may account for its use here.

[302]Gray (*Book of Job*, Pt. II, 255) makes some connection. Ziegler ("Der textkritische Wert," 287) has missed this connection; he calls it a "vertical dittography."

disclaimer in 34:10 rather than God. This verse is turned into a personal defense by Elihu in the spirit of 32:22.[303]

§93. Job 34:15b

πᾶς δὲ βροτὸς εἰς γῆν ἀπελεύσ-	34:15b	ואדם על עפר ישוב
εται ὅθεν καὶ ἐπλάσθη		
And every mortal would return to the earth, from which also he was formed.		And man would return to the dust.

Dhorme has already noted that this addition is a gloss based on Gen 3:19.[304] Gen 2:7 may have provided some influence as well.

ἕως τοῦ ἀποστρέψαι σε εἰς	Gen 3:19b	עד שובך אל האדמה
τὴν γῆν ἐξ ἧς ἐλήμφθης·		כי ממנה לקחת
ὅτι γῆ εἶ καὶ εἰς γῆν ἀπ-	Gen 3:19c	כי עפר אתה ואל עפר תשוב
ελεύσῃ		
Until you return to the earth from which you were taken, because you are earth, and to earth you will return.		Until you return to the ground, since you were taken from it; for you are dust, and to dust you will return.

καὶ ἔπλασεν ὁ θεὸς τὸν	Gen 2:7a	וייצר יהוה אלהים את
ἄνθρωπον χοῦν ἀπὸ τῆς γῆς		האדם עפר מן האדמה
And God formed the man of dust from the earth.		And Yahweh God formed the man out of dust from the ground.

Πλάσσειν and אדם appear in both 2:7a and 34:15b. אל עפר תשוב in Gen 3:19c and על עפר ישוב in 34:15b are translated similarly, including the less frequent rendering of שוב with ἀπέρχεσθαι.[305]

§94. Job 34:20

κενὰ δὲ αὐτοῖς ἀποβήσεται τὸ	34:20a	רגע ימתו וחצות לילה
κεκραγέναι καὶ δεῖσθαι ἀνδρός		יגעשו עם ויעברו
ἐχρήσαντο γὰρ παρανόμως ἐκ-	34:20b	ויסירו אביר לא ביד
κλινομένων ἀδυνάτων		
But to cry and to beg a man will result in nothing for them,		In a moment they die; at midnight the people are shaken and

---

[303] For a similar assertion, see Wis 6:22e: καὶ οὐ μὴ παροδεύσω τὴν ἀλήθειαν.

[304] Dhorme, Book of Job, 515.

[305] Cf. Wis 15:8 where the argument is also based on the Genesis passage.

for they have acted lawlessly
in turning aside the weak.[306]

pass away, and the mighty man
is taken away by no human
hand.[307]

The additional G clause in 34:20a is drawn from 15:31b, 35b, where Eliphaz is recounting the woes that eventually befall the wicked. Since Job has met calamity, he must surely be wicked.

μὴ πιστευέτω ὅτι ὑπομενεῖ	15:31a	אל יאמן בשו נתעה
κενὰ γὰρ ἀποβήσεται αὐτῷ	15:31b	כי שוא תהיה תמורתו

Let him not believe that he will survive, for his destiny will be emptiness.

Let him not trust in emptiness, deceiving himself, because his recompense will be emptiness.[308]

ἐν γαστρὶ δὲ λήμψεται ὀδύνας	15:35a	הרה עמל וילד און
ἀποβήσεται δὲ αὐτῷ κενά	15:35b	

And he will conceive sorrows, and his destiny will be emptiness.

They conceive malice and bring forth emptiness.

Elihu is now making a similar case for God's judgment of the wicked. To bring home the point that the result of the wicked man's cry for help will be emptiness, 15:31b, 35b are borrowed. This is the reverse of 13:16a, where Job says καὶ τοῦτό μοι ἀποβήσεται εἰς σωτηρίαν.

The phrase ἐκκλινομένων ἀδυνάτων in 34:20b can be explained by a reading of ויסורו אבירים לא ביד,[309] but it has been influenced by 24:4a.

ἐξέκλιναν ἀδυνάτους ἐξ ὁδοῦ δικαίας	24:4a	יטו אביונים מדרך

They have turned aside the weak from the just way.

They turn aside the poor from the road.

Job bitterly complains in G 24:4a that God lets the wicked get away with everything, including "turning aside the weak from the just way." Elihu now indirectly charges Job with the same crime.

---

[306]Literally, "The weak being turned aside."

[307]This translation is an effort to deal with the Hebrew as it stands (see also *RSV*). For the various efforts to restore the Hebrew, see the commentaries.

[308]As in 34:20, this translation reflects the Hebrew as it is. It is quite probable that G saw it in its present state. Gray (*Book of Job*, Pt. I, 140) translates the Hebrew as is and says, "This v., too, in Hebrew is questionable, but satisfactory emendation is not forthcoming." For various efforts, see the commentaries.

[309]So Beer, *Der Text*, 218.

§95. Job 34:23

(Not in old Greek)	34:23a	כי לא על איש ישים עוד
ὁ γὰρ κύριος πάντας ἐφορᾷ	34:23b	להלך אל אל במשפט
For the Lord sees all things.		Because he does not appoint a time (1. מועד) for any man to go before God in judgment.

It is difficult to account for G of this verse. The first colon has been supplied by KR, but the old Greek (34:23b) was probably also based on 34:23a, reading something like כי אל על איש ישים לבו (עיניו). Even so, the translator has gone to 28:24 for help.

αὐτὸς γὰρ τὴν ὑπ᾽ οὐρανὸν πᾶσαν ἐφορᾷ	28:24a	כי הוא לקצות הארץ יביט
εἰδὼς τὰ ἐν τῇ γῇ πάντα ἃ[310] ἐποίησεν	28:24b	תחת כל השמים יראה
ἀνέμων σταθμὸν	28:25a	לעשות לרוח משקל
For he sees everything under heaven, knowing all the things in the earth which he made: the weight of the winds.		For he looks to the ends of the earth and sees all that is under the heavens. He gave to the wind its weight.

Chap. 28 is the extended discussion on wisdom. The only one who really knows where to find it is the one who "sees everything under heaven." It would appear that 28:24a is a summary of both Hebrew cola. Αὐτὸς γὰρ comes from Hebrew 28:24a, and τὴν ὑπ᾽ οὐρανὸν πᾶσαν ἐφορᾷ comes from Hebrew 28:24b. The second G colon (28:24b) is constructed with the help of Hebrew 28:24a. Εἰδώς may be translating ידע of 28:23b a second time (see §4); τὰ ἐν τῇ γῇ is from הארץ; πάντα may be a second reading of כל in 28:24b. Ἃ ἐποίησεν is from לעשות in 28:25a.[311] Now, from 28:24a the G-translator has borrowed πάντας (πᾶσαν) ἐφορᾷ for 34:23b. Additional help may have been provided the translator from 34:21.[312]

αὐτὸς γὰρ ὁρατής ἐστιν ἔργων ἀνθρώπων	34:21a	כי עיניו על דרכי איש
λέληθεν δὲ αὐτὸν οὐδὲν ὧν πράσσουσιν	34:21b	וכל צעדיו יראה
For he sees the works of men, and nothing that they do has escaped him.		For his eyes are upon the ways of man, and he sees all his steps.

[310] ἃ in A‍א.

[311] Dhorme (*Book of Job*, 411) agrees with this last statement.

[312] Dhorme (*Book of Job*, 520) says G 34:23b sums up v 21. Beer (*Der Text*, 218) says, "Doch vgl. V. 21."

This verse is paraphrased in G. The first colon is stated positively, and the second is reversed to a negative sentence. If the translator used the Hebrew of 34:21a-b, both cola could have been summarized by 34:23b; but if he followed G, only 34:21a could have been used since 34:21b is quite different from 34:23b.

§96. *Job 34:24*

ὁ καταλαμβάνων ἀνεξιχνίαστα	34:24a	ירע כבירים לא חקר
ἔνδοξά τε καὶ ἐξαίσια ὧν οὐκ ἔστιν ἀριθμός	34:24b	ויעמד אחרים תחתם
Who comprehends unsearchable things, both glorious and extraordinary things, without number.		He breaks the mighty without inquiry and sets others in their place.

The translation of this verse is based on 9:10, which in turn has almost the same words (both Hebrew and Greek) as 5:9.

ὁ ποιῶν μεγάλα καὶ ἀνεξιχνίαστα	9:10a	עשה גדלות עד אין חקר
ἔνδοξά τε καὶ ἐξαίσια ὧν οὐκ ἔστιν ἀριθμός	9:10b	ונפלאות עד אין מספר
Who does great and unsearchable things, both glorious and extraordinary things, without number.		Who does great things beyond understanding and marvelous things without number.
τὸν ποιοῦντα μεγάλα καὶ ἀνεξιχνίαστα	5:9a	עשה גדלות ואין חקר
ἔνδοξά τε καὶ ἐξαίσια ὧν οὐκ ἔστιν ἀριθμός	5:9b	נפלאות עד אין מספר

The translation of this verse is the same as 9:10. The presence of לא חקר in 34:24a has prompted the translator to bring in most of 9:10a-b (5:9a-b) to complete the line and to ignore the remainder of the Hebrew.[313]

§97. *Job 35:3a*

ἢ ἐρεῖς τί ποιήσω ἁμαρτών	35:3a	כי תאמר מה יסכן לך[314]
	35:3b	מה אעיל מחטאתי

[313]So Dhorme (*Book of Job*, 521) and Beer (*Der Text*, 218).
[314]לך is found in indirect discourse which is translated as direct discourse.

| Or that you say, "What sin am I doing?" | That you say, "What does it profit me; what more advantage do I have than if I had sinned?" |

The old Greek, preserved in Codex A,[315] has combined the Hebrew cola taking כי תאמר (ἢ ἐρεῖς) from 35:3a, reading אעיל as אפעל in 35:3b,[316] and loosely translating מחטאתי as ἁμαρτών.[317] The translator, however, has been influenced by three other verses. One is 34:8a, which is out of place due to the KR interpolations. It is really translating 34:6b.

| οὐχ ἁμαρτὼν οὐδὲ ἀσεβήσας | 34:8a(6b) | אנוש חצי בלי פשע |
| Even though I am not sinning nor have acted wickedly. | | My wound from the arrow is incurable, though I am sinless. |

As discussed above (§90) 34:8a was influenced by 33:9a where אני זך בלי פשע is translated διότι λέγεις καθαρός εἰμι οὐχ ἁμαρτών.

| εἰ ἐγὼ ἥμαρτον τί δύναμαί σοι[318] πρᾶξαι | 7:20a | חטאתי מה אפעל לך |
| If I have sinned, what can I do to you? | | Though I have sinned, what can I do to you? |

εἰ ἥμαρτες τί πράξεις	35:6a	אם חטאת מה תפעל בו
εἰ δὲ καὶ πολλὰ ἠνόμησας τί δύνασαι ποιῆσαι	35:6b	ורבו פשעיך מה תעשה לו
If you have sinned, what will you do? And if you have committed many lawless acts, what are you able to do?		If you have sinned, what (harm) do you do to him? Even if your transgressions are many, how do you (hurt) him?

It has already been pointed out (§91) that G does not know how to handle the root סכן. Its presence in 35:3a and the rather difficult Hebrew of both cola have prompted the translator to deal with the text differently, which he has done with the assistance of 34:8a(6b); 33:9a; 35:6, and 7:20a.

---

[315]Bא* are alone in omitting this line. Holmes and Parsons (*Vetus Testamentum Graecum*, 3, *ad loc.*) list A and 20 MSS for it. Swete (*The Old Testament in Greek*, 2. 585) adds אc.aC as witnesses to it.

[316]G translates פעל in Job by ποιεῖν four times out of six.

[317]The omission of מה יסכן לך could have happened accidentally through homoeoteleuton (מה . . . מה), but it is more probably deliberate in light of the pattern established in the book of avoiding the translation of סכן.

[318]B has δυνήσομαι for δύναμαί σοι.

§98. Job 35:10b

ὁ κατατάσσων φυλακὰς νυκ-τερινάς	35:10b	נתן זמרות בלילה
Who appoints night-watches.		Who gives songs in the night.

Schleusner says: "Ordinans *vigilias* nocturnas: ubi non legerunt שמירות, sed sic acceperunt in sua mente per commutationem literarum ז et ש."[319] There is, however, the possibility that this choice was influenced by 7:12.

πότερον θάλασσά εἰμι ἢ δράκων	7:12a	הים אני אם תנין
ὅτι κατέταξας ἐπ᾽ ἐμὲ φυλακήν	7:12b	כי תשים עלי משמר
Am I the sea, or a sea monster, that you have set a watch over me?		Am I the sea, or a sea monster, that you set a watch over me?

Job bursts forth in complaint against God in chap. 7: "What kind of person would God set a watch over?" Now, in G 35:10 Elihu says: "The wicked man does not ask, 'Where is God my maker, who sets night-watches (over man).'"

§99. Job 36:5-17

These verses are being treated as a unit because they represent a collocation of selected Hebrew phrases not observed to this extent in the Book of Job. Driver has already set forth the kernel of this idea in his philological discussion of these verses, but his remarks are incomplete.[320] The verses will be presented in the order in which they appear in the old Greek with their Hebrew parallels. An explanation will follow. The KR inserts are, of course, omitted, thus leaving the old Greek a continuous whole, as it was originally intended.

5a γίγνωσκε δὲ ὅτι ὁ κύριος οὐ μὴ ἀποποιήσηται τὸν ἄκακον		הן אל כביר ולא ימאס 5a
10a ἀλλὰ τοῦ δικαίου εἰσακούσεται		כביר כח לב 5b
12a ἀσεβεῖς δὲ οὐ διασῴζει παρὰ τὸ μὴ βούλεσθαι εἰδέναι αὐτοὺς τὸν κύριον		לא יחיה רשע 6a
		ויגועו בבלי דעת 12b
12b καὶ διότι νουθετούμενοι ἀνήκοοι ἦσαν		ויגל אזנם למוסר 10a
		ואם לא ישמעו בשלח יעברו 12a
14a ἀποθάνοι τοίνυν ἐν νεότητι ἡ ψυχὴ αὐτῶν		תמת בנער נפשם 14a

[319]Schleusner, *Novus thesaurus*, 5. 479.
[320]Gray, *Book of Job*, Pt. II, 273-274.

14b ἡ δὲ ζωὴ αὐτῶν τιτρωσκομένη
ὑπὸ ἀγγέλων

15a ἀνθ᾽ ὧν ἔθλιψαν ἀσθενῆ καὶ
ἀδύνατον

15b κρίμα δὲ πρᾳέων ἐκθήσει

17 οὐχ ὑστερήσει δὲ ἀπὸ δικαίων
κρίμα

14b וחיתם בקדשים

15a יחלץ עני בעניו

6b ומשפט עניים יתן

7a לא יגרע מצדיק עיניו

And know that the Lord will not cast off the innocent. But he will hear the just, but the ungodly he will not deliver because they do not want to know the Lord, and because, when warned, they were disobedient. Therefore, may their soul die in youth, and their life be destroyed by angels, since they oppressed the weak and helpless. But the judgment of the meek he will carry out, and justice will not be lacking for the righteous.

Behold, God is mighty, and he does not refuse (the just?). He is mighty in strength of heart.[321] He does not keep the wicked alive, and they die without knowledge. And he opens their ears to instruction, but if they do not listen, they perish by the sword. They expire in youth, and their life ends among temple prostitutes. He saves the unfortunate through their affliction, and gives judgment to the afflicted. He does not withdraw his eyes from the righteous.

The word γίγνωσκε (36:5a) may be a second translation of דעות in 36:4 rather than a paraphrase as Dhorme suggests.[322] However, G-Job does tend to avoid ἰδού for (ה)הן so that it may be an arbitrary lexical choice.[323] Dhorme has, however, correctly noted the indebtedness of 36:5a to 8:20a.[324]

8:20a ὁ γὰρ κύριος οὐ μὴ ἀποποιή-
σηται τὸν ἄκακον

הן אל לא ימאס תם

For the Lord will not cast off the innocent.

Behold, God will not reject the upright.

The truncated Hebrew has caused the translator to cast about for help. The similarity of language in 8:20a has led him to bring in the Greek from that verse. The object of ימאס may have been originally תם in both 36:5a and 8:20a, but a conclusive argument for it cannot be made from G. In addition to 8:20a, there is one other passage in Job that may have influenced the translator at this point.

[321]This faulty Hebrew text (5a-b) has been patched up in various ways. G was, again, probably working with the existing text and doing the best he could with it, although his work in the following section goes beyond the call of duty.

[322]Dhorme, Book of Job, 539.

[323]Old Greek has הן or הנה 42 times and translates with ἰδού only 11 times. The same word occurs in new Greek seven times and is translated ἰδού seven times.

[324]Dhorme, The Book of Job, 539. So also Ziegler ("Der textkritische Wert," 291).

τὰ δὲ ἔργα τῶν χειρῶν σου 14:15b   למעשה ידיך תכסף
μὴ ἀποποιοῦ
But do not reject the works of   You would yearn for the work
your hands.   of your hands.

G 36:10a is supplied as a parallel to 36:5a with no regard for the Hebrew of
36:5b. The colon was probably provided with the help of 9:15a.

ἐὰν γὰρ ᾧ δίκαιος οὐκ εἰσ- 9:15a   אשר אם צדקתי לא אענה
ακούσεταί μου
For though I be righteous, he   Though I were right, I could
will not hear me.   not answer.

Chap. 27 also contains statements of God's refusal to respond to the
unjust.

ἢ τὴν δέησιν αὐτοῦ εἰσακού- 27:9a   הצעקתו ישמע אל
σεται ὁ θεός
Or will God hear his prayer?   Will God hear his cry?

ἢ ὡς ἐπικαλεσαμένου αὐτοῦ 27:10b   יקרא אלוה בכל עת
εἰσακούσεται αὐτοῦ
Or will he hear him when he   Will he call upon God at all
calls upon him?   times?

The G-translator has put into Elihu's mouth a couplet (36:5a, 10a) which
directly refutes Job's negative statements that God will not listen to just
people.
　　The addition beginning with παρά in 36:12a was prompted by 21:14b.

ὁδούς σου εἰδέναι οὐ βούλομαι 21:14b   ודעת דרכיך לא חפצנו
I do not wish to know your   We have no desire to know
ways.   your ways.

Job argues in chap. 21 that the ungodly one gets along quite well even
though he tells God he wants nothing to do with him. Elihu now says in G:
"The ungodly will not be saved when they say this to God." Hebrew
36:12b and particularly בבלי דעת may have been the point of departure to
21:14b.
　　G 36:12b is a paraphrase of the Hebrew 36:10a, 12a, but 36:14 is
equivalent to 36:14 in Hebrew. The idea of angels mortally wounding
people is derived from 33:23, which contains similar phraseology.[325] In
36:14b, קְדֵשִׁים is being read as קָדְשִׁים.
　　G 36:15b has no relation to Hebrew 36:15b, but it does match 36:6b of
the Hebrew, which is not otherwise translated in the old Greek. Likewise,

---

[325]See the discussion in §88.

the next colon in old Greek (36:17) is taken from Hebrew 36:7a, to which it corresponds quite well, including the translation of יגרע by ὑστερήσει as in Num 9:7. Κρίμα should be reading משפט or דין as in Hebrew 36:17 instead of עיניו of 36:7a; consequently κρίμα may come from Hebrew 36:17.

§ 100. Job 36:21a

ἀλλὰ φύλαξαι μὴ πράξῃς ἄτοπα[326]	36:21a	השמר אל תפן אל און
But watch out, lest you do that which is wrong.		Watch out, do not turn to iniquity.

This verse has been affected by 27:6b where Job avows his innocence.

οὐ γὰρ σύνοιδα ἐμαυτῷ ἄτοπα πράξας	27:6b	לא יחרף לבבי מימי
For I am not conscious within myself of having done anything wrong.		My heart does not reproach (me for) any of my days.

The paraphrase of 36:21a is legitimate, but it was probably influenced by 27:6b.

§ 101. Job 36:24a, 25b

μνήσθητι ὅτι μεγάλα ἐστὶν αὐτοῦ τὰ ἔργα	36:24a	זכר כי תשגיא פעלו
ὅσοι τιτρωσκόμενοί εἰσιν βροτοί	36:25b	אשר שררו אנשים[327]
Remember that his works are great, however many mortals are dispatched.		Remember to extol his work, of which men have sung.

Dhorme has given the correct parallels for the Greek and Hebrew lines but has not followed through on the idea of *angels* doing the wounding or dispatching (τιτρώσκειν).[328]

ἡ δὲ ζωὴ αὐτῶν τιτρωσκομένη ὑπὸ ἀγγέλων	36:14b	וחיתם בקדשים
And their life be destroyed by angels.		And their life ends among temple prostitutes.

[326] B: ἄδικα.
[327] This is Hebrew 36:24b.
[328] Dhorme, *Book of Job*, 551.

G probably derived τιτρωσκομένη from שׁררו, but the lexical choice was influenced by 36:14b.

§102. Job 37:16b

ἐξαίσια δὲ πτώματα πονηρῶν	37:16b	מפלאות תמים דעים
And extraordinary falls of the wicked.		The miraculous works of him who is perfect in knowledge.

G represents a homiletical addition gaining its initial thrust from מפלאות but deriving its final form from 18:12.

πτῶμα δὲ αὐτῷ ἡτοίμασται ἐξαίσιον	18:12	ואיד נכון לצלעו
But an extraordinary fall is prepared for him (the ungodly).		And destruction is ready at his his side.

Dhorme is correct in assuming that G is reading רעים for דעים in 37:16b, but his postulate of a double translation of מפלאות, treated as from נפל for πτώματα, is unnecessary in light of 18:12.[329]

§103. Job 37:19b

καὶ παυσώμεθα πολλὰ λέγοντες	37:19b	לא נערך מפני חשך
And let us stop talking so much.		We cannot draw up our case because of darkness.

The Hebrew is most difficult. Dhorme thinks G has paraphrased it,[330] but it is more likely that the translator simply could not get sense from the Hebrew. It is possible that G has followed a precedent from 29:9a.

ἁδροὶ δὲ ἐπαύσαντο λαλοῦντες	29:9a	שרים עצרו במלים
And mighty ones stopped talking.		Princes refrained from speaking.

Job says in 29:9a, that in the old days, when God was still with him, men stood in hushed silence when he walked in. Elihu now says in G that man should stop speaking in God's presence.

---

[329] Ibid., 568. Kennicott (*Vetus Testamentum Hebraicum*, 2. 517) lists one MS as having רעים. For a similar aphorism in Hebrew, cf. Ps 34:22 (Ps 112:2 the contrary) and LXX-Prov 1:18b and Wis 3:19.

[330] Dhorme, *Book of Job*, 570.

§ 104. Job 38:1-2

μετὰ δὲ τὸ παύσασθαι Ἐλιοῦν τῆς λέξεως	38:1a	
εἶπεν ὁ κύριος τῷ Ἰὼβ διὰ λαίλαπος καὶ νεφῶν	38:1b	[331] ויען יהוה את איוב מן הסערה ויאמר
τίς οὗτος ὁ κρύπτων με βουλήν	38:2a	מי זה מחשיך עצה
συνέχων δὲ ῥήματα ἐν καρδίᾳ ἐμὲ δὲ οἴεται κρύπτειν	38:2b	במלין בלי דעת

And after Elihu had stopped speaking, the Lord spoke to Job through a whirlwind and clouds: "Who is this that hides counsel from me, and holds words in his heart and supposes to hide them from me?"

And Yahweh answered Job from the whirlwind and said: "Who is this that obscures counsel by words without knowledge?"

The first colon in G is interpolated to provide a transitional sentence. The translator has brought it in, however, from 36:2, where Elihu says:

μεῖνόν με μικρὸν ἔτι ἵνα δι-δάξω σε	36:2a	כתר לי זעיר ואחוך
ἔτι γὰρ ἐν ἐμοί ἐστιν λέξις	36:2b	כי עוד לאלוה מלים

Wait for me yet a little, that I may teach you, for I still have something to say.

Wait for me a little, that I may instruct you, for there are yet words to be said on God's behalf.

Λέξις in 36:2b translates מלים. The translator is making the Hebrew explicit with ἐν ἐμοί since the actual words come from Elihu on behalf of God. Now, in 38:1a, G says that Elihu has finished his λέξις.

The second addition, νεφῶν in 38:1b, occurs also in 40:6.

ἔτι δὲ ὑπολαβὼν ὁ κύριος εἶπεν τῷ Ἰὼβ ἐκ τοῦ νέφους	40:6	[332] ויען יהוה את איוב מן סערה ויאמר

And the Lord answered further and spoke to Job from the cloud.

And Yahweh answered Job from the whirlwind and said:

Νεφῶν is added at 38:1b and νέφους at 40:6. The clouds are common enough in the book (six times), and it is only natural that God should

[331] Qĕrēʾ: מן
[332] Qĕrēʾ: מן

speak from them. In 38:1b, λαίλαπος and νεφῶν appear where Hebrew has only הסערה; λαίλαπος is dropped and only νέφους is found at 40:6 where סערה appears.

The third expansion is the extra colon in 38:2b. Dhorme says that συνέχων is expletive as in 7:11; 10:1; 34:14.[333] G may have been reading עצה (38:2a) the second time as עצר, since ῥήματα represents במלין, and ἐν καρδίᾳ may stand for בלי read as בלב. The word κρύπτειν (38:2b) does not represent מחשיך (38:2a) but מעלים in 42:3a.

τίς γάρ ἐστιν ὁ κρύπτων σε βουλήν	42:3a	מי זה מעלים עצה
φειδόμενος δὲ ῥημάτων καὶ σὲ οἴεται κρύπτειν	42:3b	בלי דעת
For who is he that hides counsel from you? And who keeps back words and supposes to hide them from you?		Who is this that hides counsel without knowledge?

G of 42:3a follows the Hebrew explicitly (the σὲ is added from the context); 42:3b, however, is based on 38:2b.[334] Instead of συνέχων, 42:3b has φειδόμενος. This may represent a reading of מחשיך based on מחשיך of 38:2a.[335]

These two verses, 38:2 and 42:3, have been handled somewhat as a unit by G. Each verse has influenced the other, but the treatment was not uniform.

§ 105. Job 38:7

ὅτε ἐγενήθησαν ἄστρα	38:7a	ברן יחד כוכבי בקר
ᾔνεσάν με φωνῇ μεγάλῃ πάντες ἄγγελοί μου	38:7b	ויריעו כל בני אלהים
When the stars were made, all my angels praised me with a loud voice.		When the morning stars sang together and all the sons of God shouted for joy.

Gard has dealt with the relation of בני אלהים/ἄγγελοι under the heading: "The Removal of References to 'Sons of God' and to Human Emotions or Mental Processes Applied to God." He says of 1:6 and 2:1:

G realizes that בני אלהים denotes "sons of divinity, sons of deity" and does not refer to the human concept of son. The translator does object, however, to the

---

[333] Dhorme, *Book of Job*, 574-575.

[334] Ibid., 645.

[335] חשך is translated by φείδεσθαι four times in Job, but it is always *qal* in form.

possibility that בני אלהים could have a mythological connotation and thereby undermine the Old Testament concept of monotheism. He therefore changes to οἱ ἄγγελοι τοῦ θεοῦ "the angels of God."[336]

What Gard fails to note is that there is already ample tradition in the Pentateuch for בני אלהים to be translated as ἄγγελοι. There is evidence for it at Gen 6:2.[337] Ἀγγέλων θεοῦ is the original reading in Deut 32:8 for בני אלהים.[338] The phrases υἱοὶ θεοῦ and ἄγγελοι θεοῦ appear side by side in LXX-Deut 32:43.[339] Ἄγγελοι, therefore, represents an old Alexandrian explanation of בני אלהים, which is simply followed by the translator of Job.

The rest of 38:7 is different. G has subordinated 38:7a to 38:7b. The first colon is thus simplified and the second amplified, with a resultant different meaning. Ἐγενήθησαν is probably reading ברא for ברן (רנן) as Dhorme suggests.[340] There is phraseology similar to 38:7b elsewhere in the OT which could have influenced the translator of Job.

καὶ ἀνέστησαν οἱ Λευεῖται ἀπὸ τῶν υἱῶν Καὰθ καὶ ἀπὸ τῶν υἱῶν Κόρε αἰνεῖν κυρίῳ θεῷ Ἰσραὴλ ἐν φωνῇ μεγάλῃ εἰς ὕψος	2 Chr 20:19	ויקמו הלוים מן בני הקהתים ומן בני הקרחים להלל ליהוה אלהי ישראל בקול גדול למעלה
And the Levites of the sons of Kath and of the sons of Korah stood up to praise the Lord God of Israel with a loud voice, on high.		And the Levites of the sons of Kohath and of the sons of Korah arose to praise Yahweh the God of Israel with a loud voice, on high.
αἰνεῖτε αὐτόν πάντες οἱ ἄγγελοι αὐτοῦ	Ps 148:2a	הללוהו כל מלאכיו

---

[336] Gard, *Exegetical Method*, 44.

[337] See J. W. Wevers, *Genesis* (Septuaginta I; Göttingen: Vandenhoeck und Ruprecht, 1974) 108. He opts for υἱοί as the original reading.

[338] See P. W. Skehan ("Qumran and the Present State of Old Testament Text Studies: The Masoretic Text," *JBL* 78 [1959] 21) for the reading בני אלוהים for בני ישראל long suspected from the LXX ἀγγέλων θεοῦ.

[339] 4QDeut has והשתחוו לו כל אלהים, which is not in MT (see J. de Waard, *A Comparative Study of the Old Testament Text in the Dead Sea Scrolls and in the New Testament* [Grand Rapids: Eerdmans, 1966] 13-16, for a presentation of the data). This Hebrew colon is translated with two Greek lines of which P. W. Skehan, in a forthcoming publication in DJD, states that καὶ ἐνισχυσάτωσαν αὐτῷ πάντες ἄγγελοι θεοῦ represents the oldest form of the LXX text, and that the introduction of προσκυνησάτωσαν and υἱοὶ θεοῦ is the result of recensional activity dating back to about the turn of the era.

[340] Dhorme, *Book of Job*, 577. Ἐγενήθησαν could be an inner G corruption of ἐγεννήθησαν, which better represents ברא.

αἰνεῖτε αὐτόν πᾶσαι αἱ δυνά- μεις αὐτοῦ	Ps 148:2b	הללוהו כל צבאו
Praise him, all you his an- gels, praise him, all you his hosts.		Praise him, all you his an- gels, praise him, all you his hosts.

The entire translation of 38:7, from "sons of God" to "angels praising God," and "praising God with a loud voice," has solid literary tradition behind it which may have been utilized by the translator.

§ 106. Job 38:14

This verse in G is the translator's theological amplification of the Hebrew.

ἢ σὺ λαβὼν γῆν πηλὸν ἔπλασας ζῶον	38:14a	תתהפך כחמר חותם
καὶ λαλητὸν αὐτὸν ἔθου ἐπὶ γῆς	38:14b	ויתיצבו כמו לבוש
Or did you take earth and make of the clay a living crea- ture and place him with the power of speech upon the earth?		It is changed as is clay by the seal and dyed (1. ותצטבע) as though a garment.

The words חמר and חותם in 38:14a have given the translator cause to depart from the Hebrew and give instead this homily on creation. חותם has been read חית, probably through a visual error, but the idea of man being made from clay and general references to clay are relatively common in the book.

ἐξ ὧν καὶ αὐτοὶ ἐκ τοῦ αὐτοῦ πηλοῦ ἐσμεν	4:19b	אשר בעפר יסודם
Of whom we also are from the same clay.		Whose foundation is in the dust.
μνήσθητι ὅτι πηλόν με ἔπλασας	10:9a	זכר נא כי כחמר עשיתני
Remember that you made me clay.		Remember that you made me as clay.
τὸ δὲ σῶμα πήλινον	13:12b	לגבי חמר גביכם
And your body (like a body of) clay.		Your defenses are defenses of clay.
ἴσα δὲ πηλῷ ἑτοιμάσῃ χρυσίον	27:16b	וכחמר יכין מלבוש
And prepare gold as clay.		And pile up clothes like clay.
ἥγησαι δέ με ἴσα πηλῷ	30:19a	הרני לחמר
And you consider me as clay.		He has thrown me into the clay.

ἐκ πηλοῦ διήρτισαι σὺ ὡς καὶ ἐγώ	33:6a	הן אני כפיך לאל
ἐκ τοῦ αὐτοῦ διηρτίσμεθα	33:6b	מחמר קרצתי גם אני
You are formed from the clay as I also am. We are formed from the same clay.		Look, I am toward God as you are; I too was formed from clay.[341]

G now argues that the ultimate evidence of the superiority of God's wisdom over Job's is God's ability to form man from the dust, give him human speech (λαλητόν), and place him on earth. The creation account in Genesis 2 uses ἔπλασεν, ἄνθρωπον, ζῶσαν, and ἔθετο. In addition, Zophar asks at 20:4b: ἀφ' οὗ ἐτέθη ἄνθρωπος ἐπὶ τῆς γῆς? The translator has taken an admittedly obscure passage and turned it into a defense of God's greatness by pointing out the crowning achievement in God's creation of the world.

§ 107. Job 38:37b

οὐρανὸν δὲ εἰς γῆν ἔκλινεν	38:37b	ונבלי שמים מי ישכיב
And has bowed heaven down to earth.		And who can turn over the waterskins of heaven?

The background for G lies in poetic passages elsewhere in Scripture.

καὶ ἔκλινεν οὐρανοὺς καὶ κατέβη	2 Sam 22:10a	ויט שמים וירד
And he bowed the heavens and came down.		And he bowed the heavens and came down.
καὶ ἔκλινεν οὐρανὸν καὶ κατέβη	Ps 18:10a (LXX 17:10a)	ויט שמים וירד
And he bowed the heavens and came down.		And he bowed the heavens and came down.
κύριε κλῖνον οὐρανούς σου καὶ κατάβηθι	Ps 144:5 (LXX 143:5)	יהוה הט שמיך ותרד
Lord, bow down your heavens and come down.		O Yahweh, bow down your heavens and come down.

These passages reflect a common poetical statement about God which has been introduced at 38:37b in lieu of the delightful metaphor of "tipping over the waterskins of heaven."

---

[341] For this translation, see *RSV*; Dhorme (*Book of Job*, 488) and Gray (*Book of Job*, Pt. I, 284) translate similarly. *NAB* has "Behold, I, like youself, have been taken from the same clay by God." Pope (*Job*, 247) treats לאל as an oath.

§ 108. Job 39:26b

ἀναπετάσας τὰς πτέρυγας ἀκίν- ητος καθορῶν τὰ πρὸς νότον Having spread her wings, star- ing, unmoving, toward the south.	39:26b	יפרש כנפו לתימן He spreads out his wings to- ward the south.
ἐκεῖσε ὢν ζητεῖ τὰ σῖτα From there, he seeks food. (29b is not in old Greek)	39:29a 39:29b	משם חפר אכל למרחוק עיניו יביטו From there, he searches for his prey; his eyes behold it afar off.

The untranslated Hebrew of 39:29b may have provided the additions of 39:26b. Ἀκίνητος is an interpretation of למרחוק, that is, the hawk can see from a distance without moving. Καθορῶν paraphrases עיניו יביטו. This simple addition makes 39:26b much more complete as a description of the activity of the hawk.

§ 109. Job 40:19b; 41:25b

πεποιημένον ἐνκαταπαίζεσθαι ὑπὸ τῶν ἀγγέλων αὐτοῦ He was created to be made sport of by his angels.	40:19b	העשו יגש חרבו Let his maker bring near his sword.
πεποιημένον ἐνκαταπαίζεσθαι ὑπὸ τῶν ἀγγέλων μου He was created to be made sport of by my angels.	41:25b	העשו לבלי חת He was made without fear.

The word ἐνκαταπαίζεσθαι was influenced by Ps 104:26 where Leviathan is the creature.

δράκων οὗτος ὅν ἔπλασας ἐμπαίζειν αὐτῷ This dragon which you formed to make sport of it.	Ps 104:26b (LXX 103:26b)	לויתן זה יצרת לשחק בו Leviathan which you formed to make sport of it.

The imagery in Job 40:19, however, is not simply that of the Almighty making sport of Leviathan (Behemoth) but that of killing him, and the killing has been deputed to the angels. Two lines of reasoning support this conclusion. The first is etymological. Παίζειν, without a preposition, means simply "to play" as in Job 40:29: "Can you play with him, as with a bird?" Ἐμπαίζειν, however, is what God did to the Egyptians (Exod 10:2; 1 Sam 6:6). It is interesting that Pharoah is called the great dragon in Ezek

29:3, and the sword is to be brought against him in Ezek 29:8. Ἐμπαίζειν is what Saul wants to avoid from the Philistines by having his armor bearer kill him (1 Sam 31:4). In 2 Macc 7:7 (ἐμπαιγμόν) and 7:10 (ἐνεπαίζετο), the word is used as a description of the martyrdom of the second and third sons. In each of these cases, the translation "mocked, mockery," is legitimate, but there is a close connection with killing. The intensified form in Job 40:19b and 41:25b (ἐνκαταπαίζεσθαι) surely means "to kill," particularly in light of the Hebrew יגש חרבו (40:19b).

The second line of reasoning is the history of the interpretation of these biblical passages by the Jews. The mythological background is the creator pursuing the primordial creature (Job 26:13; Isa 27:1; 51:9, Hebrew only). Later this activity is deputed to the angels, and the creature becomes Satan (cf. Jude 9, Michael and Satan; Rom 16:20 and Rev 12:7-9).[342] This process begins in G-Job at 26:13 where the Hebrew: "His *hand* pierces the fleeing serpent," is changed to: "He kills the apostate dragon by his *command*."[343] Furthermore, angels are considered to be messengers of destruction as agents of God (Job 33:23; 36:14; 40:11, all three in G; Isa 54:16, Hebrew; 2 Sam 24:16). This background will assist in the understanding of G in Job 40:19b; 41:25b.[344] G read העשו as a *qal* passive participle in both 40:19b and 41:25b. G then introduced the angels as agents of the action against Behemoth[345] in accord with the general interpretive principles outlined above. G probably read the same consonants now in MT at 40:19. The presence of יגש חרבו lends weight to the interpretation of ἐνκαταπαίζεσθαι as "to kill."

When the translator came to 41:25b, he brought in the expansion from 40:19b. The presence of לבלי חת (41:25b) may have reminded him of Isa 38:17[346] where Hezekiah says:

εἵλου γάρ μου τὴν ψυχὴν Isa 38:17a	ואתה חשקת נפשי
ἵνα μὴ ἀπόληται	משחת בלי
You have chosen my soul	You have kept (1. חשך) my
that it might not perish.	life from the pit of destruc-
	tion.

[342]L. Ginzberg (*The Legends of the Jews* [Philadelphia: Jewish Publication Society, 1925] 5. 43) says: "The contest between the angels and the monsters is variously described in the sources quoted above, and especially noteworthy is the description of Alphabetot. Gabriel receives the order [cf. προστάγματι, Job 26:13] from God to drag out Leviathan from the Great Sea."

[343]The shift from God as the agent to angels may account for the missing Greek in LXX-Isa 51:9-10 rather than homoioarchton as is commonly assumed.

[344]For a full discussion in the context of Job, see Pope, *Job*, 324-334.

[345]For the later Jewish practice of connecting Behemoth and Leviathan, see Ginzberg, *Legends of the Jews*, 5. 44-46.

[346]The possible use of Isa 38:15 in 3:20b is discussed in §20.

Here בלי has the nominal sense of "destruction." The translator may have connected the בלי of Isa 38:17a with לבלי in Job 41:25b (along with חת which can have the meaning of "crushed" in the verbal form) and then brought in 40:19b as the translation for it.

§110. Job 40:21

ὑπὸ παντοδαπὰ δένδρα κοιμᾶ-ται	40:21a	תחת צאלים ישכב
παρὰ πάπυρον καὶ κάλαμον καὶ βούτομον	40:21b	בסתר קנה ובצה

He lies under trees of every kind, by the papyrus and reed and bulrush.	Under the lotus trees he lies, in the covert of the reeds and in the marsh.

μὴ θάλλει πάπυρος ἄνευ ὕδατος	8:11a	היגאה גמא בלא בצה
ἢ ὑψωθήσεται βούτομον ἄνευ πότου	8:11b	ישגה אחו בלי מים

Can the papyrus flourish without water or the bulrush grow up without moisture?	Can the papyrus grow up without marsh or the reed grass flourish without water?

G has produced *three* plants in 40:21b for קנה ובצה and has followed 8:11 in doing so. Πάπυρος translates גמא in 8:11a, but πάπυρον in 40:21b has no counterpart. The G-translator may have thrown it in, since he did not know what to do with צאלים in 40:21a. 8:11b has βούτομον for אחו and ἄνευ ὕδατος for בלא בצה in 8:11a, but בצה in 40:21b becomes βούτομον. Κάλαμον is equivalent to קנה, but the other two plants have been borrowed from 8:11 without regard for the Hebrew of 40:21b.[347]

§111. Job 41:3a

ἢ τίς ἀντιστήσεταί μοι καὶ ὑπομενεῖ	41:3a	מי הקדימני ואשלם

Or who shall resist me and stay alive?	Who has confronted him (1. הקדימו) and remained safe (1. וישלם)?

τίς σκληρὸς γενόμενος ἐναν-τίον αὐτοῦ ὑπέμεινεν	9:4b	מי הקשה אליי[348] וישלם

---

[347]Thus Beer (*Der Text*, 248) is wrong when he says, "G scheint בצה πάπυρον . . . βούτομον 2 mal zu übers."

[348]Qĕrēʾ: אליו.

Who ever resisted him and stayed alive?	Who ever withstood him without harm?

γενοῦ δὴ σκληρός ἐὰν ὑπο- 22:21a
μείνῃς
Resist (him) now, if you can endure.

הסכן נא עמו ושלם

Come to terms now with him, and be at peace.

In §57 22:21a has already been discussed as dependent on 9:4b because of a failure to comprehend סכן. G of 41:3a is following a better Hebrew text. The translator read the third singular *qal* of שלם. His translation was, even so, affected by 9:4b and 22:21a.

§112. Job 41:20a

οὐ μὴ τρώσῃ αὐτὸν τόξον χάλ- 41:20a
κειον
The bronze bow will not wound him.

לא יבריחנו בן קשת

The arrow cannot make him flee.

Dhorme links this colon with 33:23 where τρώσῃ appears.[349] That whole verse has been discussed previously (§88), and probably has some bearing on 41:20a, but the line has been lifted almost verbatim from 20:24b.

καὶ οὐ μὴ σωθῇ ἐκ χειρὸς 20:24a
σιδήρου
τρώσαι αὐτὸν τόξον χάλκειον 20:24b
And he will in no way be saved from the power of the iron weapon; let the bronze bow kill him.

יברח מנשק ברזל

תחלפהו קשת נחושה

He will flee from the iron weapon; the bronze bow will pierce him through.

The key words are יברח (20:24a), יבריחנו (41:20a), and קשת (20:24b; 41:20a). ברח does not even show up in G, but the similar Hebrew has led the translator to bring 20:24b into this passage.[350]

§113. Job 42:11

Dhorme has already noted the dependence of this interpolation upon 2:11.[351] In actuality, it has been influenced by both 2:10 and 2:11.

---

[349]Dhorme, *Book of Job*, 641.
[350]Ziegler ("Der textkritische Wert," 284) has connected these passages.
[351]Dhorme, *Book of Job*, 650.

ἤκουσαν δὲ πάντες οἱ ἀδελφοὶ   42:11a
αὐτοῦ καὶ αἱ ἀδελφαὶ αὐτοῦ
πάντα τὰ συμβεβηκότα αὐτῷ   42:11b
καὶ ἦλθον πρὸς αὐτὸν   42:11c
And all his brothers and sis-
ters heard all that had happened to him, and they came
to him.

וַיָּבֹאוּ אֵלָיו כָּל אֶחָיו
וְכָל אֲחִיתָיו

And all his brothers and sis-
ters came to him.

ἐν πᾶσιν τούτοις τοῖς συμβεβη-   2:10d
κόσιν αὐτῷ
ἀκούσαντες δὲ οἱ τρεῖς φίλοι   2:11a
αὐτοῦ τὰ κακὰ πάντα τὰ ἐπ-
ελθόντα αὐτῷ
In all these things that happened to him. . . . And when
his three friends heard of all
the evil that had come upon
him

בְּכָל זֹאת

וַיִּשְׁמְעוּ שְׁלֹשֶׁת רֵעֵי
אִיּוֹב אֵת כָּל הָרָעָה
הַזֹּאת הַבָּאָה עָלָיו

In all this. . . . And the three
friends of Job heard all this
misfortune that had come upon
him.

῎Ηκουσαν δὲ (42:11a) comes from 2:11a (וישמעו, ἀκούσαντες δὲ), but
πάντα τὰ συμβεβηκότα αὐτῷ (42:11b) is borrowed from 2:10d, where it was
inserted from 1:22a.

CHAPTER III

Conclusion

I. Misunderstandings of Greek and Textual Emendations Incorrectly Based on Greek

The implications of this monograph for Septuagintal studies in Job are far-reaching. It is obvious that the translator was not slavishly following the Hebrew before him. Not only was he quite willing to abridge the Hebrew, but he was also willing materially to modify his translation by bringing in other passages of Scripture more in keeping with his concept of the direction of the passage. He generally followed the Hebrew, but his paraphrastic approach and generous manipulation of the text through other passages creates a situation that should put considerable restraint on any efforts to emend the Hebrew text based on the Greek.

This study also demonstrates that the mentality of about 150 B.C. toward the Hebrew text (at least by some Jews) was considerably different from that evidenced in the KR of a century or so later. The very careful, literal translation of the KR is not to be observed in the earlier material of Job which makes up the OG. This data must be kept in mind in any discussion of the history of the Hebrew and Greek texts of the OT.

The rather free use of G as a basis for emendation of the Hebrew text of Job without proper consideration of the nature of the translation has been justly criticized in recent years. Beer's work on Job, which won him the task of editing Job in *BHK*, is the best example of the failure to appreciate fully the nature of G-Job.[1]

The following discussion contains references where G has been misunderstood or has been reputed to have read the Hebrew in a certain way or has been used by someone to suggest a Hebrew different from that of the MT.[2] The Hebrew may indeed require emendation at these places, but the point to be made is that the emendation cannot be posited because of what appears in G. The correct explanation for G in these verses is anaphoric translation. Only summary statements will be made here; the full presentation of the data is in Chapter II.

---

[1]G. Beer (*Der Text*) throughout this chapter except for *BHK*, which will be so noted. It is interesting that in Gerleman's work in *BHS*-Job, none of the examples I list are referred to at all. This conservative approach is to be commended.

[2]As I have indicated earlier, my research in the areas of anaphoric translation tends to support the idea that the *Vorlage* of the old Greek of Job was probably not too different from the MT.

A. JOB 2:3g

Dhorme and Gerleman agree that the addition τὰ ὑπάρχοντα is to soften the statement that God incited Satan. In reality, it was provided with the assistance of 2:4c.

B. JOB 3:9c

Beer assumes G either to be translating שׁחר twice (ἑωσφόρον ἀνατέλλοντα) or paraphrasing עפעפי. The two words have been brought in, however, from Isa 14:12a.

C. JOB 3:16a

Beer, *BHK*, suggests the deletion of לא before אהיה. In *Der Text* he states that G read טמון as מטא and then expanded as in 3:10. Orlinsky wants to see a positive rendering of a negative construction.[3] Both fail to note that the colon was lifted almost vebatim from LXX-Num 12:12.

D. JOB 3:17a

Beer suggests the possibility that G read דלקו for ἐξέκαυσαν and suggests that θυμὸν ὀργῆς is a double translation of רגז. Orlinsky emends G to ἐξέπαυσαν.[4] All of this discussion is meaningless in light of the fact that G is based on other passages.

E. JOB 6:21a

König believes G has supplied ἀνελεημόνως strictly from the context,[5] whereas it has come from 30:21a.

F. JOB 7:5b

Beer, followed by Dhorme,[6] believes ἰχῶρος should be read χρωτός in accord with the Hebrew עורי. Ἰχῶρος, however, was supplied at 2:8a as an object of the verb התגרד and was then imported to 7:5b as an interpretation of עורי (Job 7:5b is discussed in §12).

---

[3]H. Orlinsky, "Studies in the Septuagint," *HUCA* 29 (1958) 238.
[4]Orlinsky, "Studies in the Septuagint," *HUCA* 33 (1962) 125-126.
[5]E. König, *Das Buch Hiob* (Gütersloh: Bertelsmann, 1929) 96.
[6]E. Dhorme, *Book of Job*, 100.

G. JOB 8:19a

Beer quotes A. Merx as reading מְשׁוּבַת for מְשׂוֹשׂ following G (καταστροφή). C. Siegfried reads מִשָּׁאת;[7] Beer opts for מְסוֹס. But G is not reading a different text. The problematic Hebrew has sent him to several OT passages from which he brought in the phrase καταστροφὴ ἀσεβοῦς.

H. JOB 9:26

Beer says G probably read חלפו as הלא and identifies יטוש with Aramaic יטוס. However, because of the *hapax legomenon* יטוש, G went to Prov 30:19 for his verbal form (πετομένου), which he brought along with other words into 9:26.

I. JOB 10:13

Beer says that G appears to be a double translation of כי זאת עמך. This is another case, however, where a verbatim translation has been imported, in this case from 42:2.

J. JOB 11:12b

Beer calls γυναικός G's "Gratisbeigabe," when in fact the whole line comes from 14:1a.

K. JOB 14:2a

Beer says that G read ימל as יפל. In *BHK*, he suggests יצמח for יצא and ויבל for וימל on the basis of G. Duhm says G is reading יבל.[8] G, however, comes from Isa 40:7.

L. JOB 15:30c

Beer, *BHK*, emends ויסור to וישר or ויסער on the basis of G ἐκπέσοι and suggests פרחו or פריו for פיו because of G αὐτοῦ τὸ ἄνθος. Most commentators provide some such emendation here (correctly), but it should not be based on G, for G is following 14:2a and Isa 40:7b.

---

[7]C. Siegfried, *The Book of Job* (The Sacred Books of the Old Testament 17; tr. R. E. Brünnow; Baltimore: Johns Hopkins Press, 1893) 30.
[8]B. Duhm, *Das Buch Hiob* (Kurzer Hand-Kommentar zum AT 16; Freiburg: J. B. Mohr, 1897) 75.

M. JOB 16:16a

Beer believes G to be reading בטני or מעי, but ἡ γαστήρ is based on Lam 1:20b and 2:11b.

N. JOB 18:4c

Beer, *BHK*, believes G may have the better reading in the third colon, but it has been lifted from 14:18.

O. JOB 20:24a

Siegfried suggests "לא ימלט מפני ב because of G, but G is paraphrasing on the basis of 5:20b and 15:22a.[9]

P. JOB 22:11a

Beer quotes Merx and Bickell as emending the Hebrew to אורך חשך on the basis of G. Siegfried suggests אורך מחשך,[10] but G has been influenced by 18:5-6.

Q. JOB 22:21a

Beer needlessly assumes a reading of הסכל נא, since G's rendering is based on 9:4b and was prompted by a failure to understand סכן.

R. JOB 22:25a

Beer believes G to be a paraphrase and correctly faults Merx for seeing מצריך מציל in G. G has been influenced by Deut 33:7d.

S. JOB 27:10b

Beer, *BHK*, suggests יעתר לו for בכל עת, but G is probably dependent on 22:27a.

T. JOB 29:18

There has been much effort to produce a different Hebrew text on the basis of G. The phoenix legend has even been posited from στέλεχος φοίνικος (see Beer's discussion, Dhorme's, and Gray's[11]). All fail to note

---

[9]Siegfried, *Book of Job*, 39.
[10]Ibid., 40.
[11]Dhorme, *Book of Job*, 426-427; Driver and Gray, *Book of Job*, Pt. II, 201-204.

the dependence on 14:8. Dhorme's suggestion of זקן based on ἡ ἡλικία results from a failure to understand the way G handled the text.[12]

U. JOB 30:14a

Beer wonders if G βέλεσιν αὐτοῦ κατηκόντισέν με might be reading בחץ רבה אותי. G has been created from the context of 30:11a, 13b, 14a. It is not based on the Hebrew.

V. JOB 31:11b

G of 31:11b is an expansion based on Num 5:11-31 and not on a different Hebrew text as Bickell, according to Beer, suggests.

W. JOB 31:23a

Beer, *BHK*, suggests on the basis of G, פחד אל עצרני, but G was derived from 3:24b.

X. JOB 33:23

Beer thinks v 23 is a paraphrase. He fails to note the dependence on other passages. In *BHK*, he reads, on the basis of G, מוסרו and inserts וחטאתו יודיעהו. However, G of 33:23 must be explained as the product of the G-translator working with essentially the same Hebrew now in MT and utilizing other G passages in the process. For a full discussion, see §88.

Y. JOB 34:10c

Beer, *BHK*, suggests מעות צדק for מעול, but G is following 8:3b; 19:6a; 34:12b.

Z. JOB 36:5a

Beer, *BHK*, wants to read אל לא ימאס תמים as in G, but G has come from 8:20a.

AA. JOB 37:16

Dhorme[13] says that מפלאות was translated a second time by G as if from the root נפל, but G has been influenced by 18:12.

---

[12]Dhorme, *Book of Job*, 426-427.
[13]Ibid., 568.

BB. JOB 38:14b

Beer rejects Bickell's reading of דברים for λαλητόν, and suggests that G comes from a form of מלל, but the whole verse is a homily on man's origins in clay and is not based on Hebrew (see §106).

CC. JOB 40:21b

Beer believes G twice translated בצה, but G is based on 8:11.

II. Conjectures as to the Reasons for Anaphoric Translations

It is always difficult if not impossible to reconstruct the mentality of an ancient translator, and any such efforts must remain tentative. Yet there is sufficient evidence to suggest at least four reason for this activity in Job.

A. FAILURE TO UNDERSTAND THE HEBREW

The following verses serve only as examples of places where the Hebrew was apparently misunderstood by the G-translator.

1. The Word סכן

The G-translator apparently did not know what to do with סכן and hence, mishandled it in each of its six occurrences in Job. 15:3a has been treated as οἷς οὐ δεῖ. 22:2 follows the translation of 21:22a, again because he did not understand סכן. 22:21a has γενοῦ δὴ σκληρός where סכן stands. This phrase was borrowed from 9:4b, triggered by the presence of שלם but because of the problem with סכן. 34:9a has ἐπισκοπή for יסכן, which was lifted from 6:14b and 29:4b at least in part because of a failure to perceive the meaning of סכן. The final passage, 35:3, contains difficult Hebrew but the ever problematic סכן as well. Parts of 7:20; 34:6; and 35:6 were brought in as a result.

2. Job 11:10b

The Hebrew אם יחלף ויסגיר ויקהיל ומי ישיבנו may have a textual problem, but even with emendation (e.g., יחלף to יחתף), the Hebrew is a little obscure. As a result, the G-translator took מי ישיבנו as a point of departure to 9:12.

3. Job 11:15b

This line was difficult for the translator because of מצק. The Greek phrase ἐκδύσῃ δὲ ῥύπον was probably produced on the basis of 9:31a as a result.

4. Job 20:7a

The cryptic Hebrew כגללו has led to an insertion based on 15:21b and 20:22a.

5. Job 30:14a

There are textual problems in 30:13b which have created problems for the translator with 30:14a. 30:14a makes fairly good sense, but since the translator apparently could not relate it to the context, he created a new colon to agree with the imagery of 30:11a.

6. Job 32:13a

Κυρίῳ προσθέμενοι has probably been influenced by 13:9b because of the problematic Hebrew word ידפנו in 32:13a.

B. DESIRE TO DEVELOP A HOMILY

There are a number of cases where the G-translator has chosen to ignore the Hebrew or to take it as a base and construct from it a homiletical statement.

1. The "Just" Way

The presence of the word "way" (דרך), in a totally nontheological sense, is too tempting to the translator for him to leave as it is. As discussed in §60, there are examples of this homiletical phrase in other wisdom literature. The G-translator inserts the word "just" at 24:4a, 11b, 13b, and 28:4b. In each case, the meaning of the Hebrew is radically changed, but the translator has accomplished his purpose.

2. Man Made from Clay

The creation of man from clay hovers behind the several discussions in Job that center upon the frailty of man. This has colored the G-translator's thinking on occasion and has caused anaphoric translations. Job 4:19 contains a line completely unlike the Hebrew. The phrase בתי חמר (4:19a), influenced by 33:6, prompted an expansion on man's vulnerability. In 33:6 the first Hebrew colon is ignored, and from the second Hebrew colon two Greek cola are developed, which discuss the common lot of mankind under the imagery of clay. Likewise, 38:14 has כחמר חותם, which was misread with the resultant two cola based on the creation account in Genesis 2 (see §22).

3. Punishment of the Wicked

Job 18:12; 20:5a; and 37:16b have in common the words πτῶμα (πτώματα) and ἐξαίσιον (ἐξαίσια). In 18:12 they are based on the single

Hebrew word איד, but in 37:16b these words are borrowed, and דעים was read רעים (see §102). They are also imported into 20:5a (see §49). This has come about from a simple desire to teach divine retribution. A similar concept occurs at Prov 1:18b and Wis 3:19. The same idea may have affected the choice of anaphoric translation at 34:20a (κενὰ δὲ αὐτοῖς ἀποβήσεται). This colon was influenced by 15:35b, which in turn received its G translation from 15:31b (see §94). "For his destiny shall be emptiness," is a favorite expression of the translator.

4. God's Sovereignty

At 1:21d, G has added a full colon which has no counterpart in Hebrew. "As it seemed good to the Lord, so it has come to pass." There are other verses listed in the discussion above that may have influenced the homily (see §9). Job's resignation to the fairness of God has motivated the translator to add this precept on God's sovereignty. This same theme has probably been the cause of an insertion at 4:21a based on Isa 40:24b. God simply blows on man, and he is withered up (see §23). Man's impotency in the face of a sovereign God is set forth also in the statement, "Who will say to him, 'What have you done?'" which was imported into 11:10b from 9:12b (see §34). This question also occurs elsewhere in the OT as discussed in §34.

C. PROBLEMS WITH THE HEBREW TEXT

There are several places where the G-translator has felt compelled to go elsewhere for help because of textual problems in the Hebrew. The following verses are only examples; three come from chap. 24, a section especially plagued with textual corruptions.

1. Job 24:6a

Πρὸ ὥρας has possibly been imported from 15:32a because of the difficult בלילו. Ἀδύνατοι has come from 24:4a to provide a subject for the hapax legomenon לקש.

2. Job 24:19b

The Hebrew here does not make sense with the result that part of 24:9a (ἥρπασαν ὀρφανόν) has been brought in. יגזלו of 24:19b may have been the point of departure, accounting for ἥρπασαν.

3. Job 24:20a-b

The Hebrew here is almost impossible to do anything with. A full discussion of what G was doing can be found above (§65). The translator has gone to 34:11 for help.

4. Job 27:8b

This much discussed verse presents a problem because of ישל. G may have read something like ישאל, but more likely gave up on it and went to Prov 29:25b for help.

5. Job 28:4b

Everyone struggles with הנשכחים מני רגל. The best that can be done with it is "forgotten by the foot." G possibly read מעגל (ὁδόν) and then added δικαίαν as in 24:4, 11, but he resorted to this from desperation.

6. Job 31:23a

The Hebrew text is probably corrupt, and the translator provided a clear statement under the influence of 3:24b. Beer's emendation, פחד אל עצרני, is incorrectly based on G.

7. Job 36:5a

The interpolation from 8:20a was brought in because of the corrupt Hebrew.

D. DESIRE TO HARMONIZE

There are certain verses that suggest a desire to harmonize on the part of the G-translator (but there are others that would have lent themselves to harmony and yet were ignored by him).

1. Job 1:14b

Τὰ ζεύγη was added at this place to harmonize with 1:3c and 42:12d where צמד/ζεύγη appears. All three passages describe the holdings of Job and so were brought into agreement.

2. Job 1:22a; 2:10d; 42:11b

G adds συμβεβηκόσιν αὐτῷ in 1:22a probably in anticipation of כל הרעה הזאת הבאה עליו (2:11a), which was then inserted in 2:10d and 42:11b to harmonize these similar accounts. Additional facets of the harmonization of these passages are discussed above (§10).

3. Job 32:1a

G has for "these three men" οἱ τρεῖς φίλοι αὐτοῦ, which is identical to G in 2:11a. There is now no doubt about the identity of the men; they are the three friends who came to Job at the beginning. Beer has wrongly assumed a reading of שלשת רעיו.

4. Job 33:4b

תחיני perhaps should be read תחוני. This reading was followed by G, but the G-translator may have changed it in the interest of harmony with 32:8b rather than having read a different Hebrew. Now ἡ διδάσκουσα appears in both verses.

5. Job 38:1-2

38:1a has νεφῶν, which is absent from the Hebrew. The word has also been supplied in G at 40:6. God is speaking in both contexts, and G wants him to be speaking from the clouds in both places. Having added "clouds" in 38:1b, he harmonizes by adding the same word at 40:6.

These samples are sufficient to suggest the four reasons set out above for anaphoric translations. There may have been other reasons, but these four at least prompted this translational technique.

It is of further interest to note the sources of the translator's interpolations. I have dealt with 113 passages which, I have attempted to show, were involved in this technique. Approximately 144 verses in Job were suggested as possible sources for the translation, and 67 in the rest of the OT. These references can be broken down into the Pentateuch, 25; Former Prophets, 6; Poetical Books, 12; Latter Prophets, 24 (only 2 in the Twelve).[14] These statistics show that although the G-translator was familiar with the rest of the LXX, particularly the Pentateuch and Isaiah, most of the anaphoric translations come from within Job itself.

---

[14] I have made several references to books outside the Hebrew canon (Wisdom in particular), but since the date for the LXX of each of these books is usually placed subsequent to 150 B.C. (a probable date for the old Greek of Job), the G-translator of Job could not have used them for anaphoric translations. The authors of those books either followed G-Job or utilized Alexandrian Jewish vocabulary and ideas common to them and the old Greek of Job.

BIBLIOGRAPHY

I. GENERAL WORKS

Barthélemy, D. *Les devanciers d'Aquila.* VTSup 10. Leiden: Brill, 1963.
———. "Redécouverte d'un chaînon manquant de l'histoire de la Septante," *RB* 60 (1953) 18-29.
Beer, G. *Der Text des Buches Hiob Untersucht.* Marburg: Elwertsche Verlagsbuchhandlung, 1897.
Bickermann, E. J. "Some Notes on the Transmission of the LXX." In *A. Marx Jubilee Volume.* Ed. S. Lieberman. New York: Ktav, 1950. Pp. 149-178.
Blommerde, A. C. *Northwest Semitic Grammar and Job.* Rome: Pontifical Biblical Institute, 1969.
Budde, K. *Das Buch Hiob.* HAT 1. Göttingen: Vandenhoeck & Ruprecht, 1896.
Cross, F. M., Jr. *The Ancient Library of Qumran and Modern Biblical Studies.* Rev. ed. New York: Doubleday, 1961.
———. "The Contribution of the Qumran Discoveries to the Study of the Biblical Text," *IEJ* 16 (1966) 81-95.
Dahood, M. "Nest and Phoenix in Job 29, 18," *Bib* 48 (1967) 542-544.
De Waard, J. *A Comparative Study of the Old Testament Text in the Dead Sea Scrolls and in the New Testament.* Grand Rapids: Eerdmans, 1966.
———. "Translation Techniques Used by the Greek Translators of Ruth," *Bib* 54 (1973) 499-515.
Delitzsch, F. *The Book of Job.* Tr. F. Bolton. 2 vols. Grand Rapids: Eerdmans, 1949.
Dhorme, E. *A Commentary on the Book of Job.* Tr. H. Knight. London: Nelson, 1967.
Dieu, L. "Le texte de Job du Codex Alexandrinus et ses principaux témoins," *Mus* 13 (1912) 223-274.
Dillman, A. *Hiob.* Leipzig: Verlag von S. Hirzel, 1891.
Driver, S. R., and Gray, G. B. *A Critical and Exegetical Commentary on the Book of Job.* ICC. Edinburgh: T. & T. Clark, 1921.
Duhm, B. *Das Buch Hiob.* Kurzer Hand-Kommentar zum AT, 16. Freiburg: Mohr, 1897.
Eissfeldt, O. *The Old Testament: An Introduction.* Tr. P. R. Ackroyd. New York: Harper & Row, 1965.
Fohrer, G. *Das Buch Hiob.* Gütersloh: Mohr, 1963.
Freedman, D. N. "The Elihu Speeches in the Book of Job," *HTR* 61 (1968) 51-59.

Gard, D. H. "The Concept of Job's Character according to the Greek Translator of the Hebrew Text," *JBL* 72 (1953) 182-186.

_____. *The Exegetical Method of the Greek Translator of the Book of Job.* SBLMS 8. Philadelphia: Society of Biblical Literature, 1952.

Gehman, H. S. "Adventures in Septuagint Lexicography," *Textus* 5 (1966) 125-132.

_____. "Exegetical Methods Employed by the Greek Translator of 1 Samuel," *JAOS* 70 (1950) 292-296.

_____. "The Theological Approach of the Greek Translator of Job 1-15," *JBL* 68 (1949) 231-240.

Gerleman, G. *Studies in the LXX. I, The Book of Job* (LUÅ, N.F.1 43.2, 1946).

Ginzberg, L. *The Legends of the Jews.* 5 vols. Philadelphia: Jewish Publication Society, 1925.

Gordis, R. *The Book of God and Man.* Chicago: University of Chicago Press, 1965.

Gray, G. B. "The Additions in the Ancient Greek Version of Job," *Exp* 19 (1920) 422-438.

Greenberg, M. "The Stabilization of the Text of the Hebrew Bible, Reviewed in the Light of the Biblical Materials from the Judaean Desert," *JAOS* 76 (1956) 157-167.

Guillaume, A. *Studies in the Book of Job.* Ed. J. MacDonald. Supplement II to ALUOS. Leiden: Brill, 1968.

Gundry, R. H. *The Use of the Old Testament in St. Matthew's Gospel.* Leiden: Brill, 1967.

Hatch, E. *Essays in Biblical Greek.* Oxford. 1889. Reprinted at Amsterdam: Philo Press, 1970.

Heater, H., Jr. "A Septuagint Translation Technique in the Book of Job." Ph.D. diss., Catholic University of America, 1976.

_____. "Textual Harmonizations in 1QIs[a] and LXX." M.A. thesis, Catholic University of America, 1967.

Jellicoe, S. "Hebrew-Greek Equivalents for the Nether World," *Textus* 8 (1973) 1-19.

_____. *The Septuagint and Modern Study.* Oxford: Clarendon Press, 1968.

Kahle, P. *The Cairo Geniza.* London: Oxford University Press, 1947.

Kedar-Kopfstein, B. "The Interpretative Element in Transliteration," *Textus* 8 (1973) 55-77.

Kenyon, F. G. *The Text of the Greek Bible.* London: Duckworth, 1937.

Kiessling, N. K. "Antecedents of the Medieval Dragon in Sacred History," *JBL* 89 (1970) 167-177.

Kissane, E. J. *The Book of Job Translated from a Critically Revised Hebrew Text with Commentary.* Dublin, 1939. Reprinted at New York: Harper & Row, 1958.

König, E. *Das Buch Hiob.* Gütersloh: Bertelsmann, 1929.

Lagarde, P. de. *Anmerkungen zur griechischen Übersetzung der Proverbien.* Leipzig: Brockhaus, 1863.

———. *Septuaginta Studien, I, II.* Göttingen: Dieterische Verlagsbuchhandlung, 1891-92.

Moran, W. F. "The Putative Root ͨ*tm* in Is. 9:18," *CBQ* 12 (1950) 153-154.

Muraoka, T. "Literary Device in the Septuagint," *Textus* 8 (1973) 20-30.

Nida, E. A., and Tabor, C. R. *The Theory and Practice of Translation* 3. Leiden: Brill, 1969.

Orlinsky, H. "Studies in the Septuagint of Job," *HUCA* 28 (1957) 53-74; 29 (1958) 229-271; 30 (1959) 153-167; 32 (1961) 239-268; 33 (1962) 119-151; 35 (1964) 57-78; 36 (1965) 37-47.

———. "The Textual Criticism of the Old Testament." In *The Bible and the Ancient Near East.* Ed. G. E. Wright. New York: Doubleday, 1965. Pp. 140-169.

———. "On the Present State of Proto-Septuagint Studies," *JAOS* 61 (1941) 81-91.

Pope, M. H. *Job.* AB 15. 3rd ed. New York: Doubleday, 1973.

Rabin, C. "The Dead Sea Scrolls and the History of the Old Testament Text," *JTS* (1955) 174-182.

Rahlfs, A. *Septuaginta-Studien.* 2 vols. Göttingen: Vandenhoeck & Ruprecht, 1904.

Siegfried, C. *The Book of Job.* The Sacred Books of the Old Testament, 17. Tr. R. E. Brünnow. Baltimore: Johns Hopkins Press, 1893.

Skehan, P. W. "The Biblical Scrolls from Qumran and the Text of the Old Testament," *BA* 28 (1965) 87-100.

———. "'I Will Speak Up!'" (Job 32); The Pit (Job 33)," *CBQ* 31 (1969) 380-382.

———. "The Qumran Manuscripts and Textual Criticism." *Volume du Congrès. Strasbourg 1956.* VTSup 4. Leiden: Brill, 1957. Pp. 148-160.

———. "Qumran and the Present State of the Old Testament Text Studies: The Masoretic Text," *JBL* 78 (1959) 21-25.

———. "Second Thoughts on Job 6,16 and 6,25," *CBQ* 31 (1969) 210-212.

———. "Septuagint." *NCE* 2. New York: McGraw-Hill, 1967, 425-429.

———. "Strophic Patterns in the Book of Job," *CBQ* 23 (1961) 125-142.

———. "4QLXXNum: A Pre-Christian Reworking of the Septuagint," *HTR* 70 (1977) 39-50.

Swete, H. B. *An Introduction to the Old Testament in Greek.* Rev. R. R. Ottley. Cambridge: University Press, 1902. Reprinted at New York: Ktav, 1968.

Talmon, S. "The Old Testament Text." In *Cambridge History of the Bible* 1. Cambridge: University Press, 1970, 159-199.

———. "The Transmission of the Bible in Light of the Qumran Manuscripts," *Textus* 4 (1964) 95-132.

Thackeray, H. St. J. *Some Aspects of the Greek Old Testament*. London: Allen & Unwin, 1927.

Tov, E. "Transliterations of Hebrew Words in the Greek Versions of the Old Testament," *Textus* 8 (1973) 78-92.

Walters, P. *The Text of the Septuagint*. Cambridge: University Press, 1973.

Würthwein, E. *The Text of the Old Testament*. Tr. P. R. Ackroyd. Oxford: Blackwell, 1957.

Ziegler, J. "Der textkritische Wert der Septuaginta des Buches Iob," *M Bib* 2 (1934) 277-296.

———. *Untersuchungen zur Septuaginta des Buches Isaias*. Münster: Verlag des Aschendorffschen Verlagsbuchhandlung, 1934.

II. GRAMMARS, LEXICONS, AND TECHNICAL WORKS

Biblia Hebraica. Ed. R. Kittel. Stuttgart: Württembergische Bibelanstalt, 1951.

Biblia Hebraica Stuttgartensia. Ed. K. Elliger and W. Rudolph. Stuttgart: Deutsche Bibelstiftung, 1969.

Blass, F., and Debrunner, A. *A Greek Grammar of the New Testament and Other Early Christian Literature*. Tr. and rev. R. W. Funk. Chicago: Univeristy of Chicago Press, 1961.

Brock, S. P.; Fritsch, C. T.; and Jellicoe, S. *A Classified Bibliography of the Septuagint*. Arbeiten zur Literatur und Geschichte des hellenistischen Judentums, 6. Leiden: Brill, 1973.

Brooke, A. E., and McLean, N. *The Old Testament in Greek*. 3 vols. London: Cambridge University Press, 1906-1940.

De Rossi, J. B. *Variae lectiones Veteris Testamenti*. 4 vols. Parma: Ex Regio Typographeo, 1788.

Field, F. *Origenis hexaplorum quae supersunt sive veterum interpretium Graecorum in totum Vetus Testamentum fragmenta*. 2 vols. Oxford: Clarendon Press, 1875.

Holmes, R., and Parsons, J. *Vetus Testamentum Graecum cum variis lectionibus*. 5 vols. Oxford: Clarendon Press, 1823.

Jastrow, M. *A Dictionary of the Targumim, the Talmud Babli and Yerushalmi, and the Midrashic Literature*. 2 vols. New York: Pardes, 1950.

Joüon, P. *Grammaire de l'Hébreu Biblique*. Rome: Pontifical Biblical Institute, 1923.

Kautzsch, E. *Gesenius' Hebrew Grammar*. Rev. A. E. Cowley. 2d ed. Oxford: Clarendon Press, 1909.

Kennicott, B. *Vetus Testamentum Hebraicum cum variis lectionibus*. 2 vols. Oxford: Clarendon Press, 1780.

Koehler, L., and Baumgartner, W. *Lexicon in Veteris Testamenti libros*. With Supplement. Grand Rapids: Eerdmans, 1951.

Lee-Brenton, L. C. *The Septuagint Version of the Old Testament.* London: Bagsters, 1844.

Liddell, H. G., and Scott, R. *A Greek English Lexicon.* Rev. H. S. Jones and R. McKenzie. 9th ed. Oxford: Clarendon Press, 1940.

Mandelkern, S. *Veteris Testamenti concordantiae Hebraicae atque Chaldaicae.* 2 vols. Reprinted at Graz: Akademische Druck- u. Verlagsanstalt, 1955.

Ploeg, J. P. van der, and Woude, A. S. van der. *Le Targum de Job de la Grotte XI de Qumrân.* Leiden: Brill, 1971.

Rahlfs, A. *Septuaginta id est Vetus Testamentum Graece iuxta LXX interpretes.* 2 vols. Stuttgart: Württembergische Bibelanstalt, 1935.

Schleusner, I. F. *Novus thesaurus philologico-criticus sive lexicon in LXX et reliquos interpretes Graecos ac scriptores apocryphos Veteris Testamenti.* 5 vols. Leipzig: In Libraria Weidmannia, 1821.

Swete, H. B. *The Old Testament in Greek according to the Septuagint.* 3 vols. Cambridge: University Press, 1896.

Thackeray, H. St. J. *A Grammar of the Old Testament in Greek according to the Septuagint, I, Introduction, Orthography and Accidence.* Cambridge: University Press, 1909.

Wevers, J. W. *Genesis (Septuaginta I).* Göttingen: Vandenhoeck & Ruprecht, 1974.

INDEX OF REFERENCES

146

15:35	62, 63, 112, 138	22:12	73, 74	28	2	
		22:21	74, 74n., 109n., 129, 134, 136	28:4	77, 87, 138, 139	
16:6	103	22:21-25	85	28:11	87, 88	
16:9	65	22:21-30	85	28:21	88	
16:12	22	22:22	27, 104, 104n., 105n., 106	28:23	17, 113	
16:16	63, 134			28:24	17, 113	
		22:23	104, 104n., 105	28:25	113	
17:1	63, 64, 65, 65n.			28:28	12, 13	
17:3	29n.	22:25	74, 75, 134			
17:8	92, 93	22:26	85, 86, 106 106n., 107, 134	29	90	
		22:27	75, 76, 85, 86, 105, 134	29:4	109, 136	
18:4	17, 65, 66, 134			29:9	120	
18:5-6	72, 73, 134	22:28	75, 76, 106	29:12	88, 89	
18:7	29n.	22:30	99n.	29:18	89, 90, 91, 134	
18:12	67, 68, 120 135, 137			29:19	90	
18:17	33, 34	23	80	29:22	91	
				30	92	
19:3	66, 67	24	80, 82, 138	30:5	92, 93	
19:4	67	24:1-6	77	30:6	93, 94	
19:6	3, 67, 110, 135	24:4	76, 77, 79, 112, 137, 138	30:11	94, 134, 137	
19:11	65			30:13-14	94, 134, 137	
19:13	48n.	24:6	77, 78, 79, 80, 138	30:16	35	
19:20	101			30:19	46, 124	
		24:7	79, 80, 81	30:20	47n.	
20:4	125	24:7-12	78	30:21	47, 48, 132	
20:5	38, 67, 68, 83n., 137, 138	24:7-13	77			
20:7	68, 69, 137	24:9	81, 138	31:11	58n., 94, 95, 135	
20:10	69	24:10	80, 81	31:23	95, 96, 135, 139	
20:11	106	24:11	76, 77, 78, 87, 137, 139	31:29	92, 92n., 96	
20:13	69			31:34	107n.	
20:14	69	24:13	76, 77, 137			
20:18	28n.	24:14	80, 81	32:1	96, 139	
20:22	68, 69, 137	24:14-18	80	32:4	100	
20:24	69, 70, 103, 129, 134	24:17-20	81	32:8	100, 140	
		24:19	81, 82, 138	32:13	97, 97n., 98, 137	
21:13	45	24:20	81, 82, 105, 138	32:21	98	
21:14	118			32:22	98, 99, 111	
21:16-17	51	26:13	4, 127, 127n.			
21:22	70, 71, 136			33	105	
21:24	106	27	85, 118	33:3	99, 99n.	
21:25	44	27:6	119	33:4	100, 140	
		27:7	82, 83, 83n.	33:5	100	
22	85, 101, 105	27:7-8	51, 52	33:6	46, 125, 137	
22:1-20	85	27:7-10	85	33:9	108, 115	
22:2	70, 71n., 109n., 136	27:8	83, 84, 139	33:10	105n.	
		27:9	86n.	33:21	100, 101, 105, 106	
22:4	71, 72	27:9-10	118			
22:6	79, 80	27:10	84, 85, 86, 86n., 118, 134	33:22	2, 103	
22:6-11	85			33:22-27	101, 102	
22:7	80	27:16	124			
22:11	72, 73, 134	27:18	86			

INDEX OF AUTHORS

152